McClellan and the Union
High Command, 1861–1863

McClellan and the Union High Command, 1861–1863

Leadership Gaps That Cost a Timely Victory

JEFFREY W. GREEN

McFarland & Company, Inc., Publishers
Jefferson, North Carolina

LIBRARY OF CONGRESS CATALOGUING-IN-PUBLICATION DATA

Names: Green, Jeffrey W., 1958– author.
Title: McClellan and the Union high command, 1861–1863 : leadership gaps that cost a timely victory / Jeffrey W. Green.
Description: Jefferson, North Carolina : McFarland & Company, Inc., Publishers, 2017. | Includes bibliographical references and index.
Identifiers: LCCN 2017001267 | ISBN 9781476665733 (softcover : acid free paper) ∞
Subjects: LCSH: McClellan, George B. (George Brinton), 1826–1885— Military leadership. | United States—History—Civil War, 1861– 1865—Biography. | United States—History—Civil War, 1861–1865— Campaigns. | Generals—United States—Biography. | United States. Army—Biography. | Command of troops—Case studies.
Classification: LCC E467.1.M2 G74 2017 | DDC 973.7092 [B] —dc23
LC record available at https://lccn.loc.gov/2017001267

BRITISH LIBRARY CATALOGUING DATA ARE AVAILABLE

ISBN (print) 978-1-4766-6573-3
ISBN (ebook) 978-1-4766-2709-0

© 2017 Jeffrey W. Green. All rights reserved

No part of this book may be reproduced or transmitted in any form or by any means, electronic or mechanical, including photocopying or recording, or by any information storage and retrieval system, without permission in writing from the publisher.

Front cover image of President Lincoln and General McClellan on the Battlefield of Antietam, Alexander Gardner, photographer (Library of Congress)

Manufactured in the United States of America

McFarland & Company, Inc., Publishers
  Box 611, Jefferson, North Carolina 28640
  www.mcfarlandpub.com

Table of Contents

Maps (Civil War; Eastern Theater) vi and vii
Introduction 1

ONE   Citizens and Soldiers: The United States Military Tradition   9

TWO   The Ninety-Day War and the Struggle for High Command   28

THREE   "I seem to have become the power of the land"   53

FOUR   "Now is the winter of our discontent": Winter 1861–1862   74

FIVE   "Walking on in the dark": McClellan's Attempt to Win the War with a Victory in the East   99

SIX   McClellan's Shadow   132

SEVEN   "And now, beware of rashness"   155

Conclusion 181
Chapter Notes 187
Bibliography 205
Index 211

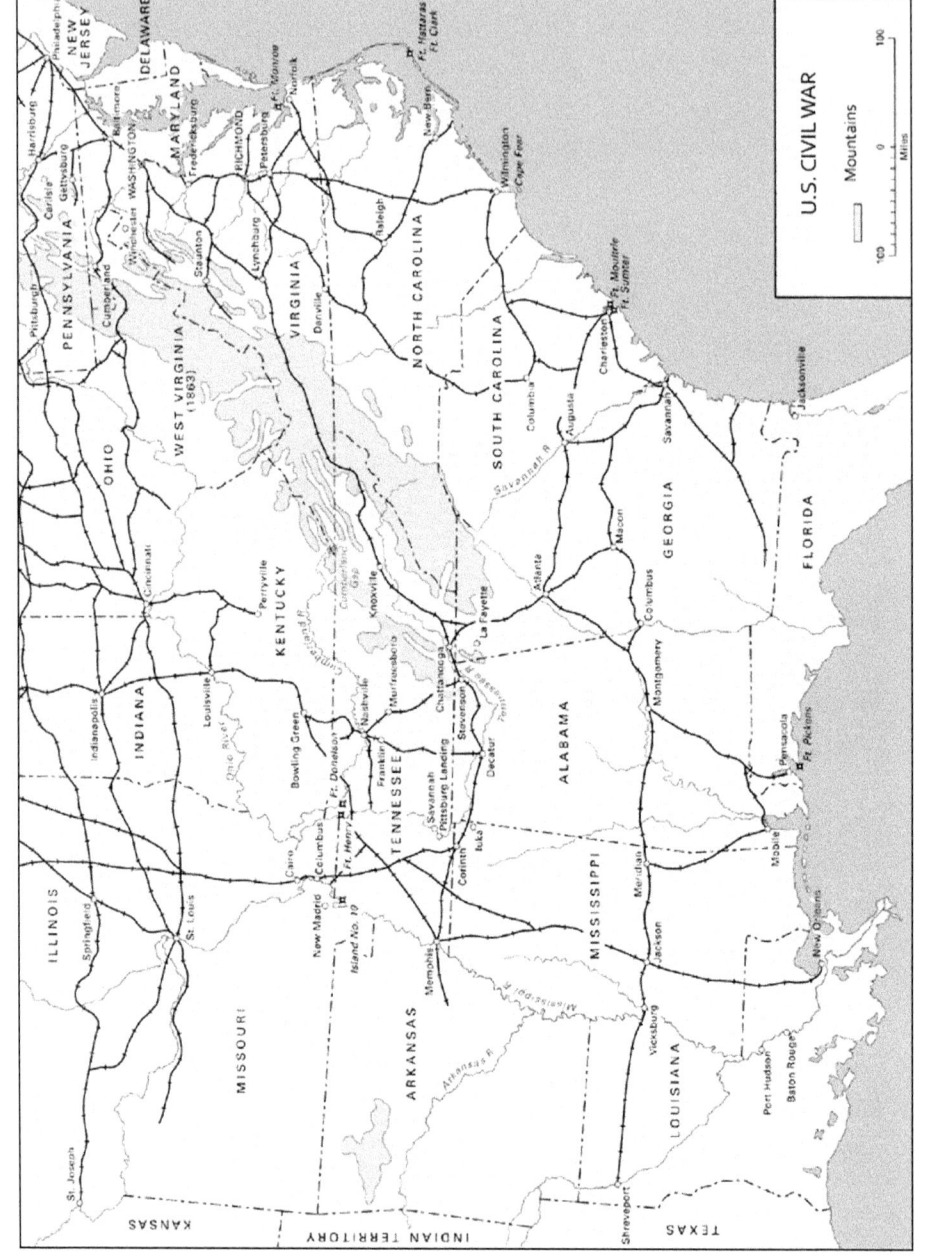

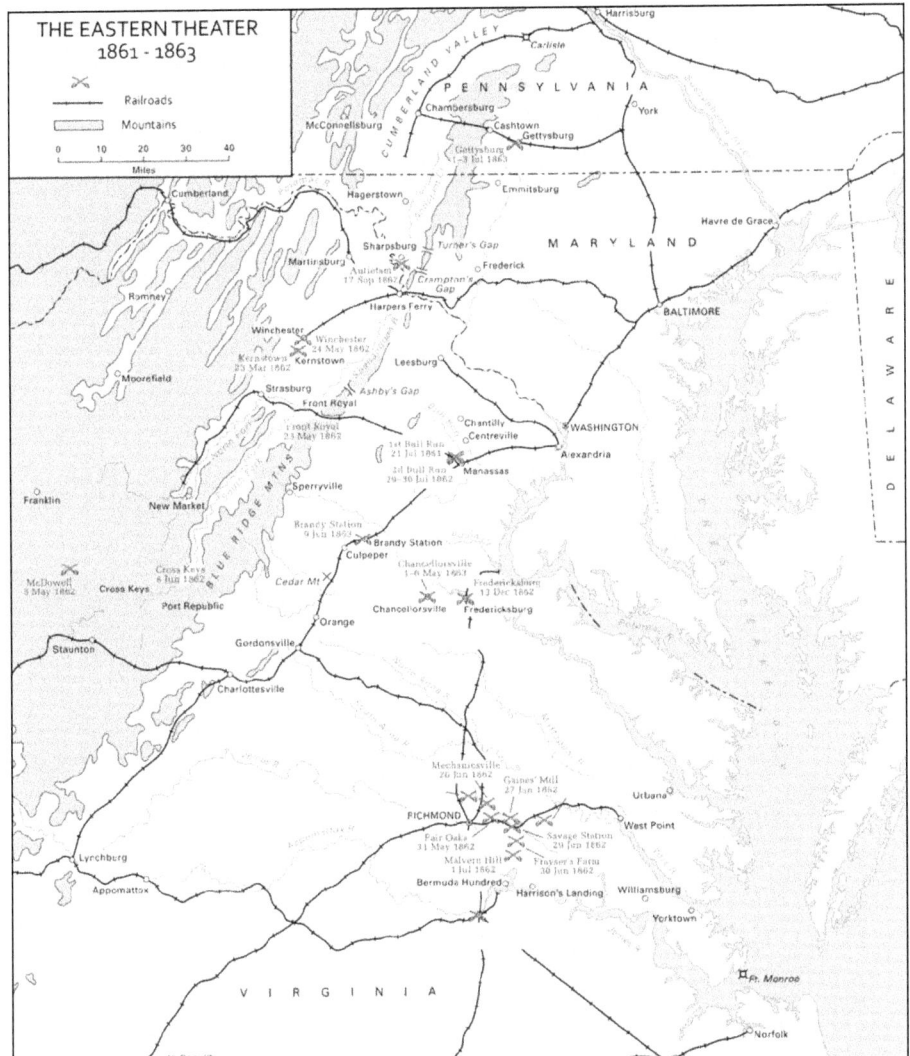

Introduction

The study of the Union's high command and Union strategy has been relatively neglected, the tendency having been to focus on battles and campaigns at the expense of high command and strategy. When the Union high command is looked at through the lens of General McClellan, and with a focus on the Union's main army, the Army of the Potomac, it can be seen that the Union lacked the high command that could have designed and implemented the Union's war aims, military strategy and operations in the first two years of the Civil War. This helps to explain why the war lasted longer than it might have and why the Union did not achieve victory a lot earlier than was actually the case.

The American Civil War is fixed in the American consciousness. The war began on April 12, 1861, with the Confederate bombardment of the Union's Fort Sumter in Charleston Harbor, South Carolina, and it is generally accepted that the war ended when General Lee surrendered to General Grant at Appomattox Court House, Virginia, on April 9, 1865. The more industrial and more densely populated North defeated the agrarian South. In the deadliest war so far in America's history, about 750,000[1] soldiers from both sides died, a greater number than died in the rest of America's wars. The Civil War battles fought and the generals who commanded the armies naturally became the focus of a lot of attention and became embedded in American culture. The Civil War saw the mass mobilization of manpower and resources for a modern war and the creation of a capitalist, modern America. The balance of political power firmly shifted from the south to the north. The political divide of the Civil War remained to some extent and was reflected in the Republican North and the Democratic South. Significantly, the war saw the death of slavery as well as the assassination of President Abraham Lincoln.

The Civil War was fought by large armies in the largest battles ever fought on American soil. The Battle of Antietam, fought in Maryland on September

17, 1862, was the single bloodiest day in American history, with about 23,000 casualties on both sides. Earlier in 1862, the Union and Confederate armies had collided near Shiloh. For two days 67,000 Union troops and 45,000 Confederates had fought for control of a small piece of land on the Tennessee River. About 23,000 casualties were suffered on both sides. From July 1 through July 3, 1863, the Battle of Gettysburg was fought in Pennsylvania. The 94,000 troops of the Union's Army of the Potomac defeated the 71,000-Confederate Army of Northern Virginia. The generals who commanded the Civil War armies became legends in their own time. The Confederate general Robert E. Lee is widely regarded as the greatest Civil War general. He seemed to represent the romantic view of the "old" south. He is also represented as a romantic figure, the last of the Napoleonic generals who had fought honorably against a numerically superior enemy. His antithesis is the Union's General Ulysses S. Grant. Grant is the untidy general who butchered Union troops as he attempted to wear down Lee's army in Virginia. Grant was methodical, but he won. Somewhere in between is the Union's General George Brinton McClellan. McClellan looked the part of the dashing Napoleonic figure. He created a formidable fighting force in the Army of the Potomac, but he failed to achieve the success he promised.[2]

The role of General George Brinton McClellan as commander of the Army of the Potomac is one of the American Civil War's most intriguing subjects. It has been studied extensively. McClellan commanded the Army of the Potomac, the Union's main army of operations, from July 26, 1861, to November 5, 1862. This army was designed to operate near Washington, a situation that put its commander under intense public and political scrutiny. McClellan was brilliant, charismatic, and arrogant, and he built the Army of the Potomac into a formidable fighting force. Some have argued that he could have won the war for the Union in 1862 if not for the political interference from President Abraham Lincoln.[3] Most have argued that he was a skilled organizer who was unsuccessful as a commander of an army on the battlefield.[4] Yet the attention that McClellan is given, with a focus on operations and battles, has distracted attention from another interesting subject, namely the reasons for and the effects of McClellan's sacking as commander of the Army of the Potomac and what this reveals about the ability of the Union's high command to direct a large-scale war.

The reason for this can be partly explained by the dominant Unionist interpretation, which argued that it was not until Grant came East and Sherman was in command in the West, that Lincoln had the military commanders he needed to win the war. The partnerships among these three men provided the Union with opportunity to enact the strategy needed to win the war from the middle of 1864 onward. Lincoln is viewed as a great commander in chief.[5] Consequently, all the efforts by other generals, prior to this important date, are seen as inconsequential and even futile. Thus McClellan is placed somewhere below Grant and Sherman in a hierarchy of Union Civil War generals. In one way this is unfair to McClellan, because the context of the war differed from 1861 and 1862 to 1864 and 1865 regarding the relative fighting capabilities of both sides. McClellan's sacking is therefore just one more painful step in the president's attempt to find a successful general.

McClellan will be used as a vehicle to explore the Union high command in the first two years of the Civil War, resulting in a focus on the Civil War's Eastern Theater. McClellan was appointed commander of the Army of the Potomac in the early stages of the war, when the Union was trying to establish a system of high command to fight on an unprecedented scale and nature in American history. The importance placed on the Army of the Potomac and its commander because of the army's proximity to Washington, the army's large size and the popular belief that it would be this army that would win the war for the Union meant that it was more tightly enmeshed in the workings of the Union's high command than any other army. McClellan seemed to be the answer to part of the problems the high command had because he seemed to be able to fight and win. It is not the purpose here to study every one of McClellan's battles and campaigns in detail because the focus will be on Union war aims, strategy and operations. However, some assessment of McClellan as a battlefield commander will naturally follow. Nor is it the purpose to try to resurrect McClellan's career or to vindicate those who regard him as a failure. McClellan's lack of success as a field commander makes it hard to rank him above Grant and Sherman, but he was not the worst Union commander and he can certainly be viewed as competent. Yet, his appointment and his conduct as commander and general in chief exposed strains within the Union's high command that would be further tested after he was sacked.

General McClellan was relieved as commander of the Army of the Potomac on November 7, 1862. Lincoln had been disappointed by his lack of a vigorous pursuit of General Lee's army after the Battle of Antietam. Lincoln even considered that McClellan may have deliberately allowed Lee to escape rather than to trap and destroy his army. Nevertheless, Lincoln used the Union victory at Antietam to announce the preliminary Emancipation Proclamation. The Proclamation had indicated a change in the Union's strategy away from the more conciliatory approach, which McClellan and many other Union officers had favored, which sought to restore the Union and not to interfere with slavery.

McClellan was replaced by General Ambrose Burnside. A group of discontented senior officers who were still loyal to McClellan worked to undermine General Burnside after the Union defeat at Fredericksburg on December 13, 1862. Their aim was to have Burnside replaced by McClellan. They achieved some success because they interfered with Burnside's plan to attack the Confederate army again. Two senior officers, Generals Franklin and Smith, wrote a letter to Lincoln that was critical of Burnside's plan. When Burnside attempted to move around Lee's army in order to get in a position to cross the Rappahannock River and attack Lee, two generals, John Newton and John Cochrane, visited Lincoln to raise concerns that they had about Burnside's ability to command the army. The result of this revolt was that Lincoln ordered Burnside not to move his army. Burnside was eventually sacked after battlefield failure and the lack of confidence in him by senior officers. He was replaced by General Joseph Hooker, however, rather than McClellan. Hooker had actively undermined McClellan and then Burnside. His plan to defeat Lee resulted in the Union defeat at Chancellorsville. Hooker blamed the defeat on three of his corps commanders. A new general's revolt began with the purpose of removing Hooker. Hooker suffered the same fate as Burnside, but Lincoln chose as his replacement General George Meade, who had enough support of the pro–McClellan faction to end the revolt. This ill-defined movement, which was comprised of an ever-changing group of senior officers, had a significant influence on the dismissal of two commanding generals and also on one major campaign.[6]

The most interesting issue about the revolt was what it revealed about the functioning of the Union's high command. In particular, senior officers in the Army of the Potomac had sought an audience with the president. The obvious question was why the chain of command was being ignored. Was this because it had not yet been fully established? Was this informed by U.S. military tradition? Senior officers in the Army of the Potomac had ignored their commanding general and had petitioned the president, the commander in chief, on a number of occasions. Why would the president allow this? Lincoln did interfere in military matters but was this just the commander in chief exercising his right to command? It certainly begs the question about how Lincoln defined the role of commander in chief during the Civil War.

The examination of McClellan and the Union's high command will inevitably bring into focus President Lincoln's role. But the aim is to study the Union's high command not from the perspective of Lincoln but that of McClellan. The Unionist interpretation of the Civil War is that Abraham Lincoln was a great president and commander in chief. Historian T. Harry Williams has best summed up this view of Lincoln: "Lincoln stands out as a great war president, probably the greatest in our history, and a great natural strategist, a better one than any of his generals."[7] According to this view, Lincoln was the self-taught military strategist who saw the path to victory more clearly than any of his generals, until General Ulysses S. Grant arrived in the East to take up the role of general in chief in 1864. This view fitted the American amateur military tradition that any American could be a great soldier just by his own natural ability and not by any formal or professional military training. However, many of the West Point–trained officers, such as McClellan, viewed the interest civilians or amateurs had in military spheres as interference that was at the least a hindrance and at worst detrimental to military strategy and operations. Did this issue affect the ability of the Union's high command to function cohesively and effectively?

The civilian/military relationship was complicated by Lincoln's determination to use his presidential powers to preserve the Union. Lincoln tried to define the role of the president by attaching the concept of "war power" to the presidency. He believed it was his solemn duty to defend the Constitution. Since the Constitution was the nation, Lincoln's view was that he could use every means to defend it. In this emergency he believed he could call out the armed forces without consulting Congress, with no formal declaration of war needed. Lincoln saw the focal point of the president's "war power" in the role of commander in chief. But the evolution of this role would create tension between Lincoln and many senior military officers.

The Union's high command comprised President Lincoln, who was also the commander in chief of the army and the navy, Lincoln's cabinet, the general in chief and senior military officers. Lincoln had a strong view about the role of the president as commander in chief in the context of the national crisis, a role provided for in the Constitution but never fully defined. This allowed Lincoln to define the functions of the commander in chief during the course of the conflict. The term general in chief was used to refer to the Commanding General of the United States Army, who was its single most senior officer. The roles and responsibilities of the general in chief were not fully defined beyond that of providing military advice to the president. Eventually, in in 1903, the position was abolished by the creation of the Chief of Staff of the United States Army. This meant that there was little to guide the civil-military relationship that was essential for the high command to work. Unless policy was put in place, the Union high command had to rely on the ability of its individual members to work cooperatively and cohesively in order to function effectively. Two sets of personality conflicts, Scott-McClellan and Lincoln-McClellan, would interfere with the effective operation of the high command and would have an impact on the Union's war aims and strategies.

The formulation and implementation of strategy is an important part of the role of the union's high command. The meaning of strategy has changed over time. What Lincoln tended to view as strategy, we would today call military operations. For the purpose of this thesis I will use the definitions that follow. "Strategy" sits in the middle of an inverted pyramid below "policy" or "war aims" and above "operations." War aims or policies inform strategy. Strategy is the deployment of military resources to achieve the desired war aim and it is put into action by military operations. "Tactics" are the domain of the battlefield and sit below operations and involve directing and deploying troops. For example, Lincoln's initial war aim was the return of the seceded states to the Union. One of the strategies employed was to use military force to secure control of the Mississippi River and compel the rebellious states to negotiate rather than face economic ruin. One of the operations used to implement this strategy was the capture of New Orleans, which blocked the mouth of the Mississippi to Confederate trade. This war aim, the return to the Union of the seceded states, is commonly referred to as a "limited" or "conciliatory" war aim. However, as the war lengthened, the Union's war aims evolved with the conflict. This created a strain within the Union's high command between those who wanted to expand the war aims of the Union to include slavery and those, like McClellan, who did not. However, there was an inherent contradiction in the Union's war aim early in the conflict between getting the seceded states to return, a limited war aim, and the destruction of the Confederate government, which was an unlimited war aim.

It is common to see a connection made between the concepts of "unlimited war" and "total war." James M. McPherson has argued that Lincoln "grasped the necessity of adopting a strategy of total war to overthrow the enemy's social and political system."[8] It is easy to see why so many have regarded the Civil War as the beginning of the twentieth century's total wars. There was mass manufacturing, mass mobilization of manpower, trench warfare, railway transportation of troops, ironclad warships, telegraph communications and huge casualty lists as a result of large battles. Mark Neely has argued, however, that while the Civil War was a modern war it did not break down the barriers between soldiers and noncombatants to the extent the two world wars in the twentieth century did.[9] It is more appropriate to describe the nature of the war the Union waged as evolving from a war of conciliation to, as Mark Grimsley has described it, a "hard war" rather than a "total war." Union policy, Grimsley has argued, moved from a limited war of restraint, in which protection was given to Confederate property, to a "hard war" policy that subjected Confederate civilians to "directed severity" so that they had to endure the horrors of war.[10] This book will be using the terms "conciliatory war" and "hard war" throughout. Certainly, McClellan and Lincoln supported limiting the impact of the war on Southern civilians, but by the second year of the war a division of opinion had emerged in the Union high command over the treatment of Southern civilians and property.

It is not the purpose here to examine the comparative merits of the Union and Confederate high command structures. However, it is worth noting that the Union and the Confederacy shared similar command problems. The Confederate president, Jefferson Davis, had the added difficulty of creating a government and military forces from scratch. This provided him with the opportunity to put into practice his views of what being president meant in regard to his role as commander in chief. It was logical and pragmatic for the Confederacy to adopt the military/political model of the United States, but Davis did not appoint a general in chief. Perhaps this innovation was based on Davis's own experience when he had been the secretary of war and had battled with general in chief Winfield Scott over who was superior in the chain of command.

Davis believed that the president was in wartime the general in chief. Davis and his secretaries of war were thus able to perform the role of commander in chief and have a strong influence on military strategy and operations.[11] Davis was well suited to the role. He had been educated at the United States Military Academy at West Point and he had experience commanding regulars and militia. In contrast, Lincoln had no military training and no military experience of any value.[12] Yet, Davis underestimated the complexity and enormity of the task in managing a war on this scale while at the same time attempting to be the Napoleonic-era leader of the nation. This type of leader was also the field commander of military forces. A Confederate general in chief was not appointed until 1865, when the action was far too late.[13]

The military task that confronted the Confederacy was as huge and as daunting as the one the Union faced. The Confederates had to defend an enormous land area including a large, exposed coastline. Davis decided he had to follow a policy to defend as much territory as possible. There were logistical issues that drove this policy and there was also the major consideration of how fragile slavery would be in the face of an invading army.[14] Davis could not trade space for time, so he made the decision to spread a cordon of troops on the border of the Confederacy. This was a problem because it meant the Confederates were weak everywhere, but it appeased states that believed they should be protected by Confederate troops. Like Lincoln, Davis had to contend with a popular push for an aggressive, offensive military strategy. Both Davis and Lincoln were under popular and political pressure to march on the respective enemy's capital because of the near proximity of the two capitals,

Richmond and Washington. Davis correctly decided against this because he did not have the military strength, but he did adopt an offensive-defensive strategy that aimed to take advantage of opportunities to bring the war to the North and threaten Union army supply lines.[15]

Both leaders had to contend with egotistical generals. Pierre G.T. Beauregard and Joseph E. Johnston were hard to handle.[16] Davis also had to manage politically appointed generals such as Gideon Johnson Pillow and David Emanuel Twiggs, who proved to be inadequate military commanders. Another factor that inhibited the working of an effective Confederate high command was Davis's unwillingness to see weaknesses and faults in his friends. General Leonidas Polk committed one of the greatest mistakes of the war when he sent troops to occupy Columbus, Kentucky, in September 1861. This rash move cost the neutrality of Kentucky and drove it into the Union. Despite this and his poor record as a commander, Davis did not dismiss him and Polk remained as a commanding officer until his death in June 1864.[17] Lincoln may not have been as tolerant as Davis was with this general. But both Lincoln and Davis were challenged with the need to find successful generals and to manage those they had in the period 1861 to 1863.

The book takes a chronological approach. The first chapter examines the military tradition of the United States and how that affected the way the Union high command responded to the Civil War. The second chapter explores the first ninety days of the war and the struggle the Union experienced to establish its war aims and strategy. It includes a focus on how Lincoln tried to define the role of the president in such a national emergency and his relationship with senior military officers. The third chapter looks at the rise of General McClellan, the McClellan/Scott feud and the struggle to define the roles of commander in chief and general in chief. Chapter Four analyzes McClellan as commander of the Army of the Potomac and as general in chief, as well as the growth of the Lincoln/McClellan conflict. Chapter Five studies the military and political tensions created by three military campaigns that eventually resulted in the sacking of McClellan. Chapter Six looks into the consequences on the Union high command of McClellan's sacking and how an influential group of pro–McClellan senior officers undermined his successor, General Burnside. The last chapter, seven, explores the ongoing problems that ensued in the Union high command in the East with the appointment of Hooker to replace Burnside and the subsequent plot to remove Hooker. This will show that the Union lacked a system of high command that could have set and implemented the war aims and strategy necessary to win the war in the first two years of the conflict and that this was accentuated by personality conflicts among the members of the Union's high command.

ONE
Citizens and Soldiers: The United States Military Tradition

When the Civil War began in 1861, the leaders of both the Union and the Confederacy looked towards the United States military tradition for guidance on how to conduct the war. The United States military tradition rested on the opposing values of the egalitarian militia and the elitist professional military. These values had been based on the experiences gained from military conflicts over two centuries, and an understanding of the events and ideas that shaped the American context is important to understanding the events of the Civil War. John Shy has argued that the consequence of this has been "a deep respect for the kind of military prowess that had become so closely bound up with the very definition of United States nationhood, a respect tinged with contempt for military professionalism which was viewed as unnecessary, ineffectual, and thus somehow un–American" as well as the view of military security in absolute terms and an optimism about the use of United States military force.[1] These views were balanced against the nation's liberal democratic ideals, which strove to limit war by establishing moral standards that restricted violence from becoming too barbaric. This view, like the first, accepted that war was part of human civilization but could be subject to reason. These liberal democratic ideals also feared standing armies because they could be used as a weapon against democratic peoples and institutions.

A defining moment for United States representations of its military tradition was the American Revolution. The popular view of the Revolution is of American citizens, in militia groups such as the "minute men," defeating British regular troops, commonly referred to as "redcoats." Military actions such as those at Lexington and Concord and the famous Battle of Bunker Hill created the paradigm that untrained American citizens, when forced to fight in a war, could defeat trained military professionals. The popular myth became accepted as fact. If the nation's citizens could repulse an enemy army then there was no need for a professional standing army, which might become involved in politics. The militia had a long and valued history in colonial North America. British settlers in America were in violent contact with Native Americans. These early British colonists were depicted as escaping the violence and political problems of Europe. The colonial governments could not fund a professional army, so they relied on the British tradition of the militia.

Some historians have described the environment that these people came to as being characterized by the extremes of uneasy truce and barbaric violence of the conflict with native North Americans. At a time when European nations were trying to limit the impact of war, particularly on civilians, the English settlers in North America had to react to the type of warfare that was typical of the Thirty Year War. English colonists fought against Native Americans in numerous military actions that were conducted as battles of survival. It was implicit in these conflicts that the military outcome was not limited to the defeat of the enemy's military forces but the total destruction of enemy settlements. The resources of the scattered populations restricted the ability of the colonists to achieve a decisive victory, which would include the total destruction or removal of the Native Americans, so that no quick victory was possible by either side.

With limited financial and human resources, twelve of the thirteen colonies passed laws for compulsory militia.[2] Every male from sixteen to sixty had to be available for militia service. Each colony had its own separate military administration. The militia was integrated into colonial life and while officers were elected, rank tended to be equated with social status. In December 1636, the Massachusetts Bay colony organized its militia into three regiments and began an organization that would become the U.S. National Guard.[3] However, the efficiency of the militia varied from colony to colony and also with the distance the militia unit was from the frontier. In the southern colonies, with their increasingly large population of African slaves, the militia became a force more concerned with internal security against slave revolt. The militia was an ad hoc defense force that accustomed the English colonists to irregular warfare and created a strong military tradition.

The early colonist conflict with Native Americans was exacerbated by European colonial rivalry in North America. England was in competition with France and Spain to control the continent's vast resources. Between 1689 and 1763 England fought in four large European wars that involved battles in North America. British regular forces were usually committed to battles on mainland Europe, so only small numbers of regulars could be spared for the defense of its North American colonies. These regular forces had to be supplemented by colonial militia. In contrast, the French colonial population was too small in comparison with the English colonists to provide an adequate military force, so the French supplemented their small military forces by using Native Americans.[4] The English colonies made use of volunteer forces to provide defense from attack. The colonial governor or the assembly selected a commanding officer, and he enlisted his men. However, enlistment periods were usually too short, officers were inexperienced, discipline was poor by European standards and there was little cooperation between the colonies to allow for any effective strategy.

Many colonials who would fight against Britain in the American Revolution gained valuable experience fighting with the British in the Seven Years War. George Washington was only twenty-two when he was given command of a force of Virginian militia. He was defeated at Great Meadows in July 1754. The next year he joined British general Edward Braddock's expedition against the French. Braddock was defeated and the survivors of the British Army included Horatio Gates, the victorious American commander at Saratoga and the iconic pioneer Daniel Boone. Despite these military setbacks, Washington's military reputation grew and in 1755 he was appointed commander in chief of the Virginia militia and given the responsibility of defending the frontier. In 1758 he was involved in General John Forbes's successful campaign against Fort Duquesne. Therefore, some facets of American colonial history were distilled into three core elements of their military tradition and formed American military policy: reliance on the militia; the use of volunteers in special circumstances; and the fear of standing armies.

The American military tradition also recognized, however, the contribution of professional military personnel. The values of the professional military is symbolized in the iconic, heroic George Washington. The war George Washington fought against the British was a political revolution but it was conducted as a conventional European war. It occurred in a time when little had changed in European methods of warfare. One of the leading military figures of this period, King Frederick the Great of Prussia, was successful because he perfected established tactical systems rather than designing new ones. The commanders of the American revolutionary armies followed the same pattern and looked to fight the war led by a professional military. The Continental Army was formed on June 14, 1775, when the Continental Congress adopted the New England Army. The next day Washington was placed in command. Congress also created four major generals and a series of staff officers, a pattern that closely followed the British model.

George Washington was part of an influential group of Americans who sought independence from Britain but without a social revolution. This political value influenced Washington's command of the Continental Army. He believed he could defeat Britain, not by a mass uprising but by raising and training a professional army. He fought his campaigns and battles in a manner that was similar to European armies of the same period. While the Americans' experience in fighting Native Americans resulted in a tendency to use open formations, this did not have a significant impact on American tactical systems. It was Washington's determination to preserve his Continental regulars that provided the base for American success in the war.[5] Russell F. Weigley has argued that Washington adopted a strategy of attrition to defeat the British. This was a risky policy because it was defensive and was based on the assumption that a protracted war could increase the chances of foreign intervention on the American side and also erode political support for the war in Britain. Certainly, Washington had no choice to fight on the strategic defense. Britain's sea power enabled it to take the offensive and to strike at will along the Atlantic seaboard. Washington was, therefore, not seeking a military victory but a political victory and this is why it was so important to avoid the Continental Army's being decisively defeated in battle.[6]

Washington acknowledged the success of the militia; he also witnessed its failure many times. The famous painting by Emmanuel Leutze of Washington crossing the Delaware leading his army on a raid on the Hessian barracks at Trenton tells only part of that story. It does not tell of the militia who failed to assist him. Washington's concern with the militia was that they were no match for regular British troops: "[W]hen opposed to Troops regularly train'd, disciplined, and appointed, superior in knowledge, and superior in Arms, makes them timid, and ready to fly from their own shadows."[7] Nathanael Greene, another American general, shared a similar view concerning the reliability of the militia: "people coming from home with all the tender feelings of domestic life" were inadequately trained so that they were "sufficiently fortified with national courage to stand the shocking scenes of war."[8]

Washington's experience as a military commander led him to the conclusion that the success of the Revolution depended on a "respectable Army,"[9] and by a respectable army he meant a European-style army. In a letter to Congress in 1776 Washington lamented the unreliable nature of the militia: "Come in you cannot tell how, go, you cannot tell when; and act, you cannot tell where; Consume your Provisions, exhaust your Stores, and leave you at last in a critical moment. These Sir are the Men I am to depend upon Ten days hence, — this is the basis on which your Case will and must for ever depend, till you get a large Standing Army."[10] Nevertheless, despite the concerns of American military commanders such as Washington, the myth of the American "minute men" came to dominate Americans' image of themselves as warriors.

John Galvin has explored the evolution of the American militia and has concluded that the common perceptions of the militia by the time of the Revolution were far from the reality. Galvin argued that by the time of the American Revolution the militia was "a well-organized, well-equipped, and relatively well-trained army of 14,000 men." The myth was that these men fought well with little equipment, training and organization. The militia myth was created when the militia concept was under attack during the nineteenth century as a means to justify its existence.[11] The creation of this myth may also reflect a need to redress the dominant view immediately after the end of the Revolutionary War. Histories during this period highlighted the success of the Continental Army and its leader, General Washington.[12] Stewart H. Holbrook has come to a similar conclusion by examining prints of the battle at Lexington. The earliest representation in 1775 depicts the British troops in their solid formation as the colonists flee before them. An 1830 depiction gave more focus on the colonists. In this print some of the colonists are firing at the British. Representations from the 1850s are dominated by the colonists, who are standing resolute and firing at the British.[13]

Even the officers of the Continental Army valued the citizen soldier so highly that they formed the Society of the Cincinnati at the end of the Revolutionary War in 1783.[14] Lucius Cincinnatus, according to Roman tradition, was appointed dictator in 458 BC and within fifteen days had rescued a besieged Roman army, celebrated the victory and returned to his farm. The most important aspect of the story was that at the end of the conflict he willingly returned to the Roman Republic the power he had been given in wartime. Cincinnatus, a farmer, soldier and politician, was represented as the model Roman. He symbolized the virtues of the citizen soldier. Many American army officers identified with this Roman republican hero.

The American colonists' victory over Britain was formalized by the Treaty of Paris on September 24, 1783. American strategy had proved successful, but the war had been lengthy as a result. With peace, Congress had to decide how best to defend the new nation. It accepted the dominant view that a militia and not a regular standing army could best achieve the defense of the nation. Congress was also influenced by prevailing concerns about the threat a standing army could pose to the young democracy and the financial strain it would place on the country's meager financial resources. Even Washington believed a "large standing Army in Peace hath ever been considered dangerous to the liberties of a country"; however, he balanced this with the view that a "few Troops" would be "indispensably necessary."[15]

The United States enshrined the value of the American militia to the American military heritage in its constitution. The debate between the Federalists, who supported a strong federal government and a standing army, and the Anti-Federalists, who sought less federal control and a strong reliance on the states militia, was reflected in the Constitution. The first ten amendments to the Constitution are referred to as "The Bill of Rights." The Second Amendment was the military policy of the young republic: "A well regulated Militia, being necessary to the security of a free State, the right of the people to keep and bear Arms, shall not be infringed."[16] Yet it is important to note that the composers of the Constitution recognized that strong central control was needed to improve the militia. A "well regulated militia" meant regulation by federal, not state, authorities. Furthermore, to strengthen the federal government the president was the commander in chief of federal forces as well as "the Militia of the several States, when called into the active Service of the United States."[17]

Washington accepted the need for a militia, but not the type he had experienced during the Revolutionary War. He wanted to enroll all males between eighteen and fifty in a nationally established militia based on the Swiss model. This militia would be involved in standardized training. Central to this model was a "special force" of well-trained militia that could be used to handle a foreign military attack until regular troops could be concentrated. Washington had support from the chairman of the congressional committee established to determine the issue. Secretary of the Treasury Alexander Hamilton preferred a national army and his recommendations were close to those of Washington.[18]

Finally, Congress agreed in 1784 to recruit a new regular army consisting of a regiment of eight companies and two artillery companies. Also, the Constitutional Convention in 1787 further defined the powers of the federal government. The Constitution strengthened the powers of that body by allowing it to raise and maintain a standing army. Yet Congress controlled the funding of the army and funding could be approved for only two years at a time. This further reflected the tension between the states, which controlled the militia, and the new federal system of government, which had power to maintain a federal army and navy. In effect, military activity was left to the states. There was still a strong feeling that an army was equated to an instrument of tyranny. One New York newspaper argued the anti-federalist sentiment of many at the time: "A free republic will never keep a standing army to execute its laws."[19]

Interestingly, the Constitution innovatively gave all executive power to the president. Consequently, the secretary for war was responsible to the president and not Congress. Furthermore, it allowed the president to be commander in chief of the army and navy. He could take personal charge of the forces in the field or he could delegate that authority. This put the military under the control of the civilian administration. Washington was elected the first president of the United States in April 1789, and in August he formed the Department of War. But while the Constitution put the military under civilian control, the election of Washington was supported by a representation of American nationalism that saw heroism in war as a high ideal.[20]

Washington had to manage his belief in regular soldiers with the popular support for a militia as the basis of American military policy. He believed that at least two and a half thousand regulars were needed to provide the background for any American military effort. Such a small force would have to rely on the militia in times of crisis. But Washington did not want the armed citizens that comprised the militia of the revolution; he wanted a new, trained militia. The Constitution valued the protection of free government to the extent that it obliged its citizens to defend it. This defined a defensive military strategy based on the militia, and regular forces would be directed to provide a police force and order in "Indian Territory." Washington was uneasy with the revolutionary nation in arms model. Yet he was also uneasy with the connection that many Americans made between the Regular Army and taxation. He was concerned as well that most Americans believed the American Revolution had demonstrated that there was no need for an expensive military.[21]

The reliance on the militia for national defense was formalized by the Militia Act of 1792: "That whenever the United States shall be invaded, or be in imminent danger of invasion from any foreign nation or Indian tribe, it shall be lawful for the President of the United States, to call forth such number of the militia of the state or states most convenient to the place of danger or scene of action as he may judge necessary to repel such invasion, and to issue his orders for that purpose...."[22] This act sought to strengthen the militia by standardizing it and placing it under increasing federal control. It achieved neither of its aims, but it did reinforce the national military policy of volunteers supporting a small force of regulars in wartime.

The young United States republic had no strategy to deal with a European military threat, other than the resort to militia. There was logic in this view. The United States was geographically distant enough from Europe to deter a European power from an attack because of the resources that would need to be deployed to give a numerical advantage. Also, the United States was spread across a large land area. This made it vulnerable to attacks at weak points, as the British had demonstrated but also made it hard for an invading army to occupy. The advance of a numerically superior European population that was prepared to deal with the Native American population violently was addressing the problem of the conflict with Native Americans on the "frontier" without the need for a large force of regulars. So with these views and the financial restraints, there appeared to be no reason to have a regular army larger than a regiment and no need at all for a navy.[23]

These issues were thrown into sharp relief by events in Europe. The French Revolution began a new phase in the conflict between Britain and France. American military policy became a series of responses to international conflict. Experience had taught Americans that European conflicts were always fought in the New World as well as Europe. Both sides made demands on American neutrality and opportunistic attacks by the Barbary pirates, who operated out of their stronghold along the Barbary Coast of North Africa, put further pressure on military planning. In 1794 America began to improve its coastal fortifications. Federalist congressmen promoted the building of six navy frigates. When America agreed to peace with Algiers, Congress still approved the construction of three frigates. The undeclared war with France in 1798 motivated Congress to build all six of the frigates. During this international crisis, Benjamin Stoddert, who became the first secretary of the navy, outlined an ambitious naval strategy that included twelve ships of the line. Congress approved six, but peace with France removed the compulsion to realize these plans.

Thomas Jefferson, who had served as Washington's secretary of state, began his presidency in 1801 by reducing military expenditure as part of a general belief in the principles of "frugal Government." He was suspicious of standing armies and viewed "a well disciplined militia, our best reliance in peace and for the first moments of war, till regulars may relieve them; the supremacy of the civil over the military authority"[24] as the best military policy. With strong support from the south and west Jefferson also had little interest in a navy. Indeed, the Jeffersonian emphasis on the militia was mirrored in its naval policy. Jefferson proposed a fleet of small, fast, armed ships, an idea inspired by the Barbary pirates. One hundred and seventy-six of these one-gun vessels were eventually built. It was envisaged that only six to eight would be operational in peacetime and the rest would become active in war and manned by naval militia.[25] Despite his mistrust of professional standing armies Jefferson created the United States Military Academy in 1801. This was recognized by Congress in the Military Peace Establishment Act of 1802, which also set the army at three thousand three hundred men. The academy and the act were designed with the political aim to reduce Federalist influence in the army and to "Republicanize" the army.

Jefferson's view of standing armies and the value of the militia was reinforced by his successor, James Madison. Madison's opinions reflected those of many at the time who argued that republics and standing armies were incompatible; yet, at the same time, they recognized the need to balance their ideals with the need for security, "to keep within the requisite limits a standing military force, always remembering that an armed and trained militia is the firmest bulwark of republics—that without standing armies their liberty can never be in danger, nor with large ones safe."[26]

The United States was not prepared for its next military conflict. The War of 1812 was a by-product of the Napoleonic Wars. The seizure of American ships and the impressment of American citizens into the British Navy increased tensions between the United States and Britain. As a result, Congress voted for war on June 4, 1812. Major General Andrew Jackson of the U.S. 2nd Division believed the war could be won by the militia. He argued the United States "has not deemed it necessary to recur to the common mode of filing the ranks of the army." Instead a "simple invitation is given to the young men of the country to arm for their own and their countries [sic] rights."[27] From the beginning, President James Madison's political objective—respect for the American flag at sea—could not be met by its military resources. With no navy, Madison decided he could achieve this objective indirectly by attacking Canada. There were only seven thousand British and Canadian regulars in Canada, which made it a tempting target for American attack. Opinion was divided, however, in America, about the war. The state of New England in particular strongly opposed it. The American attacks on Canada failed and the British navy proved the folly of the gunboat policy. As early as November 1812 President Madison recognized America lacked a high command structure and regular officers to effectively fight the British. In his State of the Nation address he recommended "a provision for an increase of the general officers of the Army, the deficiency of which has been illustrated." He continued: "I can not press too strongly on the earliest attention of the Legislature the importance of the reorganization of the staff establishment." Madison also noted the need to reform the militia.[28]

By February 1815 the war had reached a negotiated conclusion. The American victory by Andrew Jackson's militia at New Orleans near the end of the war indicated to many Americans that they had won the war. Most historians have assessed it as a draw. The fighting of the war favored neither Britain nor the United States. Indeed, the British government viewed it as a sideshow to the real war against Napoleon. The American militia, which was relied upon to form the basis of the American army, performed comparably with the Regular Army. However, the militia was not as reliable.[29]

The lesson of this war went beyond the militia and regular soldier debate. The real lesson was not the performance of the regulars at Chippewa and

Lundys Lane, because the militia and the regulars had been active for the same amount of time. The difference was in the degree of military leadership. Brigadier General Winfield Scott had trained the regulars in minor tactics. After the war Scott prepared a tactical manual for infantry, "system 1815," which was later replaced by his "system 1825." In 1834 this was modified to include elements from the Prussian drill manual. This remained standard until Captain William J. Hardee's manual just before the start of the Civil War. Consequently, Weigley has described Scott as the "preeminent figure in American military history for four and a half decades after the War of 1812."[30]

William B. Skelton has concluded that the War of 1812 "marked a major transition in the history of the military profession."[31] American setbacks in the War of 1812 added momentum to the idea of creating a professional army and for standardization. General Winfield Scott's study tour to Paris in 1815 to examine the military lessons of the Napoleonic Wars identified the theoretical support for a professional military. Scott based a new manual for infantry tactics for regulars and the army regulations of 1821 on his research in Paris. General Antoine Henrei Jomini's study of the military lessons of the Napoleonic Wars, titled *Traite des Grandes operations Militaires* (1804–05), began a fascination for the theory and practice of Napoleonic warfare by American military theorists and educators. Consequently, Jomini's *Precis de l'Art de la Guerre* (1838) had a significant impact on military practice and thought in the United States.[32]

The fear of a new war with Britain encouraged Congress, which had to meet in Blodgett's Hotel in February 1815 because the Capitol was in ruins, voted to form a peacetime army of 10,000. Secretary of War Crawford recommended the return of the General Staff. Crawford argued for "the necessity of giving the military establishment, in time of peace, the organization which it must have to render it efficient in a state of war."[33] A quartermaster general was added to the staff in Washington and the Corps of Engineers was increased. General Simon Bernard was placed in charge and began to supervise a program to build coastal fortifications. As part of further reforms, more resources were directed to the U.S. Military Academy at West Point to guarantee that a solid core of trained professional officers were available to command the Regular Army.[34] Of importance, the academy became the main entry point into the officer corps, providing cohesion and camaraderie. In an attempt to streamline military procedures, Superintendent Sylvannus Thayer, who was appointed in 1817, standardized the curriculum and rules of the academy. During his sixteen-year tenure Thayer instigated a great number of changes, which earned him the title "Father of West Point."[35]

A protégé of Thayer, Dennis Mahan, joined the Academy in 1832. He promoted the emphasis for professional study as an integral part of a professional officer corps vigorously. This would allow officers to be flexible and pragmatic in their decision making because they would be able to adapt the rules of war learned from textbook study. Mahan believed in the conservative European military tradition as the solution for America's military needs and in particular he romanticized the study of Napoleon. West Point Military Academy was an important part of this solution. West Point was not an equivalent to the Prussian "Kriegsakademie" or the French "Ecole Polytechnique." However, Mahan and his associates made important and significant contributions to American military thought.[36]

West Point developed under French influence and therefore looked to the French-Swiss military writer Henri Baron de Jomini, who had worked as a staff officer with Marshal Ney in the French Army during the Napoleonic Wars. Jomini soon progressed to Napoleon's staff, but jealousy and personal conflict forced him to leave the service of the French. In 1814 he joined the Russian Army as a staff officer for the campaigns that year. He wrote a biography of Napoleon and his *Précis de l'Art de la Guerre* (1838) was the most influential of any foreign military study on American military thought.[37] Jomini did not examine the relationship between war and society in as much depth as Clausewitz had done. Instead, he focused on the military questions of strategy, tactics and logistics. But Jomini's main focus was on operations such as turning movements and not on strategy and war aims or national policy. Clausewitz recognized the potential of war to become chaotic. Jomini defined war in terms of patterns formed by rival armies and universal rules of warfare. Clausewitz looked at the revolutionary nature of the wars of the French Revolution and Napoleon, while Jomini thought of war in terms of the limited wars of the eighteenth century. Thus the American army looked to the conservative European traditions of war.[38]

However, it is not clear how much impact the teachings of Mahan had on the students at the academy. Only 29 percent of the four-year program was devoted to military tactics and the science of war and these topics were taught only in the fourth year and allocated only nine hours of teaching time. Mathematics, science and engineering were a major part of the West Point curriculum and also determined the cadets' ranking in their class. The curriculum's emphasis on engineering reflected the fear of a European naval threat and therefore the need for coastal defenses. It is also hard to determine the level of Jominian influence on graduates from the academy and their future conduct in the Civil War. Beauregard, Lee, Halleck and McClellan studied Jomini and this may have influenced how they conducted military operations; however Sherman, another West Point graduate, believed that

Jomini did not influence his thinking or his military operations during the Civil War.[39]

Furthermore, Jomini's' *Summary of the Art of War* was not included into the West Point curriculum until 1859, which lends weight to the argument that the Jominian influence was not as significant as had generally been accepted.[40] Nevertheless, it is easy to see that the extent of Jominian influence might not be a result of how many had read it but who had read it. Certainly Halleck and McClellan were strong proponents of Jomini and these men held positions in the Union high command early in the war and were thus able to determine the strategic direction and operations of the conflict.[41]

After Mahan, Henry W. Halleck was the main exponent of Jomini's theory of war. Halleck had appropriated much of Jomini's theories in *Precis de l'Art de la Guerre* into his *Elements of Military Art and Science*. Weigley described Halleck as "the early fruition of Mahan's West Point system in an American equivalent to Jomini."[42] Halleck emphasized to the readers of *Elements of Military Art and Science* the importance of a trained army and especially a trained officer corps. In a rebuttal of the amateur soldier tradition Halleck argued the importance of foreign officers to the American Revolution because the colonial army lacked an officer corps trained in the science of war. It was this emphasis on the study of warfare as a science that was the basis of the rationale for a professional army. This view was an attack on the dominant Jacksonian emphasis on the military amateur. The Jacksonian view recognized the potential of the individual and in particular the more capable individuals, who in a time of crisis could match the best European commanders through natural ability. However, Halleck argued that not every soldier possessed the intellectual ability to achieve this, nor could the American army hope to always find a military genius to avert a military disaster. The safest and most reliable way to ensure the American army was provided with the best leadership was to have its officers study the principles of war: "War is not, as some seem to suppose, a mere game of chance. Its principles constitute one of the most intricate of modern sciences; and the general who understands the art of rightly applying its rules, and possesses the means of carrying out its precepts, may be morally certain of success."[43]

Halleck listed numerous examples from history to argue that trained armies had accomplished more that untrained armies. He referred to Washington's many complaints about the militia and went on to argue how a small number of regular troops could have prevented the Black Hawk War in 1832 and the Seminole War, and that a well-trained army of twelve thousand men, which could have advanced to the Rio Grande in 1846, might have averted the Mexican War. Halleck therefore stressed the need for an enlarged regular army that could be expanded in wartime. This was consistent with Calhoun's "Report on the Reduction of the Army." The expansible army was the main platform of the supporters of a professional army as a way of reconciling the dominant view supporting the militia tradition and the fear of a large standing army. Halleck, like Jomini and Mahan, was a believer in the offensive. This aggressive approach to war required highly trained troops. The warfare of the offensive thus became equated to the warfare of professionals. Halleck had argued that the importance of the militia was its ability to fight well on the defensive.[44]

However, an expansible army required an appropriate high command system. Halleck, like others before him, was concerned that the United States was lacking in this crucial area. Conflicting authority divided the system in place. This was the main concern between the secretary of war and the commanding general. The Corps of Engineers and the Quartermaster's Department were independent organizations, over which the commanding general of the army had little authority. Also there was little in the way of units higher than regiments and a lack of generals to provide a sense of high command. Halleck proposed the creation of a professional general staff corps comprising officers with special staff training.[45]

John C. Calhoun was appointed secretary of war on December 8, 1817. Calhoun had been a keen supporter of war against Britain and he now had to fight proposals to cut army strength and remove the General Staff and the military academy. These proposals were given less priority when the tensions between Native Americans and European settlers near the border between Georgia and the Spanish colony of Florida escalated into the First Seminole War in December 1817. Andrew Jackson was placed in command of U.S. troops. The movement of Jackson's army, a mixture of regulars and militia, was ultimately successful in removing the threat to American territory, even though the American army had invaded Spanish territory and captured Spanish forts. These actions did not have any serious diplomatic consequences with Spain because negotiations for the United States' purchase of Spain's Florida territory were well advanced. The Adams-Onis Treaty ceded Florida to the United States in 1819. For the U.S. Army, the breakdown in logistics had been the significant lesson of this war and the War of 1812. The main logistical problem was the reliance on civilian contractors who proved to be unreliable. Congress, in response to Calhoun's recommendation, created, for the first time since the Revolutionary War, a Subsistence Department, under the control of a commissary general of subsistence.[46]

United States strategy was increasingly influenced by the expanding American frontier into Native American territory. The Regular Army, sometimes aided by the militia or locally raised units, played a role in the Age of Manifest Destiny. Indeed, Calhoun's reforms complemented President Monroe's foreign policy announced as part of his annual message to Congress on December 2, 1823. In what became known as the Monroe Doctrine, Monroe informed the Old World powers that the American continents were no longer open to European colonization and that America would "consider any attempt on their part to extend their system to any portion of this hemisphere as dangerous to our peace and safety."[47]

The antebellum period of 1781–1860 saw the increased professionalism of the officer corps and the replacement of the traditional militia units by volunteer forces of the national guard. Calhoun believed that regular troops and not militia provided the best means to protect the frontier. However, to maintain a regular army with a force capable of defending the entire frontier and seacoast was beyond the manpower and financial resources of the nation. Congress was eager to reduce the Regular Army and pressured the secretary of war to reduce the army to six thousand. Calhoun planned to cut the Regular Army by reducing the number of troops in companies and not cut regiments so that the army could be rapidly expanded for war to a force of approximately nineteen thousand. The "expansible army" concept, which had also been espoused by Hamilton, was a compromise between the need for a regular army and the reliance on the militia. Calhoun therefore defined national military strategy as based on the navy as the first line of defense, behind which would be the army. In March 1821 Congress reduced the Regular Army from eight regiments of infantry to seven—four regiments of artillery, a rifle regiment, a regiment of light artillery and a corps of artillery comprising eight battalions. Congress had ignored the idea of an expansible army, possibly because a simplistic form of isolationism, the fear of European-modeled standing armies and the fear that some states still had over federal control of their militia during wartime all weighted against the reforms.

But the command structure was revised and an Eastern Division under Brigadier General Winfield Scott and a Western Division under Major General Jacob Brown replaced the Northern and Southern divisions. To facilitate a more effective high command structure in time of war, Calhoun moved General Brown to Washington to hold a position, which would be called the "commanding general of the army." Major General Alexander Macomb succeeded General Brown in 1828. In 1841 Major General Winfield Scott, who in 1847 became the first three-star general since George Washington, took over the position he would hold until the early part of the Civil War in 1861.[48]

Even in the late 1820s some Americans were still concerned about the size of standing armies. President Andrew Jackson, in his first inaugural address on March 4, 1829, referred to "standing armies as dangerous to free governments in time of peace, I shall not seek to enlarge our present establishment, nor disregard that salutary lesson of political experience which teaches that the military should be held subordinate to the civil power." While he was suspicious of standing armies, Jackson had a positive view of the militia, which he saw as the "bulwark of our defense ... which in the present state of our intelligence and population must render us invincible."[49]

Tensions between European settlers and Native Americans culminated in the Second Seminole War in 1832. General Scott left Washington in 1836 for Florida to take command of a maneuver from Tampa. Logistical problems hampered American military movements. However, unlike the first war, the logistical difficulties were reduced to the transportation of troops. Scott was removed from active operations when he was unjustly blamed for delays in military operations. The war was concluded in 1842 after Colonel William J. Worth campaigned through the summer of 1841, which prevented the Indians from raising and harvesting crops. Worth's strategy was to ruthlessly destroy the Indian communities and food supplies. This strategy reflected the guerrilla warfare nature of the conflict. Significantly, this mode of warfare was representative of American views about it, which had been shaped by many decades of irregular warfare between themselves and Native Americans. Weigley has argued that as a consequence of this, Americans came to see war as a conflict for total victory.[50] Shy has argued that the frequency of warfare with Native Americans cannot be exaggerated and that Americans saw warfare as retribution for violence, not as protection from violence.[51]

The westward movement of the frontier inevitably pushed America into conflict with its southern neighbor, Mexico. The Oregon Trail led many American settlers into Upper California, but most American emigration into Mexican territory was to Texas. In March 1836, American settlers proclaimed their independence from Mexico. The settlers knew this would force the Mexicans, commanded by General Antonio Lopez de Santa Ana, to seek to crush what was from the Mexican perspective a rebellion. The American militia garrison at the Alamo was destroyed. However, in April General Sam Houston's Texan army defeated Santa Ana at San Jacinto. This was the decisive battle of the "Texas Revolution." An American army under General Gaines, which had been positioned on the frontier of Louisiana, moved into Texas and occupied Nacogdoches to prevent any Mexican reinforcements from swinging the military balance back in favor of the Mexicans. For almost ten years Texas remained an independent nation, keen to be annexed by the United States but delayed because annexation was linked to the divisive issue of slavery. This problem was further complicated by the domestic debate over slavery. Many in the north saw the attempt to annex Texas as a means of extending slavery. During this time, Mexico refused to recognize the independence of Texas. The border remained tense, marked by fierce raids by both sides.[52]

James K. Polk's election as president in November 1844 provided the catalyst for the U.S. annexation of Texas. In his inaugural address, Polk regarded "the question of annexation as belonging exclusively to the United States and Texas." This was part of his plan to extend the United States: "by all constitutional means the right of the United States to that portion of our territory which lies beyond the Rocky Mountains."[53] In March 1845 Congress formally admitted Texas into the union. Mexico responded by severing diplomatic relations. Polk hoped to resolve the crisis through a negotiated settlement that would also include the purchase of Upper California. When negotiations broke down in February 1846, Bvt. Brigadier General Zachary Taylor advanced to the Rio Grande. Taylor's army of about four thousand troops, many of whom were regulars, was victorious at Palo Alto and Resaca de la Palma. In this army were West Point graduates George C. Meade and Ulysses S. Grant. Congress declared war on May 13, 1846, and approved the increase of the army from 8,500 to 15,450. The president was authorized to call for 50,000 volunteers for either one-year service or the duration of the war.[54]

American strategy had one clear objective: to take all Mexican territory north of the Rio Grande and west to the Pacific. Concerned that General Scott was taking too long in his preparations to move an army to Mexico, Polk promoted Taylor and placed him in command of the U.S. Army in Mexico. In August Taylor moved on Monterrey with six thousand troops, including a West Point graduate who had recently been elected to Congress, Colonel Jefferson Davis. Taylor captured Monterrey, but with significant losses because he decided on an assault on the city's defenses. Taylor's decision to fight at Buena Vista was also costly, but it did fit well with the American public's representations of heroic, masculine combat. Indeed Taylor, who had a dislike of professional military, had fought in a manner that was consistent with the tradition of Bunker Hill. His operations in northern Mexico were too far from the political center of Mexico to have any political impact on deciding the war, but the heroic status that Taylor had acquired as a result of his victories was perceived as a threat to the Democrat President Polk. Therefore the decision was made to reduce Taylor's army by redeploying its regulars, under Scott, to the main maneuver toward the Mexican capital.

General Scott's invasion of Mexico via Vera Cruz finally began in March 1847. He had a clear strategic objective, namely the capture of the capital of

Mexico, and he skillfully and successfully maneuvered his army to Mexico City, which surrendered on September 14. Scott's thorough preparation for the movement of his army allowed him to make brilliant turning movements, such as at Cerro Gordo and Pedregal. In contrast to Taylor, Scott avoided costly battle in favor of maneuver. This was very much in the eighteenth century tradition, rather than the warfare of Napoleon, who sought the decisive, costly battle at every opportunity. Robert E. Lee described Scott's attention to detail: "He sees everything and counts the cost of every measure." Scott acknowledged the contribution of the troops, particularly the regulars and the West Point graduates. One of these graduates, Ulysses S. Grant, evaluated the success of the campaign as "due to the troops engaged.... But the plans and the strategy were the general's."[55]

The Mexican War also reinforced brevet second lieutenant of engineers George B. McClellan's negative views of the militia. He complained in his diary: "I have seen more suffering since I came out here than I could have imagined to exist. It is really awful. I allude to the sufferings of the Volunteers. They literally die like dogs. Were it all known in the States, there would be no more hue and cry against the Army, all would be willing to have so large a regular army that we could dispense entirely with the volunteer system. The suffering among the Regulars is comparatively trifling, for their officers know their duty and take good care of the men."[56] He was also critical of the undisciplined behavior of the volunteers towards Mexican civilians and the inability of volunteer generals to command their troops.[57]

The Treaty of Guadalupe Hidalgo formally ended the war. The United States agreed to pay compensation of fifteen million dollars to Mexico and to assume all unpaid claims by Americans against Mexico. Mexico for its part recognized the Rio Grande as the new border and ceded New Mexico and Upper California to the United States, thus losing almost half of its territory to the United States. The U.S Army became occupied in the administration and exploration of this immense territory.

The Mexican War solidified Scott as one of the most important influences on the U.S. military and its strategic planning. His lengthy and distinguished service, his translating several French military manuals into English, and his writing of a three-volume training and drill manual seemed to be surpassed by his quick and spectacular victory over Mexico. In 1855 he received the honor of promotion to lieutenant general. Significantly, 130 future Civil War generals served under Scott in Mexico.

The Mexican War had important consequences for the officer corps. The officer corps valued planning for future wars and formal education as well as the more traditional representations of leadership, which included courage, military bearing and a natural brilliance.[58] Robert E. May has argued that the Mexican War finally established the officer corps favorably with American civilians. May has noted that West Point had been criticized for the aristocratic values it exposed and the waste of public money on graduates who sought careers in private enterprise. Some state politicians had even gone so far as to move to abolish it. However, the heroic achievements of the West Pointers in Mexico destroyed this negative attitude. The Mexican War added an aura to West Point, which helped to turn it "into a breeding ground for Manifest Destiny apostles."[59]

An extreme representation of Manifest Destiny was filibusters. Before 1900, the term referred to American adventurers who raised or participated in private ventures that involved invading or planning to invade countries the United States was at peace with. This practice was contrary to international law and the laws of the United States. The most famous filibuster was William Walker, who invaded Mexican Lower California in 1853–54 and in 1855 fought in the Nicaraguan Civil War. He eventually became Nicaragua's president. As a social phenomenon it has been explained as a product of the southern military tradition or a consequence of the disruption caused by the Californian Gold Rush. For students at West Point, it is easy to see the empathy for filibusters in the heroic image of the officer and the desire for military adventure. Some officers who participated in filibusters would later serve as generals in the Civil War. P.G.T. Beauregard was keen to join Walker in Nicaragua. However, Walker's 1856 sacking of Granada convinced Beauregard not to support him. In 1857 George B. McClellan, Johnson Kelly Duncan, Gustavus Smith and Lovell, all of whom would serve as generals in the Civil War, corresponded about joining Walker in Nicaragua. When this failed to be realized, Lovell and Johnson in 1858 negotiated sending four thousand filibusters to support Mexican liberals in the Mexican Civil War. As late as 1860, Major James Longstreet wanted to raise a regiment of volunteers for an expedition into Mexico to take Chihuahua.[60]

On the eve of the Civil War, the United States military tradition did not prepare the nation for the scale and intensity of the conflict. The citizens' right to bear arms and the obligation of the citizens to defend the Constitution and democracy motivated people in the north and the south to fight but did not prepare them for the type of war they would fight. The United States had modeled its military institutions, from the militia to the Regular Army, on European models. The impetus toward a stronger regular army, a high command structure supported and staffed by professional and trained officers, was stymied by the political values of the American Republic. The values of professional officers were seen to be at odds with those who believed in the amateur military tradition. This divide would hinder the Union's high command from working cohesively, a situation complicated by the political tensions between the federal government and the states. The reforms Calhoun had strived for, as well as the idealistic goals of Mahan, Halleck and Scott, had floundered because the United States was not, at this point in its history, a unitary political entity such as the United Kingdom, France and Prussia. The increasing professionalism of Regular Army officers had helped to develop a pool of trained professionals who would be capable of leading armies, but there would not be enough of these to meet the scope of the conflict even in 1861. Indeed, the scope of the war was beyond the best endeavors of those who had advocated having an expansible army and would place military and political strains on the United States high command as it tried to deal with the conflict.

Two

The Ninety-Day War and the Struggle for High Command

When the Civil War began in April 1861 the political leaders in the North and its citizens expected a quick war with little loss of life. Secretary of State William H. Seward predicted "there would be no serious fighting after all; the South would collapse."[1] With greater resources and a moral cause, many people looked to the U.S. military heritage and were not worried about lack of military preparedness or the lack of training for the troops. The American military heritage held that battles and wars were won by superior causes and backed by courage, manliness and natural ingenuity. These factors were more than enough to overcome lack of military training and lack of military professionals. The leaders and the citizens in the South shared similar views. During the first ninety days of the war these values and beliefs would be tested by the realities of the war and challenged by the small, professional officer corps as the Union high command came to terms with how to defeat the rebellion and, more immediate and pressing, how to protect the capital of Washington.

The election of Abraham Lincoln in November 1860 to the presidency of the United States was the catalyst that sparked a political crisis over the long-standing issue of the expansion of slavery into the new territories in the West. Lincoln and his party were opposed to the expansion of slavery into these areas. Many slave states felt threatened to the extent that they broke away from the United States and organized themselves into a "Confederacy." Many inside and outside the United States believed Lincoln's political problems to be so endless and insurmountable that he would accept the collapse of the union. The Confederates were keen to take over U.S.-held forts in their territory. Lincoln advised the governor of South Carolina that he intended to resupply Fort Sumter, South Carolina, with provisions only. The local Confederate military commander, General Pierre G.T. Beauregard, began the bombardment of Fort Sumter on April 12, 1861. This event is commonly regarded as the beginning of the Civil War. The fort surrendered on April 14, 1861, and its garrison was transported to a U.S. fleet outside Charleston Harbor to be taken to New York. The Confederate attack helped President Lincoln's efforts to preserve the Union because the Confederates had appeared to act as the aggressor. Consequently, Lincoln proclaimed, on April 15, that the states of South Carolina, Georgia, Alabama, Florida, Mississippi, Louisiana and Texas were in a state of insurrection against the Constitution of the United States. In essence, he had declared war on the rebellious southern states but in fact he never did for fear that such a move would have recognized the legitimacy of the Confederate government.

The United States Regular Army was in no position to provide a quick military solution to the crisis. Its small size meant that it did not have the strength to make an immediate response. This was how many of America's political leaders, with a mistrust of a large standing army and the Constitution, intended it. The Regular Army was deliberately kept small so that it could not be used against the liberties of American citizens. The U.S. Army was structured into departments that were created by Secretary of War John C. Calhoun and later expanded by Secretary of War Davis in 1853. The Regular Army was divided into seven war departments, six of which were west of the Mississippi. This reflected the role it was playing as an ad hoc police force on the frontier. Each department had developed into a powerful institution by 1861. While this administrative structure was efficient in peacetime, it proved to be clumsy and ineffective in organizing hundreds of thousands of troops in the conflict ahead. With only 1,080 officers and 14,926 troops, however, the Regular Army was inadequate to force the states of the newly formed Confederacy to return to the union.[2] There were eight hundred and eighty-six West Point graduates on the active list. The effectiveness of the U.S. Army to deal with the crisis was weakened by the resignation or dismissal of two hundred and ninety-six active officers. One hundred and eighty-four of these decided to serve the South. General in Chief Winfield Scott was one of a number of prominent southerners who fought for the union.[3]

The small Regular Army could be used in two ways. First, it could be held together as an elite force similar to the elite guards units of European armies. This would be similar to the manner in which Washington had used the Continental Army in the American Revolution and how General Scott had fought the Mexican War by keeping regulars and volunteers separate. Second, the regulars could be used as a cadre for the volunteers and dispersed among them to provide leadership, knowledge and experience. The scale of

President Abraham Lincoln, February, 1861 (Library of Congress).

the mobilization was beyond Calhoun's "expansible army" concept and there was a shortage of officers. With no plan, the Regular Army was used in both ways as a pragmatic response to the crisis. The Union army mirrored United States armies from the past. It would be a combination of regulars, volunteer and militia. The volunteers began as a mainly state force and the militia were state forces until they were mustered into federal service. However, the militia had become dilapidated to the extent that they were ineffective. Russel H. Beatie has concluded they "would never be a truly federal force."[4]

The decision was made to keep the small Regular Army intact and not to disperse it through the volunteer units. This policy was initially criticized by those who believed that regular troops could have helped to develop much more discipline and training in volunteer units. However, Lincoln did not expect a long war and most of the regular troops remained on the frontier until new trained units could replace them. There was also a concern that a breakdown in morale would occur with the dismantling of regular regiments. Regular officers in 1861 were loath to accept a commission in the volunteers because they had to first resign a regular commission unless the War Department specially released them. This did not mean, however, that trained officers could not gain advancement in the Regular Army by first serving in the volunteers. U.S. Military Academy graduates Ulysses S. Grant and William T. Sherman asked for volunteer command when they reentered the military.[5]

Lincoln's military solution for the constitutional crisis was firmly based in the American military tradition of the citizen soldier. At this early stage of the conflict many in the North harbored the traditional American mistrust of regular armies. An article in *Harper's Weekly* represented this belief when it attacked the need for a standing army and concluded, "Hereafter, let every citizen pay homage at least to his country that he will understand how to handle a musket in her defense."[6] Since Congress was not in session Lincoln had the opportunity to use the powers of the president without referring to the legislative branch of government. To support the weakened Regular Army, Lincoln asked the loyal states, on April 15, 1861, to furnish 75,000 militiamen to serve for three months. This was the maximum period permitted under law and at the time, it seemed adequate based on the assumption that there were large numbers of Union supporters in the South who would eventually force the rebellious states back into the Union. Others saw the need for a larger military response. The veteran General John E. Wool had called for an army of 200,000 troops to take Richmond and hold it. General William T. Sherman had called for a similar-sized force in Kentucky. At the time, both were ridiculed.[7] This militia force that was being recruited could not have been a force for conquest, but it would protect the capital. The Northern states responded enthusiastically to the call-up, with 100,000 men enlisting. This was seen as an indication of the strength of the ideal of the citizen-soldier and as evidence, as the *New York Times* reported, "of our qualities as a military people. All that remains for us to do is to add to our native genius that which knowledge alone can give."[8]

In his proclamation calling for the militia, Lincoln defined a limited military response from the Union: "I deem it proper to say that the first service assigned to the forces hereby called forth will probably be to re-possess the forts, places, and property which have been seized from the Union; and in every event, the utmost care will be observed, consistently with the objects aforesaid, to avoid any devastation, any destruction of, or interference with, property, or any disturbance of peaceful citizens in any part of the country."[9] He perceived a war limited by the extent of Union military activity in the South and with limited impact on the civilian population and private property. Lincoln was also mindful of the number of states undecided about remaining with the Union. Eight slave states were still with the Union. Missouri, Kentucky, Maryland, and Delaware were undecided and both sides moved carefully to avoid pushing them into the opposing camp.

The size of the Union military task was not fully grasped by the Union command. The lessons of America's military past had demonstrated how hard it was to conquer the vast territory. The distance from northern Virginia to New Orleans was 1,000 miles and the distance from the Chesapeake Bay between Maryland and Virginia to the Mississippi River at Memphis was 900 miles. The area of the seceded states was nearly a million square miles.[10] Geography severely complicated the Union military task. Britain, which had considerable military resources at its disposal, had twice failed to defeat the Americans. By his own authority, and perhaps with the realization that the military effort might last longer than three months, Lincoln was forced on May 3 to call for an additional forty-two thousand three-year volunteers and increased the Regular Army by twenty-three thousand without the authorization of Congress. The volunteers were organized into forty regiments and were to serve for three years or the duration of the war. These volunteers, unlike the militia, would be under the laws and regulations of the U.S. Army. Lincoln also ordered the navy increased by eighteen thousand sailors. He had acted boldly. According to the Constitution, Congress alone has the power to raise and support armies. But Lincoln believed that the Constitution gave the president the power to do whatever was needed to protect the nation in this emergency. The Union high command was not equipped to handle the enthusiastic response to the president's call for volunteers. The efficiency of militia units varied from state to state. Many militia units elected their company officers, and state governors commissioned majors and colonels. These were state units, however, not Federal units.[11]

According to the Constitution President Lincoln was the commander in chief of the United States Army and Navy and, also according to the Constitution, had the power to "make War," which gave him the authority to direct military operations. This meant that the U.S. had civilian control over its military in wartime. This combination of the political with the military ensured that political influences affected military decisions. Precedent also gave the president the power to make both political and military decisions. President James Madison had determined strategy and selected army commanders in the War of 1812. President James K. Polk had directly commanded the war with Mexico. Success had justified and endorsed this practice. One of the most important roles the president had as commander in chief was the appointment of military commanders. The combination of the military and political roles meant that some military commands were treated as political in order to strengthen public support for the war.[12]

Lincoln was determined to give the war effort broad political support, so he appointed generals from among politicians. This strategy was particularly important in the first months of the war. In order to gain the support of Democrats, Lincoln commissioned large numbers of leading Democrats as generals, most notably Benjamin F. Butler. The North's large number of foreign-born citizens provided an opportunity to appoint ethnic leaders such as Carl Schurz, Franz Sigel, and others as generals. The West Point–trained officers disdained the practice and the term "political general" became associated with incompetence. In recognition of the need for trained officers, Lincoln, however, gave the majority of appointments of the forty volunteer regiments to officers on active duty or to West Point graduates such as George B. McClellan. Most historians agreed that the political generals were more hindrance than help. However, McPherson was also correct to conclude that political generals were "an essential part of the process by which a highly politicised society mobilised for war."[13]

Thomas J. Goss takes a position similar to McPherson's. He has examined the political nature of the war, with his aim "a revision of the historical approach to the examination of generalship." He has argued for broader criteria to judge the performance of Civil War generals than just battlefield success. Goss agreed that the combat record of political generals was poor. However, he argued that the Civil War was a political war; political considerations were as important and necessary as military ones and therefore political generals made significant political contributions to strengthen support for the war effort. This was particularly important in the first years of the war.[14] Goss's thesis is interesting for its linking of political, military and social factors, but Lincoln had to judge his generals on their success on the battlefield or risk losing the war.

Lincoln had no military experience except service in a militia unit in a minor Indian war, and he had no formal military education, in contrast to the Confederacy's president, Jefferson Davis. It was logical and responsible of President Lincoln to seek the military advice of the commanding general. On April 1, 1861, Lincoln wrote General Scott to ask him for "comprehensive daily reports to me of what occurs in his Department, including movements by himself, and under his orders, and receipt of intelligence?" Scott reported to Lincoln with regularity.[15] The objective of this letter was to establish a formal line of communication between the civilian administration headed by the president and the military commanding general because no established process existed for military guidance to the civilian administration. Most of Scott's reports during this period concerned military routine and administration, but Lincoln was interested in knowing Scott's plan to suppress the rebellion.[16]

The Union general in chief, Winfield Scott, was a veteran of two wars and widely regarded as the finest soldier in the United States. He was born in 1786 and, at seventy-five when the war began in 1861, was physically incapable of commanding a field army. Yet he was only one of two men alive at the time who had commanded army formations large enough to be referred to as an army.[17] Although the president was commander in chief, he delegated his command of his armies to the general in chief. As general in chief, Scott reported to the president through the secretary of war. The post was not legislated and had developed from the tradition of retaining the senior general officer of the army in Washington. With little authority, the general in chief would struggle to control the army.[18] Harry T. Williams has observed there were no officers in the first year of the war who were capable of "efficiently administering and fighting a large army." "Old Fuss and Feathers" predicted a three-year conflict that would involve enormous manpower. Yet even this early in the conflict there were indications that Scott would struggle with his duties.

In October 29, 1860, Scott had sent President Buchanan advice on the political situation in a paper entitled "Views Suggested by the Imminent Danger of a Disruption of the Union by the Secession of One or More of the Southern States."[19] Scott warned that the political divisions could result in destructive wars and "the fragments of the great republic ... form themselves into new confederacies, probably four." Scott recognized from his knowledge of the Southern population that there was a "danger of an early act of rashness preliminary to secession" by the seizure of isolated Federal forts throughout the South. Scott recommended that these forts be immediately garrisoned so that they could not be taken by surprise.[20] What was most important, Scott hoped (rather than reasoned) to avoid the dangers of civil conflict: "With the army faithful to its allegiance and the navy probably equally so, and with a Federal Executive, for the next twelve months, of firmness and moderation, which the country has a right to expect—moderation being an element of power not less firmness—there is good reason to hope that the danger of secession may be made to pass away without one conflict of arms, one execution, or one arrest for treason."[21]

General Winfield Scott (Library of Congress).

On March 3, 1861, in letter entitled "The Wayward Sisters," Scott outlined four strategies to resolve the political crisis. First, he advised conciliation and the adoption of the Crittenden proposals, as he thought, "my life upon it, we shall have no new case of secession; but, on the contrary, an early return of many, if not of all the States which have already broken off from the Union."[22] Such an optimistic view was based on the assumption of a strong pro–Union view in the South. Second, he advised an economic solution: The collection of duties on foreign goods outside the ports the government had lost control of or a blockade of them. Third, the South could be conquered by a Federal army of three-hundred thousand troops but at an enormous loss of life and the devastation of the conquered territory. Scott estimated the military option would cost at least $250,000,000 and the conquered territory would need to be garrisoned for generations. Scott warned of a lengthy war and also the problem of how to win the peace. Fourth, the Federal government could do nothing, merely watch the states "depart in peace."[23] Scott did not advise the president which of the four options he preferred, but it seems from his emphasis on the monetary cost, loss of life and destruction of the military option that he preferred to resolve the crisis through negotiation.

But Lincoln had a more immediate and pressing problem. He called a meeting on Monday, April 14, to discuss the attitude of Pennsylvania, the most exposed of the loyal states and the second most important in terms of wealth, population and military power in the context of the possible scenario of the secession of Virginia and Maryland. Lincoln invited General Scott, Pennsylvanian governor Curtin and Alexander McClure, the chairman of the Military Committee of the Senate. They met in the White House at 10:00 a.m. on the day Fort Sumter surrendered. After the meeting, Scott reassured McClure that with fifteen hundred men in Washington the capital was not in danger of attack from General Beauregard's Confederate army. Scott admitted that at this time Beauregard had more troops at Charleston than the Union had on the continent east of the frontier. McClure calculated that Beauregard's army could be transported by sea, and in a few days it would be in Washington. McClure became aware of "the utterly hopeless condition of the government." In view of this information, he again asked Scott whether Washington was in danger. Scott answered, "No, sir, the capital is not in danger, the capital is not in danger." Scott admitted that the capital was not a defensible city but, to reassure those present he pointed out the window to a sloop of war on the Potomac. McClure looked out the window and beyond the sloop to Arlington Heights on the Virginia bank of the Potomac, from which one or two batteries of out modeled Confederate artillery could destroy the sloop in half an hour. He must have also realized that the White House could be hit from the same position. McClure again asked, "General, is not Washington in great danger?" Scott straightened himself up and with crushing dignity answered, "No, sir, the capital can't be taken; the capital can't be taken, sir." Lincoln, who had listened silently but with interest to the discussion, reacted to Scott: "It does seem to me, general, that if I were Beauregard I would take Washington." Governor Curtin and McClure were "profoundly impressed with the conviction that the incompetency of General Scott was one of the most serious of the multiplied perils which then confronted the Republic."[24]

After the secession of Virginia from the Union, Scott, a Virginian, had remained loyal to the union he had served for fifty years.[25] Scott would have preferred another West Pointer and native Virginian, Robert E. Lee, to be the field commander of the Union army. But in a major blow to Scott, on April 20, 1861, Lee had resigned from the United States Army to follow his native state of Virginia as it left the Union. West Point provided a solid basis for a professional officer corps, but it did not prepare them for the higher art of war, which included staff organization. The staff of the army comprised Scott and the heads of the military departments and the various bureaus. The failing of this structure was that no one had made any preparations for war in particular or the process to expand the army to meet the needs of the war.[26]

Secretary of War Simon Cameron directed the mobilization of the Union army. This task was so all-consuming that Lincoln directed the design of the new structure for the expansion of the Regular Army to Secretary of the Treasury Salmon Chase. Chase needed military advice, so he formed an advisory committee of regular officers. Lincoln appointed the three-man committee, which comprised Adjutant General of the Army Colonel Lorenzo Thomas, Major Irvin McDowell and Captain William B. Franklin. Within two weeks the officers presented their recommendations, which Chase accepted and Lincoln approved. The three officers designed a uniform Federal system for the enlistment of regulars and volunteers, which was communicated as General Orders number 15 and 16. Franklin's efforts were noticed and he was promoted to colonel on May 14, 1861. Major Irvin McDowell was rewarded when his supporter Salmon Chase recommended him to General Scott for a promotion to brigadier general and to command the anticipated operation against the Confederates in Virginia.[27] Secretary of War Cameron and Ohio governor William Dennison had also supported Chase.

General Scott's concern was that there were few officers who had commanded in the field or a military unit as large as a brigade. The Confederates had taken most of the officers who held higher ranks (although Scott did have some promising West Point graduates such as William T. Sherman, George B. McClellan, William B. Franklin, Winfield S. Hancock, Joseph Hooker, Henry W. Halleck and Edwin V. Sumner, who with time and experience would provide good service).[28] This left Scott with no clear-cut candidate for the position. He had recommended Joseph K.F. Mansfield for the command. Lincoln considered Mansfield too old for it and went against Scott's recommendation; on May 28, 1861, he appointed McDowell to command the newly created Department of Northeastern Virginia.[29] McDowell was forty-three and had graduated in the middle of his class at West Point in 1838. He had served on the border with Canada and in the Mexican War. He had spent most of his time in the army as a staff officer and consequently this bought him to the attention of General Scott.

Lincoln's decision to take military action was a dramatic and bold move by the new president. Lincoln was aware that few of the Republican Party leaders at the time had faith in him as president. The party did not have a policy to deal with the crisis and was divided on the best solution for the problem: Seward, who at this time had a skeptical, almost condescending attitude towards Lincoln, "ridiculed" the idea of a civil war. Chase preferred "peaceful disunion" to civil war, while Cameron regarded war as inevitable. The president could count on the support of cabinet members James Harlan, William Dennison and Caleb B. Smith, but he had no precedent to draw upon and therefore he was left with a policy that did not go beyond the generalities of the Constitution.[30] Added to these concerns was the vulnerable situation of the capital because it was enclosed by slave states, Virginia to the south and Maryland to the north. Union control of Maryland was critical to protect Washington from Confederate attack because this would enable a free flow of troops and supplies to the capital.

In Washington many of its citizens were concerned about the safety of the city. Horatio Nelson Taft, a senior member of the United States civil service whose children were playmates with the Lincoln children, heard the rumors that Virginia would leave the Union, which made him feel "we are surrounded by enimies [sic]" and that "reports from various quarters indicate that danger is imminent of an attack upon the City."[31] Baltimore, which had one-third of Maryland's population, had weak support for the Union. The railroad tracks of the Baltimore and Ohio Railroad had been damaged and the management of the railroad refused to transport Union troops on its trains.[32] The mayor of Baltimore had divided loyalties and the police chief was sympathetic to the South.[33]

Baltimore was strategically important because it was a major railroad junction for the capital for troop reinforcements from the Northern states. General Scott had feared a Confederate attack across the Potomac directed towards Baltimore and their then attacking Washington from the north.[34] Scott's fear was unrealistic considering the strength and level of preparedness of the Confederate forces at the time. Considering the importance of Maryland for the security of Washington, an important strategic decision was made two weeks into the conflict. This was to secure the rear of Washington.

On April 19 Scott appointed his reliable friend Robert Patterson of Pennsylvania as major general of volunteers in the service of the Federal army. Patterson was placed in command of the Department of Washington, which also included Delaware, Pennsylvania and Maryland. His objective was to "post the volunteers of Pennsylvania all along the road from Wilmington, Del., to Washington City, in sufficient numbers and in such proximity as may give a reasonable protection to the lines of parallel wires, to the road, its rails, bridges, cars, and stations." Scott saw the importance of opening secure communications between Washington and the loyal northern states and land routes through Maryland to allow reinforcements to reach Washington and to clear the Harrisburg-Baltimore-Washington railroad.[35] Troops could reach Washington through Annapolis and march overland until Patterson could build an army based in Philadelphia to move on Baltimore.[36] Patterson's delay in moving on Baltimore and concerns over the size of his military department resulted in its breakup into three more realistic commands. Patterson was given the Department of Pennsylvania, which included Pennsylvania, Delaware and northern Maryland. The remainder of his previous command was divided into the Department of Washington and the Department of Annapolis.[37]

The first violence of the Civil War after the surrender of Fort Sumter occurred in Baltimore during clashes between Union troops and secessionist sympathizers. In response to Lincoln's call for troops, a regiment of troops arrived in Baltimore on its way to Washington. At noon on April 19 the 6th Massachusetts and a Pennsylvania militia unit arrived at President Street Station, Baltimore. The troops had to change trains for a southbound station as there was no direct railroad to Washington. Rail cars that transferred passengers between the two stations had to be pulled by horses. An angry mob blocked the route and broke windows on the cars. The troops realized they could proceed no further and got out of the cars and marched in formation towards Camden Station. As they proceeded a crowd attacked them with a shower of missiles. The troops increased the tempo of their march and pistol shots were fired at them from within the crowd. In response, the order was given to the troops to fire. The mayor of Baltimore placed himself at the head of the column, believing that his presence would deter the mob from further attacks, and begged the captain not to fire again. He was wrong and was forced to kill a man when his patience was exhausted.[38] In the "Baltimore Riot" four troops were killed and thirty-one wounded, while twelve civilians were killed and an unknown number wounded.[39] The violence was enough for the *New York Times* to report, "Civil war has commenced."[40]

The report of the Baltimore Police Commissioners concluded "that it was utterly impossible from the state of the public mind that any more forces from other States could, by any probability, then pass through the city to Washington without a fierce and bloody conflict."[41] Mayor Brown and the governor of Maryland, Hicks, advised President Lincoln: "Under these circumstances it is my solemn duty to inform you that it is not possible for more soldiers to pass through Baltimore, unless they fight their way at every step."[42] Controversially, just after noon on April 20, Brown and Hicks were informed that more Union troops were on their way to Baltimore over the Northern Central Railroad. It appeared that the governor approved the destruction of bridges along the railroad to prevent the troops reaching Baltimore. Union troops, which would have arrived later in the day, were persuaded to return to Philadelphia and Lincoln told Brown and Hicks, "For the future troops must be bought here, I make no point of bringing them through Baltimore."[43]

This was a political decision that avoided the sensitive issue of Federal troops fighting civilians, and was linked to the bigger political balancing act of not wanting to push Maryland towards secession, an important consideration. However, it was argued that Lincoln needed to be more decisive on such a vital issue as the security of the capital. Patterson ordered General Benjamin F. Butler who commanded the 8th Massachusetts to Washington via Annapolis together with the 7th New York. He seized a ferry at Havre de Grace and on the night of April 21 Butler and his regiment arrived at Annapolis. He was requested to halt one regiment and "report to Lieutenant-General Scott for instructions."[44]

Lincoln made a strong political statement on April 27, 1861, in response to the attacks on Union troops in Baltimore by instructing the commanding general "to suspend the writ of Habeas Corpus for the public safety" along the line of troop movements between Philadelphia and Washington. Lincoln justified his action to Scott as being constitutional because "you are engaged in suppressing an insurrection against the laws of the United States."[45] This began a series of suspension of Habeas Corpus at different parts of the country and eventually on September 15, 1863, he suspended Habeas Corpus throughout the Union. These decisions created a debate over the constitutional right of the president to take such an action.[46] Some critics went as far as to denounce the acts as despotic and dictatorial. Yet Lincoln was fully aware of the dire political and military situation that confronted him at this time. The federal armory at Harpers Ferry on the Potomac had been occupied by Southern troops. To the south of Washington a small Confederate army held the strategically important road and railroad junction at Manassas Junction only 27 miles from Washington. The railroad from Washington to Baltimore was closed and General Benjamin Butler was still at Annapolis in Maryland.

At this time, Patterson commanded more troops than any Union officer. Scott had ordered Patterson "by force to occupy Baltimore and reopen regular communications between Washington and Philadelphia by rail and wires." Scott proposed a four-pronged advance on Baltimore from Relay House, York, Have de Graced and Annapolis.[47] However, Patterson always found a reason to delay the movement. At Annapolis, Butler was keen to advance. On May 6, he informed Scott that he had occupied the station at the Relay House, which was nine miles from Baltimore, with the Eighth New York Regiment. Concerned about rumors of some units of Maryland militia in his vicinity, he ordered up a battery of artillery and the 6th Regiment Massachusetts. He concluded, "I find the people here exceedingly friendly, and I have no doubt that with my present force I could march through Baltimore." Then he added, "I trust my acts may meet your approbation, whatever you may think of my suggestions."[48]

Butler was aware that Scott would not approve his plan to march on Baltimore, so he obtained confirmation from Scott that his command encompassed the city.[49] He did not tell Scott of his bold, though politically dangerous plan. With almost one thousand troops, Butler headed by train towards Washington but then cut the telegraph wires and headed back towards Baltimore. Butler's troops arrived in Baltimore by train at 6:00 p.m. on May 11 and moved towards Federal Hill, which commanded the area. As they moved up the hill heavy rain from a thunderstorm pelted the troops and reduced the chances of a violent confrontation with secessionist sympathizers. Butler established his headquarters in a German tavern and informed General Scott on May 15, 1861. General Scott was angered by the actions of the untrained militia general and in particular that he had not been informed of the operation.[50] Butler was relieved of his command and sent to Fortress Monroe in Virginia. General George Cadwalader assumed command and began to peacefully neutralize Baltimore.[51] Interestingly, Butler appealed to Simon Cameron, the secretary of war, instead of his superior officer, saying he desired "a personal interview with you and with the President before I accept further service."[52] Butler would receive no explanation from Scott or Lincoln, but this was his usual practice. However, in his orders to Butler for his new command at Fortress Monroe, Scott asked Butler to "be sure to submit your plans and ask instructions from higher authority. Communicate with me often and fully on all matters important to the service."[53] Butler's reckless actions had secured Baltimore and Annapolis. When the Maryland legislator voted in favor of what was, in effect, neutrality, the threat to the rear of Washington had been removed.

In the Union high command, the debate over the issue of military action in Virginia tested the command structure. In early May 1861, Salmon P. Chase had been transfixed by the strategic importance of Manassas Junction. He was in favor of its immediate occupation by Union forces. On May 3, he had met with General McDowell to work on a plan to occupy Virginia. Both were aware of the reluctance of General Scott to move into Virginia while it was still technically part of the Union. The vote by Virginia on May 23 to secede from the Union removed the constitutional question and Scott's affections for his home state as objections to a military movement into the state. The establishment of the Confederate capital at Richmond, which occurred before

Virginia voted to secede, added to the attraction of such a plan. Scott considered the plan too risky but he did sanction the occupation of Arlington Heights, on the Virginia shore of the Potomac, to protect the capital and the president. On May 16, McDowell planned to operate inside Virginia by first occupying Alexandria and Manassas and then attacking Richmond from Fort Monroe between the York and James rivers.[54] On May 23, the Union army finally crossed the Potomac and by May 24 had occupied Arlington Heights and Alexandria.

The first military action of the war was a small-scale action at Philippi in western Virginia on June 3, 1861. Union forces under Major General George B. McClellan had moved into the area to support the pro–Union majority. No one was killed and few were wounded, but it did provide excellent publicity for Major General McClellan and tended to reinforce the popular view that quick military action could achieve decisive results. The first large-scale military action of the war demonstrated that neither side was prepared and had not trained their troops sufficiently for a major battle. On the left of the Union line to protect Washington was the politically appointed Major General Benjamin F. Butler's force, located at Fort Monroe on the end of a peninsula between the James and York rivers in Virginia. Butler had attempted to push back Colonel John B. Magruder's Confederates but he was defeated at Big Bethel, Virginia, on June 10, 1861. The Union defeat further highlighted the clash between the professional officers over appointing "amateur" commanders and added pressure on the Union high command for a successful military action on the front that was to the south of Washington. An article titled "Civilians in Military Command: Views and Impressions Current in Military Circles in Washington" gave a public voice at the time to the minority who disagreed with the popular view about fighting wars with amateurs. It criticized the policy of appointing civilians or militia officers to command and asked a rhetorical question: "Is this war we are engaged on, or merely an immense national militia parade, wherein all the posts of honor are to be assigned on political and personal grounds."[55]

On June 25 Lincoln called a meeting with General Scott, Quartermaster General Montgomery Meigs, Major General John A. Dix and the cabinet to consider the military situation. Major General Dix had been secretary of the treasury under President James Buchanan from January to March 1861. Lincoln recognized his political influence with Democrats and appointed him a major general of the Union army. Lincoln was concerned with the presence of Confederate general Thomas J. Jackson's Confederate army in the Shenandoah Valley, a location that would allow it to strike into Pennsylvania and turn Union forces that were deployed to the south of Washington.

On June 29, 1861, an important meeting to discuss Union strategy was finally held when the president met with his cabinet and Generals Scott and McDowell. Scott had verbally instructed McDowell to prepare and present a plan to attack the Confederate troops under General Beauregard at Manassas in Virginia.[56] McDowell presented the plan he had communicated in writing to Scott about June 24.[57] Scott was concerned that Union troops in McDowell's army were still too untrained for battle and for weeks had urged caution. He disagreed with making Richmond the objective of the maneuver and with the line of march.[58] Scott's solution to the question of how to defeat the rebellion became the first military strategy for the Union. It reflected President Lincoln's limited war aims with the April 15 call-up of the militia. On May 3, 1861, General Scott wrote General George B. McClellan in response to McClellan's letter of April 27 in which he advised Scott to concentrate large numbers of troops in Ohio and told him "the movement on Richmond should be conducted with the utmost promptness, & could not fail to relieve Washington as well as to secure the destruction of the Southern Army."[59] Scott took the time to reply to McClellan's plan of operation and passed both McClellan's plan and his criticism to the president. He did not need to do this and, while we do not know why, it was the prelude to the future antagonism between these two men.[60] Scott did not agree with the need for hasty action. Indeed, he preferred a plan that could take a year to defeat the rebellion.

It is in this May 3 letter to McClellan that Scott outlined the main points of what would be referred to as his "Anaconda Plan." Scott never took the opportunity to write a detailed plan of operation and it seems that what we have is only a preliminary plan based on the political and military situation in 1861. Scott described his three-point strategy to defeat the rebellion. First, it involved a blockade of Southern ports which would strike at one of the South's weaknesses: the fact that it was not self-sufficient. Lincoln, on April 19, 1861, had already ordered the blockade of ports in the states of South Carolina, Georgia, Alabama, Florida, Mississippi, Louisiana, and Texas. This was extended on April 30 with the blockade of North Carolina and Virginia.[61] At this time the blockade was more a "paper" blockade than an actual one. Flag-Officer Stringham, the commander of the Atlantic Blockading Squadron, had on June 29 only seven ships available in the Atlantic.[62] But Lincoln had reversed a seventy-five-year-old U.S. policy on the freedom of the seas.

Second, Scott proposed strong attacks down the Mississippi River that would be "sufficiently strong to open and keep it free along its course to its mouth, [and] you will thus cut off the luxuries to which the people are accustomed." Scott explained that when the people in the South felt this pressure, without having been "been exasperated by attacks made on them within their respective States, the Union spirit will assert itself; those who are on the fence will descend on the Union side, and I will guarantee that in one year from this time all difficulties will be settled." This assumption of the existence of strong Union sentiment in the South was accepted by many in the North, including Lincoln. With a strong line of Union positions isolating the South it would be forced to negotiate. It would also give the Union time to assemble and train the large armies that would be needed if the South had to be conquered. This implied that the Union maintained a defensive position in the East. This made sense because the terrain between Washington and Richmond did not favor land operations, while the river systems in the West would allow for the movement and supply of large armies. Scott warned, "If you invade the South at any point, I will guarantee that at the end of a year you will be further from a settlement than you are now."[63] Most historians view Scott's plan as one designed to use military strategy to lead to a negotiated settlement.[64] In contrast, Geoffrey Perret has asserted that Scott's strategy did not plan a war that would last for three years as has been popularly recorded but one that would be over in 1862. To achieve this victory Scott intended a type of Schlieffen Plan by sweeping through the West while remaining on the defensive in the East.[65]

The "Anaconda Plan" had a strong Jominian influence, with its emphasis on strong points as the basis for Union military maneuver. Another assumption underpinning Scott's plan was the belief that there existed many "patriot and loyal Union friends" in the South who would help to force the rebellious states to return to the Union. This suggests that Scott either did not want to conqueror the South or believed it unnecessary because all that would be needed was to force it to see that it could not prevail.[66] This was a plan for reunion, not conquest, and was consistent with the Union war aim in 1861, which was to preserve the Union and not to destroy the South. Lincoln also supported this policy of conciliation just as much as conservative officers in the army.[67] Such a belief was more at home in Europe in the eighteenth century. However, this strategy assumed war for a year. In effect, Scott wanted not only to besiege the South but also to slowly dismember it and therefore demonstrate to the people of the South that its independence could not be achieved. This would avoid the devastation that would result from a Union invasion of the South Scott had predicted in his letter to Seward in March. The *New York Times* reported the value of Scott's plan, which included the desire to end the conflict with the least loss of life: "The main objective of the war ... was to bring the people of the rebellious States to feel the pressure of the Government; to compel them to return to their obedience and loyalty. And this must be done with the least possible expenditure of life, compatible with the attainment of the objective. No Christian nation can be justified ... in waging war in such as shall destroy 501 lives, when the object of the war can be attained at a cost of 500."[68]

Mark Grimsley has argued that such a military policy was consistent with the view that conciliation and not conquest dominated Union military policy in the first year and a half of the war.[69] Yet this strategy, with its combination of the political and the military, was more in tune with the writing of Karl von Clausewitz. A contemporary of Jomini, Clausewitz had also studied the Napoleonic Wars but had drawn different conclusions. Clausewitz defined two types of national strategy: the conquest of enemy territory or the defense of one's own and the overthrow of the enemy's political system. Scott's strategy was the first type of strategy, which usually ends with a negotiated settlement. But with the Confederate government acting more as a sovereign state, many in the Union high command came to the realization that overthrow of the Confederate government was necessary to achieve this. This was Clausewitz's second type of national strategy, which ends when one side surrenders unconditionally. This was the inherent contradiction in the Union war aims. To win the conflict the Confederate government had to be destroyed. To do this the Union would have to conquer the South or force it to surrender. Most officers at the time were prepared to support a military policy that limited the impact on civilians. The conciliatory approach impacted two key political issues—slavery and the political question of how to treat enemy civilians. Not all in the North supported this conciliatory approach. Those who favored the destruction of slavery saw the conflict as an opportunity to achieve this.[70]

However, Lincoln and other members of his cabinet were sensitive to what they saw as the dominant Napoleonic paradigm of war: short and ended by a decisive battle. The popular media pressed this view and General Scott was aware that his strategy would be politically unpopular.[71] *Harper's Weekly* reflected this popular belief in May 1861 when it confidently predicted the "war will be over by January 1862." It further espoused the "On to Richmond" strategy by highlighting the symbolic importance of the city to the Confederacy.[72] This was highlighted with a map of Maryland and Virginia titled *The Seat of the War*, clearly indicating that the most fighting and the most important battles would be fought over this area.[73] Lincoln rejected the Scott plan because it "was more a diplomatic policy than a plan of strategic action."[74] Secretary of the Navy Welles also rejected the plan because it did not include operations to invade the South.[75]

Adding further impetus to the push for an immediate military offensive were those who sought to quickly destroy the rebellion before the Confederacy could consolidate and also to punish those involved. In a letter to Secretary of War Simon Cameron, Galusha A. Grow, a prominent politician and lawyer who was Speaker of the House of Representatives from 1861 to 1863, urged the administration to "prosecute it to the bitter end, if need be, to quell insurrection and hang traitors … until the flag floats from every spot on which it had a right to float."[76] A similar view was expressed in a letter to the *New York Times* attacking the "feeble way Gen. Scott has of putting down rebellion."[77] Postmaster General Montgomery Blair also argued for immediate military action but for more pragmatic reasons even though his views were based on assumptions similar to those of General Scott.

Blair believed that early Union military action would encourage what he perceived as significant Unionist sentiment in the South and thus end the rebellion early and without the need for a war of conquest.[78] As early as May 7 the president met with representatives of a convention of governors that had recently been held at Cleveland to affirm their support to crush the rebellion and "demanded that a positive and vigorous policy should be pursued and pushed by the Administration."[79] Lincoln may also have been keen to use the ninety-day militia before their term of service had expired. While he believed that the Confederates were as untrained as Union troops, he also believed that one Confederate defeat would be enough to end the conflict.

Against the advice of General Scott and the concerns of General McDowell, the Union army was ordered to advance towards Richmond. Scott would have preferred to have moved to retake Harpers Ferry with Major General Robert Paterson's Department of Pennsylvania while McDowell's troops feinted an attack to distract Confederate forces. The Confederate evacuation of Harpers Ferry reversed the roles.[80] Lincoln had accepted a simple plan to move to Manassas, fight a battle and then see what options arose as a consequence. Without consulting McDowell, Scott decided on July 8 as the date to commence the advance.[81]

Lincoln had justified Scott's decisions so far in the conflict, including the increase in the Regular Army in his July 4 address, "Message to Congress in Special Session," in which he skillfully outlined his aims for the war. He argued that the issue "embraces more than the fate of these United States" and more specifically he raised this question: "Must a government, of necessity, be too strong for the liberties of its own people, or too weak to maintain its own existence?" Lincoln argued that the legacy of the American Revolution and the establishment of the Constitution now had to be successfully maintained. Congress approved the raising of five hundred thousand troops to serve for three years in an early admission that the war would not be over as early as many had optimistically predicted.[82]

Furthermore, the limited war aims of the Union were reaffirmed when Lincoln stated he had "no purpose, directly or indirectly, to interfere with slavery in the States where it exits."[83] Congress affirmed this view on slavery when it passed the Crittenden-Johnson resolutions. Radical Republicans who would have liked to see slavery included as a war aim accepted the resolution so as not to divide the Republican Party and weaken support for the war. In August the radical Republicans weakened the resolutions with the passing of the Confiscation Act, which provided for the seizure of property that had been used to assist the insurrection. Lincoln determined the following: "So viewing the issue, no choice was left but to call out the war power of the Government; and so to resist force, employed for its destruction, by force, for its preservation."[84] Lincoln was arguing that "war power" was derived from the presidential oath to protect and defend the Constitution. He elaborated later that "the Constitution invests its Commander in chief, with the law of war, in time of war."[85]

General McDowell had only three months to form the three types of units—militia, volunteer and regular—into a coherent fighting force. He attempted to do a lot himself and there were not enough staff officers to help him. He had almost fifty thousand troops to guard Washington. Opposing him was General Beauregard with twenty thousand troops at the rail and road hub at Manassas, Virginia. On the left of the Confederate line eleven thousand troops were deployed at Winchester in the Shenandoah Valley under Brigadier General Joseph E. Johnston. Opposing Johnston was Major General Robert Patterson's eighteen thousand Union troops.

McDowell's plan for an advance towards Richmond was sound but it had to be executed by inadequately trained troops. With thirty-five thousand troops, McDowell's objective was to rapidly advance thirty miles and outflank Beauregard's twenty-two-thousand-strong army. Union generals Butler and Patterson had to prevent the Confederate troops opposing them from reinforcing Beauregard.[86] On July 16, 1861, and almost a week after Scott's date for the start of the advance, the largest army ever assembled on the North American continent up to that time advanced towards the railroad junction at Manassas. Commanding the Third Brigade of the First Division was Colonel William T. Sherman; Colonel A.E. Burnside commanded the Second Brigade of the Second Division; and Colonel William B. Franklin commanded the First Brigade Colonel S.P. Heintzelman's Third Division. The advance of the army was reported optimistically: "It was not an army, in the strict sense of the word.... It was a gathering of armed men, making up for their deficiency in tactics and discipline by the moral bond which unite then in a common cause, and by the self-confidence which they derive from the sentiment of their individual value."[87] The army was romantically described as "Gen. McDowell's corps d'armee" in reference to Napoleon's Grande Armée and also the popular Napoleonic representation of war.[88]

The line of operation enabled McDowell to gain the advantage of the Jominian principle of interior lines. He intended to turn the Confederate left and destroy the Manassas Gap Railroad, thereby preventing Confederate forces under Johnston from reinforcing the outnumbered Beauregard. However, McDowell's delay in implementing his plan and the advantages of surprise and concentration of mass was lost. The use of electric telegraph enabled Confederate forces to concentrate at Manassas. In the Shenandoah Valley, General Johnston managed to mask his withdrawal by using cavalry as a screen. His lead brigade, commanded by Brigadier General Thomas Jackson, covered fifty-seven miles in about twenty-four hours to reach Beauregard by July 20.

The next day, McDowell began his maneuver around the Confederate left flank when five brigades crossed the Bull Run at Sudley Springs. As a diversion, three brigades of Brigadier General Daniel Tyler's division moved towards Stone Bridge on the Warrenton Turnpike. The Union flanking movement had been detected and the first attack by Union troops was disorganized, which gave Beauregard the time to form a second line of defense on a hill behind the Henry house. Union forces pushed Confederate troops hard on this line. When Brigadier General Barnard E. Bee, CSA, tried to rally his troops by shouting to them, "Look at Jackson's Brigade it stands like a stone wall," he had created the legend of "Stonewall" Jackson. At 2:00 p.m. McDowell deployed two artillery batteries at the Henry house but with poor infantry support. A regiment of Confederate infantry advanced on these batteries. The Union artillery commander mistook the blue-clad infantry for Union troops, and the Confederate troops advanced to within seventy yards of the Union artillery and fired their muskets. The Union artillery was neutralized for the rest of the battle. At 4:00 p.m. Beauregard, encouraged by the arrival of reinforcements, ordered an advance. Union troops without adequate artillery support lost cohesion and began to withdraw, becoming more disordered with the retreat. The retreat turned into a rout for part of the Union Army when the Cub Run Bridge was blocked by overturned wagons. President Davis arrived on the field and immediately instructed the Confederate right to advance towards the Centreville road. The order was never delivered and as in so many Civil War battles to come the opportunity to destroy an opposing army through a vigorous pursuit was lost. But the war would also demonstrate the myth of the Napoleonic decisive battle concluded by the destruction of the defeated army by a vigorous pursuit. Both sides committed 18,000 men to the battle.[89] McDowell's forces suffered 2,708 casualties and Beauregard lost 1,982.[90] These losses seemed enormous at the time. Some critics argued that McDowell's campaign had been doomed to fail, yet they also acknowledged that he came close to victory.

McDowell was untrained in the art of higher military science and his army was not prepared for campaigning. Herman Hattaway has stressed that both sides lacked a sound system of command and control and the second echelon of the command of both sides did not understand the plan of battle.[91] Most experts acknowledge the importance of the strategic use of railroads by the Confederates, which may have reduced the Jominian advantage of interior lines. Indeed, the Joint Committee on the Conduct of the War in its report laid the "principal cause of the defeat of the day to the failure of General Patterson to hold Johnston in the Valley."[92] The committee, dominated by Republicans who desired a more vigorous prosecution of the war, was also critical that the Union took too long to march on Manassas. These factors worked against the Union army.

However, McDowell did manage to maneuver a wing of seventeen thousand men over the Bull Run in an action that required rapid movement to achieve success. However, this he did not achieve. These criticisms of McDowell do not suggest that the Confederate leadership performed better or that this was the factor that decided the outcome of the battle. Weigley has concluded the outcome of the battle was "as much through the accidents of a battle fought by untrained troops and inexperienced commands as through these other factors."[93] The Prince de Joinville, a Frenchman, observed the battle and would have agreed that McDowell's defeat was "through the absence of organization and of discipline."[94] It is more accurate to argue that the disadvantage of the offensive and the benefit of the defensive was a common feature of Civil War battles that provided the best answer to the question of why McDowell lost the battle.

The Union defeat at Manassas had an immediate impact on the Union high command. The widespread fear that the Confederate army could march into Washington unopposed added impetus to the need to rethink the approach to fighting the conflict.[95] It convinced many who had thought in terms of a quick war that the conflict would now be a long-term struggle that would require an immense commitment of manpower resources. Significantly, it demonstrated that the Union had the capacity to sustain defeat, a quality that is so important in determining the outcome of wars. On July 22 President Lincoln called for 500,000 three-year volunteers and disbanded the ninety-day militia. The president was building a federal force rather than relying on the traditional system, which was an amalgam of state and federal control and support.[96] On July 25 Lincoln signed another act to enlist a further 500,000 troops for the duration of the war.[97] On July 23 he issued the "Memorandum of Military Policy Suggested by Bull Run Defeat," which was added to on July 27. Lincoln reinforced the need for an effective blockade, the organization and training of the new volunteer forces near Washington so that Manassas could be permanently held and in the West a joint movement from Cairo on Memphis and from Cincinnati on East Tennessee. This memorandum accepted Scott's previously held ideas except that it did not include the main part of his plan, the advance along the Mississippi. Lincoln was proposing a simultaneous advance on all fronts to achieve victory.[98] John G. Nicolay, Lincoln's chief personal secretary, summed up the beliefs of many in the Lincoln administration: "The preparations for the war will be continued with increased vigor by the Government."[99]

Significantly, more were persuaded to accept the advice of professional soldiers who would be capable of conducting the war across the vast geography of the United States. Strategically the U.S. Navy established a blockade with all manner of ships providing a solid base for a Union victory. From August 1861 the navy landed army forces at strategic points such as Savannah, Charleston and Wilmington. Joint navy-army operations would eventually convert the sea blockade into an occupation of key strategic areas that sealed off major ports in the South. Military action in the West would have significant strategic importance to the course of the war.[100]

However, always the political schemer, General Scott had publicly criticized the plan to force battle in Virginia. *Harper's Weekly* reported a conversation between Scott and the ex-governor Raymond that was critical of some members of the cabinet "who know much more about war than I do, and have far greater influence than I have in determining the plan of the campaign." It was these members of the cabinet who should be held responsible for the defeat and not him: "I shall fight when and where I am commanded. But if I am compelled to fight before I am ready, they shall not hold me responsible."[101]

The Western Theater of operations was more active in 1861 than the eastern. A Confederate advance into Kentucky violated the state's neutrality and as a result the state legislature invited Union forces into the state to remove the Confederate forces. Grant occupied Paducah and Southland at the mouth of the Tennessee and Cumberland rivers on September 6, 1861. This secured Kentucky in the Union and positioned Grant for his campaigns in 1862. Earlier, Union forces had also secured Missouri.

In western Virginia a series of military actions would have a dramatic and significant impact on the course of the war. Forty counties in western

Virginia seceded from Virginia and asked for Federal forces to protect them from Confederate troops in the Shenandoah Valley. Major General George B. McClellan, with a force of Ohio volunteers, occupied Grafton in western Virginia and then defeated invading Confederate forces at Philippi and Beverly. These victories provided the basis for the entry of West Virginia into the Union. Even the arrival of General Robert E. Lee, the principal military advisor to President Jefferson Davis and future commander of the Army of Northern Virginia, failed to remove the Union troops. Lee returned to Richmond at the end of October 1861 as a defeated general while McClellan's reputation soared.

The Union's victories in the West were significant. However, Scott and Lincoln's main concern was the front to the south of Washington. On July 22, 1861, Lincoln followed Scott's advice and summoned McClellan to Washington with a brief telegram: "Circumstances make your presence here necessary. Charge Rosecrans or some other general with your present department and come hither without delay."[102] Lincoln placed McClellan in command of the Department of Washington and the Department of Northeastern Virginia, which was named the Division of the Potomac.[103] McClellan was not Scott's first choice for command. Scott would have preferred General Halleck.[104] Stanton expressed a less optimistic view about the appointment of McClellan in a letter to ex-president Buchanan in which he made clear his fear that the young general would be undermined by the political intrigue in the capital: "General McClellan reached here last evening, but if he had the ability of Caesar, Alexander or Napoleon, what can he accomplish? Will not Scott's jealousy, Cabinet intrigues and Republican interference thwart him at every step."[105]

In the first ninety days of the war, the Union's high command struggled for solutions to the problem of organizing and administering mobilization and then the administration, command and control of a war unprecedented in size in American military history. Indeed military policy evolved incrementally. The early call in April for seventy-five thousand, ninety-day militia evolved to the July 4 call for five hundred thousand men. Lincoln had acted decisively by using the powers he saw the Constitution had given to the president in times of war. Tensions between the American ideal of the citizen-soldier and the practical need for trained officers and regular troops created strains within the army and the Union high command. The Union had decided on a limited war with the aim being the return of the rebellious states to the Union.

Yet, even at this stage of the war, President Lincoln, who after the defeat at Manassas took a more hands-on approach to the running of the war, envisaged a Union victory by simultaneous advances on all fronts to overcome the

Confederates' advantage of interior lines. This was not consistent with the limited war aim because it implied a war of conquest. The Battle of Manassas was the rejection of Scott's strategy to win the conflict. The president rejected the strategy of a defensive war in the East and an offensive along the line of the Mississippi in the West. In this case, the tension between popular will in a democracy and military policy resulted in an advance by an unprepared army. Yet the view, however rash, that the war could be won by a single decisive battle, had to be tested. Lincoln also rashly replaced McDowell. Lincoln had relied on the advice of General Scott but in key decisions, such as the appointment of McDowell to command the Union Army to advance into Virginia and the decision to advance into Virginia itself with a raw army, he had ignored him. It is interesting how the blame for the defeat at Manassas has been shifted from Lincoln to McDowell and impatient Northerners who supported the "On to Richmond" strategy. After failing to accept Scott's advice on these two occasions Lincoln accepted his advice on another important matter: that General McClellan should come to Washington to command the Union's army in the East.

Three

"I seem to have become the power of the land"

The appointment of General McClellan as commander of the Department of the Potomac began a turbulent period in United States military history. Major General George Brinton McClellan is one of the most controversial figures in that history. He represented the American ideal of individualism, which valued the importance of the individual in times of crisis, but he also represented the values of the elite officer corps, who believed that the nation's salvation in war rested with professionally trained officers and soldiers and not with highly motivated amateurs. In times of national peril all nations look for a great man to lead them to victory. Many viewed McClellan as the nation's Napoleon. In the three months after he arrived in Washington, McClellan was able to use his organizational genius to build a grand army around Washington. He would also supplant General Scott as the general in chief of the armies of the United States of America. Yet, McClellan would add tensions to an evolving high command structure that was struggling from the defeat at Manassas, the demands of a large war and the strategy required to achieve victory, as well as how the president as commander in chief related to the nation's highest-ranking soldier, the general in chief.

This chapter is not a study of McClellan, but he is central to any examination of the development and functions of the Union high command and its strategy in the East simply because he commanded the Union's main army of operations in the East, the Army of the Potomac. Also, he was at one time both the commander of this army and the general in chief. Furthermore, he is widely acknowledged as the creator of the Army of the Potomac. It is of importance that his relationships with fellow officers as well as Lincoln and the cabinet provided the basis for some success but also for great disaffection. The United States Constitution gave civilians control over the military in wartime. Samuel P. Huntington has described civilian control as "subjective civilian control," which meant its success depended on the personal relationship between the president and his military leaders.[1] McClellan became general in chief at a time when there was for the first time a clear distinction between Soldier and Civilian. As the first West Point–trained officer to serve as general in chief, McClellan was a departure from U.S. military tradition.[2]

Major General McClellan began his military career when he entered the military academy at West Point in June 1842, when he was fifteen. He graduated in July 1846, second in his class of fifty-eight. McClellan was made second lieutenant in the Company of Engineers, where he gained a reputation as a good organizer. On September 26, 1846, McClellan's company left New York to fight on the Rio Grande River in the war with Mexico. He proved to be a brave soldier and after the Battle of Churubusco was promoted to first lieutenant. Like so many U.S. soldiers, he contracted dysentery and malaria. With the U.S. victory in 1848, McClellan had learned many military lessons from the American commander General Winfield Scott. What was important was that he observed Scott's decisions to use turning movements and siege tactics instead of frontal attacks. After that war he became an instructor at West Point. The War Department sent him and two other officers to Europe to investigate military organization. While on the tour he observed the closing stages of the Crimean War. Sears has argued it was at this stage in McClellan's life, as a member of the officer corps of the Regular Army, that he formed the view that civilians could not understand war and should not be trusted to direct it.[3] In 1857 he left the army and accepted the position of chief engineer of the Illinois Central Railroad. He then became the president of the Ohio and Mississippi Railroad.

When Major General George Brinton McClellan arrived in Washington on July 26, 1861, he was thirty-four years old. In contrast, Lieutenant-General Scott was seventy-four, Colonel Samuel Peter Heintzelman was fifty-five and Brigadier General Irvin McDowell was forty-two. Many in the North, eager to avenge the defeat at Manassas, saw in him qualities he did not possess. The perceived similarities between the short "Little Mac" and Napoleon continued to Jena and Austerlitz but not to Waterloo. Also, he was a Democrat and the importance of this was significant because it was evidence that Northern Democrats would defend the Union.[4] McClellan assumed command of the Division of the Potomac, which was created by General Orders Number 47 of July 25, 1861. This new military command comprised the Military Department of Washington and Northeastern Virginia.[5] This was a break from the traditional U.S. military organization because it was a geographic command rather than a military department.

Three—"I seem to have become the power of the land"

General George Brinson McClellan (Library of Congress).

At this early stage of his command, McClellan, surprisingly, displayed a lack of understanding of military protocol, a situation that would provide the basis for future tensions in the Union high command. It is surprising considering the formal military education he had received and at which he had done so well and his military experience in the war with Mexico. When he commanded the Department of the Ohio he had written directly to the president to advise him on the delicate political and military position in Kentucky, to lay out his plans for military action and to petition for more arms.[6] Military protocol required that he communicate with General Scott, who would then advise the relevant civilian or military authorities.

When McClellan arrived in Washington on Friday, July 26, one of the first things he did was to visit General Scott that evening. The next day, he reported to Adjutant General Lorenzo Thomas, who gave him orders to visit the president. The president welcomed McClellan and placed him in command of all Union troops in the vicinity of Washington. Lincoln then asked him to return to the White House for a cabinet meeting at 1:00 p.m. without General Scott and without informing Scott of the president's request.[7] McClellan then met with General Scott, his immediate superior. In what should have been a productive meeting to discuss the military situation, Scott became angry when he learned of McClellan's invitation to attend that afternoon's cabinet meeting. For this breach of military protocol Scott kept McClellan until it was too late to attend the meeting.[8] From their discussion McClellan was concerned Scott knew less about the defensive condition of the city and more about Union army stragglers in the city. Scott then ordered McClellan to ride around the city and send stragglers to their regiments.[9]

As ordered, that afternoon McClellan examined the Union troops around Washington. The estimated fifty thousand troops were, as McClellan had described it, spread out chaotically. On the Virginia bank of the Potomac the brigade organization of General McDowell still existed. Many other regiments were encamped on low ground near the river and were not in the best defensive positions. On the Maryland side of the Potomac, two regiments were stationed near the Chain Bridge, but there were no troops on the Tennallytown Road or on the roads entering Washington from the south. These units were not placed in the best defensive position. No pickets were placed on the roads and no attempt had been made to organize into brigades. No defensive works had commenced and on the Maryland side there was nothing to stop the Confederates from occupying the heights, which would place them within artillery range of Washington. Of more concern to McClellan was the morale of the troops: "Many soldiers had deserted, and the streets of Washington were crowded with straggling officers and men, absent from their stations without authority, whose behavior indicated the general want of discipline and organization."[10]

McClellan concluded the current military situation was "fraught with great danger." The defeated Union army did not resemble an army but a collection of "undisciplined, ill-officered, and uninstructed men" who were so demoralized by their defeat that they would run at the first shot. McClellan also asserted there were not enough troops in quality and quantity to protect the city, and the period of service of most of the troops had expired or would expire in a few days. Also, the civilian leadership of the nation was demoralized. Finally, he was "not supreme and unhampered, but often thwarted by the lieutenant-general."[11] However, McDowell's brigade and divisional structures were still intact. There is no doubt McClellan had painted a picture worse than the reality of the situation to underline the enormity of his task and also to emphasize that he was the only man capable of creating an army out of the survivors of Manassas.

After only a few days in the capital, General Scott asked McClellan what his plans were for his command. McClellan wished to have his command organized as an army and not a geographic division. The traditional U.S. military structure of departments meant that if a commander moved his troops into the geographic area of another department then the command of his troops passed to that command. Therefore, if McClellan moved his army to another department, he would be subordinate to its commander. McClellan's first step to reorganize his army was to form the infantry into brigades of four regiments. Eventually he planned to form divisions of three brigades. The delay was to enable general officers to gain the required experience to command larger formations. Therefore, he did not want to recommend appointments to Major-General until after they had experience of active service.[12] Scott was critical of all the recommendations except the formation of brigades.[13]

McClellan quickly began the task of organizing into an army the defeated Union troops who had fought at Manassas and the stream of new recruits arriving daily at the capital. Order was achieved in the city by the appointment of a provost-marshal, Colonel A. Porter, who was supported by some regular troops. Colonel Porter and his troops strictly carried out their duties and Union troops quickly returned to their formations. By August 4, 1861, Porter was able to boast, "I have Washington perfectly quiet now, you would not know there was a regiment here. I have restored order very completely already."[14] The new troops that arrived in the capital were formed into temporary brigades and placed in camps for the purpose of equipping, instruction and discipline under the direction of General Silas Casey, a veteran officer with a reputation for strict discipline. Once in fit condition they were transferred to brigades serving across the Potomac.[15] Casey also initiated programs to improve the officer corps. On September 20 he established two boards of inquiry to examine the qualifications of officers. This move was aimed at weeding out the "amateur" and political officers who had been appointed to command state militias. His frequent parade ground inspections and reviews helped to maintain discipline and created a strong sense of purpose in the army.

On the evening of July 30, 1861, McClellan had begun to document for the president his views on how the Union could win the war. At this early stage of his command McClellan must have been solicited by the president to present his ideas. He had also been working on a bill that would allow him to appoint as many civilian and military aides as he pleased.[16] This bill became law on August 5, 1861.[17] The basis of his thinking was the creation of a large army. He wanted this army staffed by "the right kind of Genl officers." The scope of the document went beyond McClellan's theater of operations and examined the wider strategic challenges of the war. In this context Lincoln was seeking advice on matters he should have sought from General Scott. Yet McClellan was comfortable with his behavior. In a letter to his wife he observed how the "Presdt, Cabinet, Genl Scott & all deferring to me—by some strange operation of magic I seem to have become *the* power of the land."[18]

McClellan distinguished between an "ordinary war" and "this contest," which had "become necessary to crush a population sufficiently numerous, intelligent and warlike to constitute a nation; we have not only to defeat their armed and organized forces in the field but to display such an overwhelming strength, as it will convince all our antagonists, especially those of the governing aristocratic class, of the utter impossibility of resistance."[19]

McClellan identified Virginia as the main battleground and also envisioned secondary military operations along the Mississippi, into Missouri, Tennessee and Texas. Even in this early stage of the war McClellan insightfully identified railroads as a "new and very important element into war."[20] For his main army of operations in Virginia, McClellan asked for 273,000 men. This idea was the beginning of the creation of the Army of the Potomac. The objective of his army would be to occupy Richmond and then to take Charleston, Savannah, Montgomery, Pensacola, Mobile and New Orleans. This part of McClellan's plan contrasted with Scott's plan to defeat the South with an emphasis on a defensive strategy in the East and an offensive in the West aimed at gaining control of the Mississippi; however, like Scott he did imply a negotiated peace once the landed aristocracy in the South and the Confederate army had been defeated. McClellan intended to win the war himself and with his "main Army of operations." This belief fit his representation of himself as the savior of the nation.[21] T. Harry Williams rejected this plan as unrealistic.[22] Sears has argued McClellan's strategy was a criticism of Scott's because it required the five-hundred thousand troops Congress had recently approved to be assigned to his advance into Virginia.[23] Kenneth P. Williams saw the strategy as nothing more than an opportunity for McClellan to create tension between himself and Scott that would eventually turn to hostility.[24]

On Friday, August 2, 1861, McClellan personally delivered his memorandum to the president. The next day, McClellan read it at a 10:00 a.m. cabinet meeting. His plan was more considered than the one he had outlined in a letter to Scott on April 27. His emphasis on the capture of Confederate cities, in particular Richmond, to end the war must have appealed to those in the cabinet who saw victory in terms of conquest and not by gaining a favorable military position achieved by holding strategic positions. Scott's "Anaconda" eastern defensive strategy planned for a Union victory but only after lengthy war fought mainly in the West. McClellan offered a shorter war won by a decisive Napoleonic battle in the East. As a result, McClellan had deliberately placed himself in disagreement with his direct superior officer but also laid the seeds of expectation that would haunt him in the future.

Whether the Confederates were to be conquered quickly or forced to surrender after a lengthy struggle, the Union required a large army to effect either strategy. There was a strong agreement on the need for a large military effort. Both Scott and McClellan had advised Lincoln of the need for hundreds of thousands of troops to fight the war. This number would need to be financed at a scale unprecedented. Section 8 of "An Act to Provide Increased Revenue from Imports, to Pay Interest on the Public Debt, and for Other Purposes" provided for "a direct tax of twenty million dollars ... annually laid upon the United States." In accordance with the Constitution the direct taxes were apportioned among the states and according to their respective numbers.[25] While this act was regarded as the first federal income tax, it was the fifth time the federal government had resorted to this mode of revenue raising. Indeed, Congress found most of its work done for it in drafting the act because it was able to revise the Acts of 1813 and 1815 for the current legislation.

The tensions in the Union high command, between Scott and McClellan, were increasing. McClellan believed that Scott had been trying to undermine his authority by inviting him to accept that General Emory be made inspector general of "*my* army & *the* army." McClellan declined the offer, aware that he had "disgusted the old man." This would not be the last time he believed he had been undermined from above. Adding to the friction between the two generals was McClellan's ambition to replace Scott. McClellan's ego saw in Scott's old age the opportunity to replace him when Scott retired.[26] On August 4 McClellan attended a dinner with the president and forty other guests, including Prince Napoleon. With General Scott leaning on him, McClellan felt that many had identified the contrast between "the old veteran (Scott) & his young successor."[27]

Eventually, a disagreement over the level of the Confederate military threat to Washington provided the catalyst for the breakdown in relations between Scott and McClellan. McClellan wrote Scott on Thursday, August 8, to reinforce his view of an imminent Confederate attack on Union positions on the western bank of the Potomac and also a Confederate attempt to cross the Potomac at some point north of Washington. McClellan believed General Beauregard had 100,000 men at his disposal and he reasoned, "Were I in Beauregard's place, with that force at my disposal, I would attack the positions on the other side of the Potomac, and at the same time cross the river above this city in force."[28] McClellan's assessment of the Union's military strength was alarming; "I feel confident that our present army in this vicinity is entirely insufficient for the emergency, and it is deficient in all the arms of the service-infantry, artillery, and cavalry."[29] This was a strong criticism of Scott's more optimistic view that the capital was safe. McClellan urged Scott to reduce all garrisons in the rear of Washington to a minimum and suggested that all available troops be sent to Washington. All new regiments and volunteers should also be sent to the capital without delay until at least 100,000 men were available to defend the city. Furthermore, he argued, "military necessity" demanded that the departments of North East Virginia, Washington, the Shenandoah, Pennsylvania and Fort Monroe should be merged into one department "under the immediate control of the Commander of the main army of operations, and which should be known and designated as such."[30] In accordance with the concept of unity of command, McClellan's request made military sense, and perhaps Scott would have accepted McClellan's proposal if this was the reason. Instead, McClellan tried to justify his proposal by fear and the suggestion that Scott had neglected the defense of the capital.

This letter was delivered to Scott on August 8, 1861, and also on the same day and in another breach of military etiquette Thomas M. Key, a volunteer aid of General McClellan, delivered a copy to the president. A military threat to the capital seemed logical in the context of the Union defeat at Bull Run and the chance of a Confederate advance towards Washington to take advantage of their victory. McClellan's assessment of the strategic situation recognized "the vital importance of rendering Washington perfectly secure, and its imminent danger, [which] impel me to urge these requests with the utmost earnestness, and that not an hour be lost in carrying them into execution."[31] McClellan must also have known the psychological weight a threat to the capital would have on the president and cabinet and that this would polarize opinion between Scott and himself to the extent that the president and the cabinet could lose confidence in Scott's advice. McClellan had most likely reached the opinion that Scott was a hindrance to himself and to the Union: "but that confounded old Genl always comes in the way—he is a perfect imbecile. He understands nothing, appreciates nothing & is ever in the way." He also expressed a much harsher, emotive view: "I do not know whether he is a *dotard* or a *traitor*! I can't tell which."[32] After only two weeks in Washington, McClellan had not only planned to concentrate the Union's military resources under his command but also to replace Scott as general in chief.

McClellan's organized mind must have anticipated a reaction to his letter. Sometime on August 8, perhaps in the afternoon, he had "a row with Genl Scott until about 4 o'clock." This may have occurred with the daily meetings that Scott and McClellan had been having with Lincoln and his cabinet. Later that same afternoon Seward discussed with McClellan his "pronunciamento" against "Genl Scott's policy." But while McClellan had fleeting thoughts of resigning if he still had to work with Scott, he was nevertheless determined to remove Scott.[33] His letter to Scott on August 8 was his "bombshell," designed to create a "stampede in the Cabinet." He had anticipated that within a day he would be given the authority to work independently of Scott.[34] Such a fracture in the Union high command would have made it even more dysfunctional than the personalities of its two top generals had made it.

The next day Scott responded to McClellan's criticism in a letter to Secretary of War Simon Cameron. Scott was annoyed McClellan had not discussed with him his concerns over the safety of the capital; on the other hand, Scott had presented all his military views and opinions to McClellan "without eliciting much remark." Scott believed the capital was safe because of the number of Union troops in the capital, the forts and the obstacle of the Potomac River itself. Moreover, more troops were arriving in the capital daily. As a result, he had "not the slightest apprehension for the safety of the Government here." Scott added that his physical condition had affected his ability to command as well as he should to the extent he felt he had "become an incumbrance to the Army" and he should be "giving way to a younger commander." He concluded: "Accordingly, I must beg the President, at the earliest moment, to allow me to be placed on the officers' retired list, and then quietly to lay myself up—probably forever—somewhere in or about New York. But, wherever I may spend my little remainder of life, my frequent and latest prayer will be, 'God save the Union.'"[35] We will never know if Scott intended to make way for McClellan or if he intended to put pressure on Lincoln to reestablish his authority as the Union's general in chief. Either way, the president could not afford to have the Union's most senior and respected general resign so soon after the defeat at Manassas, nor could he have his two top generals feuding.

Lincoln must have discussed the situation with McClellan, perhaps on Friday, August 9, 1861, because on Saturday, August 10, McClellan wrote the president to assure him that he "would abstain from any conduct that could give offence to General Scott or embarrass the President or any department of the Government." Furthermore, to try to heal the differences between Scott and himself, McClellan decided to "yield to your request and withdraw the letter referred to."[36] On the same day, the president visited Scott at his home to discuss the "patriotic purpose of healing differences." Out of respect for the president, Scott considered his request; however, he could not withdraw the letter because the "original offense," as he termed it, had been the result of a breakdown of military protocol to the extent "that freedom of access and consultation have, very naturally, deluded the junior general into a feeling of indifference toward his senior." Also, Scott was not only concerned with McClellan's access to the president and the cabinet but also the support he appeared to receive.[37] On August 12, 1861, Scott wrote his reply to the president's request that he withdraw his resignation. The letter was addressed to the secretary of war and from there it was passed on to the president. Scott informed the secretary of war, "I deeply regret that, notwithstanding my respect for the opinions and wishes of the President, I cannot withdraw the letter in question...."[38] The president could not accept Scott's resignation. Rather than respond to the letter, he simply kept it.

Four days after McClellan had withdrawn his letter of August 8, he wrote Gideon Welles, secretary of the navy, about "additional information" that could place Washington in danger. McClellan believed the Confederates would attempt to move from Aquia Creek into Maryland. This operation "would place Washington in great jeopardy." McClellan urged Welles that "the strongest possible naval force be at once concentrated near the mouth of Aquia Creek and that most vigilant watch be maintained."[39] McClellan had ignored his apology to Scott and military etiquette. He also still viewed Scott as "the most dangerous antagonist I have—either he or I must leave here—our ideas are so widely different that it is impossible for us to work together much longer."[40]

As a sign of McClellan's growing power and influence, he was able to break with tradition and form an army, not a geographical department, under his command. On August 20, 1861, he was able to announce that General Orders Number 15 of August 17, 1861, placed him in "command of the Army of the Potomac, comprising the troops serving in the former Departments of Washington and Northeastern Virginia, in the valley of the Shenandoah, and in the States of Maryland and Delaware." The order also announced the appointment of sixteen officers to the staff of the army.[41] For now he had had his way over the disagreement with Scott over departments and armies. But there was nothing to clarify the question about what would happen if he moved his army into another military department.

However, the concerns of Lincoln and his cabinet over the security of the capital were still there for McClellan to exploit. The political situation in Maryland must have been at the back of their minds. General Butler had secured Maryland and Baltimore in April and General Banks had managed to maintain the peace. The fear that the Maryland legislature would pass an ordinance of secession was just as strong in August as it had been in April. Frederick Schley, the editor of the *Examiner*, warned Secretary of State William H. Seward of such a plot. Schley's assessment of the political balance was "there are twenty-two senators, of whom twlve [sic] is the requisite majority to enact a law. Of the present senators eight are loyal and reliable, leaving fourteen in whom I have no faith and I speak the sentiment of many." He urged Seward to arrest the secessionist senators to protect the state from violence.[42] In a letter to Secretary of War Cameron, on September 8, McClellan again raised the possibility of a Confederate attack on Baltimore to cut the lines of communication to Washington and to encourage an insurrection.[43] With a threat militarily to Washington from Virginia and a political threat on Washington's lines of supply, the Union high command was prepared to take bold and decisive action.

In early September President Lincoln, Secretary of State Seward and the assistant secretary of state, Frederick Seward, met with McClellan and General Banks at Rockville to discuss the political situation in Maryland and in particular the alarming prospect that the Maryland legislature, which was scheduled to meet on September 17, could pass an ordinance of secession.[44] General Dix in Baltimore had received a visit from Seward a day or two earlier so that he would be fully informed of the situation. They formed a plan, but it was not put on paper. The least number of people were informed. They were all concerned about removing a democratically elected body, but they also believed that if the Maryland legislature passed the secession ordinance it would plunge the state into anarchy by inviting in the enemy. They therefore felt it morally necessary to dissolve the legislature. Generals Banks, Dix and McClellan believed that loyal members of the legislature could do as they wished. However, secessionists would be turned away from the meeting at Frederick.[45]

On September 11, 1861, Secretary of War Cameron instructed General Banks to prevent the passage of any act of secession by the Maryland legislature by arresting any number of its members. On the same day, General Dix was ordered to arrest six active secessionists, three of whom were members of the Maryland legislature. The prisoners were taken to Fort Monroe and then to New York.[46] Also on the same day, General Dix sent a list of the Maryland legislature members to Seward and McClellan and had marked the names of those he considered should be arrested. The next day fourteen civilians were arrested.[47] General Banks then ordered Lieutenant Colonel Thomas B. Ruger, commanding the Third Wisconsin Regiment at Frederick to ensure that any meeting of the legislature at any place or time should be prevented and the remainder of the legislature arrested, including the presiding officers of the two houses, secretaries, clerks and all subordinate officials.[48]

The decisive action of the Union high command had stopped attempts by Maryland to secede. Interestingly, General Scott appears to have had no knowledge of the plan nor did he have any input into its execution. As lieutenant general of the United States Army, he should have been involved but he was not invited. Perhaps Lincoln had pushed Scott to the side with the knowledge of his letter of resignation or perhaps McClellan's campaign of ignoring Scott had had the intended results. Whatever the reason for ignoring military etiquette, McClellan had worked with Lincoln and Seward in a major political operation without Scott. Indeed, the success of the operation seemed to vindicate McClellan's position as the foremost military commander in the U.S. Army at that time.

McClellan continued to communicate directly with Secretary of War Cameron. On September 13, 1861, McClellan appealed to Cameron to reinforce the Army of the Potomac by sending all available troops to counter a perceived Confederate concentration and eventual movement on Washington. He also argued for the reinforcements because "the decisive battle of the War is soon to be fought in this vicinity." He estimated that the Confederate strength opposing him was twice as large as his own and sought half of General Frémont's fifty thousand troops at St. Louis because the safety of the nation required it.[49] In response to breaches of military etiquette, Scott on September 16 issued General Order number 17, which sought to address "irregularities in the correspondence of the Army which need prompt correction." In effect Scott sought adherence to the military chain of command: "It is highly important that junior officers on duty be not permitted to correspond with the General-in-Chief or other commanders on current official business, except through intermediate commanders; and the same rule applies to correspondence with the President direct, or with him through the Secretary of War, unless it be by the special invitation or request of the President."[50] On the same day, Scott sent a message to McClellan requesting information on the strength of his command.[51]

McClellan ignored the request from Scott but was happy to supply the information to members of the cabinet. Gideon Welles, secretary of the navy, recalled a meeting at General Scott's rooms opposite the War Office. In the Welles diary the entry is dated February 25, 1863, but he did not date the actual meeting. McClellan refers to a meeting on September 27, 1861, and this is most likely the meeting referred to by Welles.[52] In attendance were President Lincoln, General Scott, General McClellan, Secretary of War Cameron, Secretary of State Seward and himself. During the meeting a question arose concerning the number of Union troops in and around Washington. Cameron could not answer the question, and neither did McClellan. Scott said he had received no reports. The president was concerned at the response from his two most senior soldiers. Seward then read from a small piece of the paper details about the troop strength, the several commands and the total of the whole force. Seward asked McClellan to confirm the figures he had read out. McClellan responded that the numbers "approximated the truth." General Scott was angered:

> I am in command of the armies of the United States, but have been wholly unable to get any reports, any statement of the actual forces, but here is the Secretary of State, a civilian, for whom I have great respect but who is not a military man nor conversant with military affairs, though his abilities are great, but this civilian is possessed of facts which are withheld from me. Military reports are made, not to these Headquarters but to the State Department. Am I Mr. President, to apply to the Secretary of State for the necessary military information to discharge my duties?[53]

Seward tried to explain to Scott that he obtained his figures by vigilance, attention and by keeping a daily count of the arrival of troops. Scott was not convinced with the explanation offered and he must have concluded that McClellan and Seward were working against him. The old general told Seward, "If you in that way can get information, the Rebels can also, though I cannot."[54] The detailed account of the meeting by Welles contrasts to McClellan's own record. McClellan makes no reference to the incident regarding troop strength, but he does mention the conflict between Scott and himself and in doing so he represents Scott as the instigator of the conflict. McClellan stated that Scott "raised a row" with him before they went into the meeting. At the end of the meeting McClellan sensed that Scott had been trying to avoid him. He walked up to Scott, looked him in the eye and said, "Good morning, General Scott." In McClellan's mind Scott had thrown down the glove and he had taken it up and so "war is declared."[55]

The rift in the Union high command Lincoln had hoped to heal had deteriorated and it was not all General McClellan's fault. Scott complained to Cameron on October 4 of McClellan's continued communication with the president and cabinet members. Scott believed McClellan's neglect was close to disobedience. He felt only a young general in chief could control him.

Scott foresaw that McClellan intended to replace him as general in chief and he advised Cameron he intended to stay in his post until General Henry W. Halleck could arrive to replace him.[56] By this time McClellan had also become disillusioned with Lincoln and his cabinet, which would add further strains on the embryonic high command. This reflected his previously held belief that civilians could not be trusted to direct a war because they did not have the formal education to understand it. He was "disgusted" by "these wretched politicians—they are a most despicable set of men." Seward, the secretary of state, was "the meanest of them all—a meddling, officious, incompetent little puppy," and Lincoln "is nothing more than a well meaning baboon."[57]

In direct defiance of Scott, McClellan pressed ahead with the organization of the army into divisions. Scott had directed McClellan not to organize anything larger than brigades. On October 15, 1861, McClellan could report the reorganization of the Army of the Potomac into twelve divisions comprising three infantry brigades and artillery and cavalry.[58] He appointed McDowell, who had commanded the Union army at Manassas, to command a division and claimed later it was one of his greatest mistakes, because McDowell had worked to have him replaced. Samuel Heintzelman was the only other officer to retain command after Manassas. The other ten divisional commanders were either at Manassas or joined the army after the defeat. Seven were West Point graduates. Selected as division commanders were Banks, Porter, Stone, Franklin, Buell, McCall and Hooker. These men formed the army's core leadership. They were professionals and most had served under Scott in Mexico. They supported McClellan's cautious and limited war philosophy in that they did not want to see slavery become a war aim of the Union.[59] McClellan was now determined to "force the issue" with Scott over the policy rift between the two. McClellan simplified the rift as a choice between Scott's policy of "inaction and the defensive" and his own, which centered on a decisive battle fought with his own main army of operations.[60]

On Wednesday, October 16, 1861, the president and Seward visited McClellan in what McClellan notated as a friendly, informal meeting. There is no record of what was said except McClellan's own recollection that he was interrupted by Lincoln and Seward, "who had nothing very particular to say, except some stories to tell."[61] Two days later, on Friday, October 18, the cabinet met and after Lincoln read a draft letter accepting General Scott's offer to resign, they decided to accept General Scott's resignation. They also determined not to follow Scott's recommendation to appoint General Halleck as general in chief. McClellan heard the next day the cabinet had rejected Scott's recommendation to appoint Halleck and he happily announced to his wife he would "be Comdr in Chf within a week."[62]

The growing impatience for battle was exerting more pressure on both Lincoln and McClellan. On October 21, 1861, McClellan ordered an engagement with the Confederates that would have disastrous consequences. He directed General Charles P. Stone to make a "slight demonstration" on the Maryland side of the Potomac and opposite to the Confederate-held Leesburg while a large force was shifted across the river to flank the position. Colonel Edward Baker was given the job of holding the attention of the Confederates on the river near Ball's Bluff. Baker unwisely deployed most of his troops across the river to dislodge the Confederates. Union forces were routed and Baker was killed in the action.[63] The battle angered abolitionists and Radical Republicans Governor John A. Andrew and Senator Charles Sumner of Massachusetts because of the large loss of troops from their state and they were further angered when they learned that Stone had returned two escaped slaves to their owners.

The defeat at Ball's Bluff was militarily insignificant but politically it was embarrassing to Lincoln. When Congress met on December 3, 1861, it established the Joint Committee on the Conduct of the War. Congress had sent a clear message that it was unhappy with the way in which the Union high command was conducting the war. The committee, dominated by Radical Republicans—a group of Republicans who sought to have the abolition of slavery included into the Union's war aims, and who were also keen for the army to fight the war much more vigorously—were determined to investigate the Union defeats at Manassas and Balls' Bluff as a means of exerting political pressure on the Union high command. While Stone became the scapegoat for the Ball's Bluff defeat, McClellan must have realized he was its real target. In effect the committee aimed to try to exert the influence of Congress on Union military policy, strategy and operations. Lincoln, as commander in chief, had been defining the role of the president in wartime as circumstances arose and without the need to confer with Congress. The chairman of the committee was Senator Ben Wade from Ohio. He was a strong opponent of slavery and was determined to use the committee to push abolition as a Union war aim. While the committee could put pressure on the Union high command, it had no real power. At best, it could make suggestions to the president and secretary of war. At another level, these were amateurs who were keen to investigate the actions of any professional generals who did not win victories fast enough and who did not support abolition.[64]

The Radical Republicans sought to put pressure on the Union high command by targeting General Scott. In their view the Union defeat at Ball's Bluff was evidence that Scott had outlasted his usefulness. On the evening of October 26, 1861, Lincoln was petitioned by Senators Trumbell, Chandler and

Wade to press for a battle. Lincoln then went to General McClellan's office, where he spoke with Colonel Key. Colonel Key also spoke in favor of a grand battle to "clean out the enemy." Lincoln asked Key what McClellan thought about it and he answered, "The General is troubled in his mind. I think he is much embarrassed by the radical difference between his views and those of General Scott." This was not the case. McClellan did not want to fight a battle for the purpose of just fighting. McClellan had his concerns over the Union chain of command increased by the defeat. Until his concerns were allayed, he could not consider a major advance of the army. But by seeming to agree with the Republican senators McClellan added pressure to remove Scott. The colonel left when McClellan entered his office. When told of the meeting with the senators, McClellan reported that Wade preferred a defeat to a delay because defeat could easily be reversed by the swarms of recruits arriving daily in the capital. Lincoln reminded McClellan of the political reality of a democracy at war but advised him, "You must not fight till you are ready."[65] Determined to add more political pressure, Senators Wade and Chandler visited Secretary of State Seward the next evening and petitioned him to force the Army of the Potomac to battle. They repeated their reasoning of the previous day, that a defeat was no worse than delay and "a great deal more trash."[66] The pressure on General Scott had become too much. Under attack from McClellan and the Radical Republicans and believing he did not have the support of Lincoln and the cabinet, Scott wrote to Cameron on October 31, 1861, and for a second time offered to resign: "I am compelled to request that my name be placed on the list of Army officers retired from active service."[67]

Lincoln and his cabinet unanimously agreed to place McClellan in command of the U.S. Army as general in chief. The part of the text of this order announcing the retirement of General Scott was published in *Harper's Weekly* on Saturday, November 16, 1861. The article gave the impression that this was Scott's first and only offer to resign.[68] At four o'clock on the afternoon of October 31, Lincoln and his cabinet visited Scott at his house. The president read the following order: "On the first day of November, A.D. 1861, upon his own application to the President of the United States, Brevet Lieutenant-General Winfield Scott is ordered to be placed, and hereby is placed, upon the list of retired officers of the army of the United States, without reduction in his current pay, subsistence, or allowances." Lincoln then added, "The President and unanimous Cabinet express their own and the nation's sympathy in his personal affliction." He recognized Scott's "long and brilliant career" and "faithful devotion to the Constitution, the Union, and the Flag, when assailed by parricidal rebellion." Scott, with his customary gentlemanly honor, responded to the president. Then the president, followed by the cabinet, shook Scott's hand and left.[69]

The text that appeared in *Harper's Weekly* was taken from General Order, Number 94, November 1, 1861, the last paragraph of which advised, "The President is pleased to direct that Major General George B. McClellan assume the command of the Army of the United States."[70] Promptly General McClellan issued General Order, Number 19, also on November 1, 1861, to take command of the armies of the United States.[71] The president had reviewed this order prior to its publication. Curious as to how McClellan would handle the workload as general in chief and commander of the Army of the Potomac, Lincoln remarked, "I should be perfectly satisfied if I thought that this vast increase of responsibility would not embarrass you." McClellan responded that he felt it was a great relief: "I feel as if several tons were taken from my shoulders today. I am now in contact with you and the Secretary. I am not embarrassed by intervention." Lincoln added that the workload of the two positions "will entail a vast labor upon you." McClellan confidently and quietly replied, "I can do it all."[72]

McClellan was now commanding all U.S. armies as well as the Army of the Potomac. This gave him command of his army wherever it went. But, as yet, his army had not gone far at all. Small operations towards Munson Hill on September 29 and the Confederate withdrawal to Manassas had not dampened the Northern public's desire for an advance by McClellan's army. One of the unintended consequences of the McClellan-Scott feud had been the increase in support for the "On to Richmond" strategy. McClellan also believed that the Army of the Potomac would not be in a state to move until late November 1861.[73] Also reflected in this debate was the Union policy on the conduct of the war. Radical Republicans had sought to expand the Union's war aims to include slavery. By implication this meant that the Confederacy would need to be totally defeated. At this stage of the war, most in the Union high command thought in terms of a conciliatory war policy. Scott's "Anaconda" strategy seemed to offer conciliation because it aimed to achieve a negotiated end to the war even though it intended Union conquests in the West. Even McClellan's strategy with a main army of operations capturing Richmond and other strategic Southern cities implied a negotiated settlement. So both Scott and McClellan saw the object of the war as the restoration of the Union with the inclusion of the Southern states, with slavery intact.

As general in chief, McClellan was able to push the conciliation policy onto all Union commanders.[74] He was quick to advise General Buell, Department of the Ohio, on November 7, 1861, that "political affairs in Kentucky is more important than that of our military operations" and that the aim of the war was "the preservation of the Union and the restoration of the full authority of the General Government over all portions of our territory." He then advised of the limited nature of the war: "The inhabitants of Kentucky may rely upon it that their domestic institutions will in no manner be interfered with,"[75] In a second letter to Buell, he elaborated: "It should be our constant aim to make it apparent to all that their property, their comfort, and their personal safety will be best preserved by adhering to the cause of the Union."[76]

Various incidents had put strains on this conciliatory policy, none more so than Major General John C. Frémont's command of the Western Department at St. Louis. His management of this department was plagued by accusations of corruption and mismanagement. Isolated from the political leaders in Missouri, he issued a proclamation assuming administrative powers over the state government.[77] Controversially, on August 30, 1861, he declared, "The property, real and personal, of all persons in the State of Missouri who shall take up arms against the United States, or who shall be directly proven to have taken an active part with their enemies in the field, are declared to be confiscated to the public use, and their slaves, if any they have, are hereby declared freemen."[78] Freeing the slaves was not part of Union policy and Missouri was delicately balanced between Unionists who were antislavery and those who believed slavery should not be touched. Lincoln wrote Frémont on September 2, 1861, anxious that his declaration did not comply with an Act of Congress approved on August 6, entitled "An Act to Confiscate Property Used for Insurrectionary Purposes." Lincoln enclosed a copy of the act. Finally, Frémont's military inactivity and mismanagement gave Lincoln the opportunity to replace him on October 24, 1861.[79]

All through November 1861, Lincoln continued his habit of visiting McClellan on a daily basis. Occasionally McClellan would be summoned to a meeting at the White House, but it was customary for Lincoln to visit McClellan at his house. This behavior was not limited to Lincoln's dealings with the new general in chief. He tended to spend a lot time in other people's offices because it enabled him to find out much information and he could also study people. The frequency of his visits to his general suggests he was trying to determine if McClellan could cope with his role as general in chief and commander of the Army of the Potomac.[80]

McClellan had turned his attention to the Union armies in the West so that they could begin an advance as early as possible in the spring of 1862. They were to advance much earlier than the Army of the Potomac and engage all Confederate forces in the West so that the Confederates could not send reinforcements to Richmond.[81] However, McClellan was concerned that the western armies were poorly organized. He divided the area into two military commands, the Department of Missouri under General Halleck, which comprised Frémont's Department of the West and also the western part of Kentucky and the Department of the Ohio under General Buell, which comprised the remainder of Kentucky and Tennessee. McClellan's orders to Halleck on November 11 were aimed at solving the internal problems in the department and reaffirming the Union's conciliatory war aims: "In regard to the political conduct of affairs, you will please labor to impress upon the inhabitants of Missouri and the adjacent States, that we are fighting solely for the integrity of the Union, to uphold the power of our National Government, and to restore to the nation the blessings of peace and good order."[82]

Halleck was given few military instructions except to concentrate his army near the Mississippi for "ulterior operations as the public interest may demand."[83] McClellan did not expect any problems with his professional relationship with Halleck, even though Halleck had been General Scott's preference to replace him as general in chief. Halleck shared McClellan's conciliatory policy towards Southerners and was not required or expected to achieve great victories.[84] Buell was directed to hold Kentucky and, in a move to placate Lincoln's sympathy towards the people of Tennessee, to prepare to move into East Tennessee. He was also reminded of the government's policy regarding the seceded states.[85]

McClellan had learned quickly the political impossibility of withdrawing troops from the West to reinforce the Army of the Potomac, as he argued in a letter to Cameron on October 31, 1861.[86] McClellan had decided to leave the troops in the West because they could be used to tie down Confederate forces that might reinforce Confederate troops in Virginia. So McClellan's plans for military action in the West were limited because he believed that the Union's most important strategic objective was to achieve a decisive victory in Virginia. Unfortunately, this meant that the advance towards Richmond, the delay of which he had previously blamed on Scott, could not begin until he received encouraging reports from Halleck and Buell. McClellan was aware of the expectations for an early advance into Virginia, and in a letter to Cameron on November 15 he appealed for the country's "confidence and patience" because he "must claim to be the best judge of the time to strike."[87]

About the middle of November 1861, Secretary of the Navy Gideon Welles and David D Porter, a lieutenant in the navy, described to Lincoln a plan to take New Orleans. New Orleans, Louisiana, was the largest city in the Southern states, with about 160,000 people. Lincoln was impressed with the idea and, along with Welles and Porter, went to see McClellan. Lincoln presented the plan to McClellan as a "fate compli." McClellan was asked to consult with Porter to draw up a plan for the attack on New Orleans. McClellan was initially disinterested but changed his opinion when he learned that the plan called for only 10,000 troops, not 50,000, to hold the city.[88] Lincoln argued the importance of gaining control of the Mississippi River. Lincoln pointed to a map and remarked, "What a lot of land these fellows hold, of which Vicksburg is the key." He concluded, "The war can never be brought to a close until that key is in our pocket."[89]

This idea was not new and had already been proposed in Scott's "Anaconda" strategy. The navy had been considering the seizure of New Orleans for some time because of its strategic value as the South's major port and because it was at the end of the Great Northern Railroad connecting the railroad hub at Jackson and the Mississippi interior to the Gulf Coast. Lincoln also identified Vicksburg as the next strategic target and in so doing established the Union's military strategy in the West into the middle of 1863. McClellan must have disliked the fact that he had not been consulted on this matter of strategy prior to its being discussed with Welles and Porter. He would have resented the fact that the president had determined military strategy in the West without his advice.[90]

This incident may have resulted in McClellan's infamous snub of the president. Perhaps it had proved to him that, as M.W.D. Kelley has concluded, the "restraints imposed or duties demanded by the President were as irksome and irritating to him as had been the consciousness of Scott's superior rank."[91] Ethan S. Rafuse agreed that McClellan had become irritated by Lincoln's daily unannounced visits.[92] If Lincoln had believed the removal of Scott and the promotion of McClellan had sealed the rift at the top of the Union high command, an incident on the evening of November 13, 1861, must have created doubts in his mind. Lincoln, Seward and Hay went to McClellan's house. The servant said that McClellan was at the wedding of Colonel Wheaton and would soon return. The men went in and waited about an hour. McClellan arrived home and was told by the porter that the president was waiting to see him. McClellan went upstairs, passing the door of the room where the president, Seward and Hay were seated. They waited about another half-hour and sent a servant to remind the general they were there. The servant replied that the general had gone to bed. John Hay represented the incident as "unparalleled insolence," "a portent of evil to come" and "the first indication I have yet seen of the threatened supremacy of the military authorities." When Hay asked Lincoln about the incident he answered "it was better at this time not to be making points of etiquette & personal dignity."[93] Ethan S. Rafuse has argued that McClellan "unconscionably ignored the porter's announcement that Lincoln was waiting"[94] without giving any reason or evidence to support the conclusion except by implication that his attendance at the wedding may have been part of the answer. Another suggestion, that McClellan could have been drunk, is equally without any evidence to support it.[95]

The major achievement of the Union high command by November 1861 was that it now had a large, well-trained army in both the East and the West; its armies were making solid progress. Lincoln had determined that the president had the power to determine military policy. Yet as Lincoln tried to define the role of the president in wartime he was still too involved in decisions that may have been better left to the military. He was commander in chief but much of these powers were delegated to the general in chief. It was this relationship between the commander in chief and his general in chief that was evolving. Lincoln had ignored Scott in favor of McClellan. This not only fed McClellan's ego but also ignored the chain of command. McClellan could not work with Scott, so he deliberately and carefully ignored the chain of command and sought to have him replaced by himself. McClellan had forged a formidable army. McClellan had sought the removal of Scott as a means to stop Scott's interfering in his plans. The clash between the Union's two most important generals was the major reason the Union lacked a cohesive military strategy. Of importance, the clash ended once and for all any chance that Scott's "Anaconda" plan could be resurrected. McClellan certainly desired to be general in chief, but he underestimated the magnitude and demands of the position. The troops of the Army of the Potomac and many of its officers were loyal to their general. There is no doubt that both Lincoln and McClellan viewed the Army of the Potomac as theirs. With a military strategy that recognized the East as the main theater of operations, this army would need to fight. But where and when would it fight? These questions would be the source of future tension in the Union high command.

Four
"Now is the winter of our discontent": Winter 1861–1862

The great review of the Army of the Potomac on November 20, 1861, was a morale-raising spectacle of Union might. The review of fifty-thousand troops took place at Munson's Hill, near Bailey's Cross Roads, about six miles from Washington on the Virginia side of the Potomac. Munson's Hill was also the target of McClellan's first limited though symbolic advance on September 29, 1861. The army was reviewed by General McClellan and his staff and his brigadier generals and their aides as well as the president, the secretary of state, the secretary of war, Colonel Scott, the assistant secretary of war and John G. Nicolay. The review, on horseback, lasted one and a half hours. Then the troops marched by and went off to their respective camps. Nicolay described it as "the largest and most magnificent military review ever held on this continent."[1] The artist's depiction of the scene in *Harper's Weekly*[2] on December 7, 1861, must have inspired awe in the North over the size and power of the Union army. Public perception was still shaped by the myth of a timely victory as a result of a decisive battle. This myth persisted despite the evidence of previous wars in North America that were long struggles. The strength of this myth put pressure on the Union high command. General McClellan had forged a formidable army, which was evident at the review. However, ironically this spectacle added pressure on the Union high command for this army not only to fight but also to fight soon. This did not suit McClellan. The when and how the army should fight was the major operational issue that caused great tension in the North and the Union high command.

With so much attention given to the Eastern Theater of the war because of the near proximity of the two capitals of Washington and Richmond, it was natural for many on both sides to see the outcome of the war as a major battle requiring the capture of the enemy's capital. The Southern press had been urging an advance towards Washington to force a battle, challenging President Davis's eastern defensive strategy. General Meade, who at this time commanded the 2nd Brigade, McCall's Division, Army of the Potomac, also believed that the only way for the war to end early was by "a most decisive and complete victory."[3] From November 1861 to the end of March 1862, the attention of the North and the Union high command was fixed on when and where a major campaign by the Union's main army of operations, the Army of the Potomac, would occur. The pressure on a democracy in wartime to maintain public support for the war pressed for an early action. This was supported by the belief of many in the United States who saw wars as being decided by heroic battles. Supporters of this view found it hard to believe that an army as large as the Army of the Potomac could not just simply march out from Washington and fight and defeat the Confederates to the south of Washington. The professional officers who commanded the army knew that war was not always about heroic charges and desperate, "fight to the last man" defense. It was about carefully planned campaigns underpinned by logistical support. The delay in launching a major campaign in the East in particular brought these divisions into sharper focus and put strain on the important relationship between the president and his main general, McClellan.

On December 1, 1861, Secretary of War Cameron published his first and last report as secretary of war. To that date, the Union military had experienced mixed results on the battlefield, but the mobilization of the Union army was an unprecedented success. The report put the Union forces at 660,971 troops.[4] Nevertheless, there were constant calls for Cameron's resignation over concerns of illegal and corrupt actions. Cameron certainly took advantage of opportunities to increase his wealth. Union troops that moved by rail from New York to Baltimore were redirected from July 1861 via Harrisburg, Pennsylvania, on the Northern Central Railroad. This saved the War Department money and also increased the Northern Central revenue by 50 percent. Cameron was the largest shareholder of its stock. His actions were most probably legal at the time but they provided ammunition for his opponents' attacks on his credibility.[5]

In his report, Cameron also raised the delicate issue of Union policy towards slaves:

> What shall be done with them? Can we afford to send them forward to their masters, to be by them armed against us or used in producing supplies to sustain the rebellion? Their labor may be useful to us. Withheld from the enemy, it lessens his military resources, and withholding them has no tendency to inducven [sic] in the rebel communities. They constitute a military resource, and being such, they should not be turned

over to the enemy is too plain to discuss. Why deprive him of supplies by a blockade and voluntarily give him men to produce them?[6]

Controversially, Cameron had also raised the emotive and politically sensitive issue of the slaves being a military resource and, by arguing that the South might arm the slaves, he was posing the question of the right of the North to do the same. Yet, this was not the paragraph Cameron had written. This was Lincoln's less politically sensitive version. Cameron had shown his draft report to Edwin M. Stanton, the War Department's legal counsel. Stanton rewrote the final paragraph to read as follows: "It is as clearly a right of the government to arm slaves when it may become necessary, as to use gunpowder taken from the enemy."[7] A copy was sent to the White House but Lincoln did not read it. The superintendent of Public Printing, John D. Defrees, a friend of Lincoln's, read the report. Alarmed by the section on arming slaves, he took a copy with him to Lincoln. Lincoln was just as alarmed as Defrees and he rewrote the paragraph and ordered all copies of the report seized. Some copies were not recovered and their contents were printed.[8]

General Meade wrote to his wife with relief that Lincoln had suppressed Cameron's attempt to force abolition onto Union military policy: "Congress and its doings I suppose you see in the papers. It appears Cameron has come out on the Abolition side, but honest old Abe made him suppress the principal part of his report."[9] Lincoln's annual Message to Congress on December 3, 1861, still emphasized that the struggle was to preserve the Union and not to free the slaves: "The Union must be preserved, and hence, all indispensable means must be employed. We should not be in haste to determine that radical and extreme measures, which may reach the loyal as well as the disloyal, are indispensable."[10] The Union high command was far from ready to formally consider slavery as a war aim, so the conciliatory policy favored by McClellan and his supporters remained the Union's official position. Yet the pressure to change the Union's policy was steadily increasing.

The pressure on Lincoln to get the Army of the Potomac to march into Virginia had also increased. He wanted more information about what McClellan intended to do so that he could better answer criticism over McClellan's inactivity. McClellan had not informed Lincoln of his decision and the reason for delaying any major operation until spring 1862. In a memorandum to McClellan, which may have been written on December 1, 1861, Lincoln proposed to McClellan a plan of advance for the Army of the Potomac. First, Lincoln asked McClellan how long it would take for the army to be ready to advance. Then he outlined an advance along two lines of operations. One, southwest of the Potomac, would move towards Centerville. Another would move from Alexandria south along the Telegraph Road and cross the Occoquan River, where it would join a force that would have landed near the mouth of the Occoquan. This combined force would move, presumably along the south bank of the Occoquan, inland to Brentville and then the railroad south of its crossing of the Broad Run near Bristoe Station.[11] Such a maneuver would threaten the rear of the Confederate position at Manassas.

The plan represented the conventional wisdom of the time, which favored a direct line of advance from Washington towards Richmond by land. The problem with the plan was the division of the Union forces into two and operating on exterior lines. This would offer the Confederate army the opportunity to use interior lines to defeat the Union forces in detail.[12] The memorandum also included a series of questions for McClellan to answer concerning the available troop strength for Lincoln's proposed advance. McClellan replied on December 10, 1861, and advised Lincoln that the Confederates were "equal forces nearly" and the earliest time the army could be ready to move would be December 15, 1861. Significantly, he added, "I have now my mind actively turned towards another plan of campaign that I do not think at all anticipated by the enemy nor by many of our own people."[13]

Lincoln may have tried to force McClellan to divulge more details about his military plans, because Lincoln's plan for the Army of the Potomac could have been based on his understanding of what McClellan's own plans were. McClellan claimed in his memoirs that at a meeting on January 12, 1862, in which was discussed his refusal to outline his war plans, he had "reminded the President that he and the Secretary of the Treasury knew in general terms what my designs were."[14] Salmon P. Chase, the secretary of the treasury, was aware of McClellan's plans because on January 11, 1862, he had told General McDowell and Colonel Key what he knew about them in strict confidence. In his journal, he did not reveal what he knew, but it seems he may have known about an attack on Richmond by water.[15] General Franklin, a division commander and a friend of McClellan's, was asked on January 10, 1862, how he would advance the Army of the Potomac. He replied he believed it should "be taken, what could be spared from the duty of protecting the capital, to York River to operate on Richmond."[16] Lincoln may have been aware of McClellan's thinking but he did not know the details of his plans. As commander in chief, Lincoln should have been informed by McClellan of the details of his plans, including the time and line of operation for the army.

McClellan's plan to take Richmond and end the war evolved over several months. In August and September 1861 McClellan was initially thinking in terms of an advance similar to McDowell's line of advance of July. He intended to move south from Alexandria and cross the Occoquan River. Then he would swing west towards Brentsville and turn the Confederate defenses at Manassas.

This plan was similar to the one proposed by Lincoln in December 1861. McClellan must have thought of General Scott's successful turning movements in the Mexican War. General S.P. Heintzelman also proposed a similar line of operation in October.[17] This line of operation was eventually rejected by McClellan. It was too much like McDowell's failed campaign and he believed the Confederate position at Centerville was too strongly defended. He also considered the result of fighting another battle in northeast Virginia. The densely wooded terrain and the rivers and streams that ran west to east provided numerous natural defensive positions for the Confederate army. He must have doubted it would provide the decisive battle he desired.

By the end of 1861 McClellan probably had formed his plan to advance on Richmond in a turning movement by water. In October he asked William F. Barry, a brigadier general and chief of artillery, for advice on the politically sensitive issue of the number of troops needed to garrison Washington. Barry informed McClellan on October 22, 1861, that 33,795 troops would be required.[18] McClellan would have asked this question only if he planned to move the Army of the Potomac from in front of Washington. General Fitz John Porter had reported to Stanton that he knew of McClellan's Occoquan Plan in September and the Urbana Plan in November 1861.[19] McClellan told General John G. Barnard, chief of engineers in the Army of the Potomac, of his intention or idea of a movement by way of the Lower Chesapeake and the Rappahannock in November 1861.[20] Admiral Louis M. Goldsborough remembered McClellan told him in December 1861 of a plan to land the army on the Rappahannock at Urbanna and march from there to West Point on the York River.[21] This was a concept similar to General Scott's Vera Cruz campaign during the war with Mexico, in which Scott turned the Mexicans by an amphibious landing that eventually resulted in the capture of the Mexican capital and an end to the war. His plan was daring and dangerous. Resting on the belief that the war would end with the capture of Richmond, it held the prospect of a timely Union victory. The risk was exposing Washington to Confederate attack while the Army of the Potomac could not cover it. This was more than a question of strategy: it was a politically sensitive issue. William Swinton concluded that the adoption of the Urbanna Plan "had a most important bearing on the relations between the Executive and the General-in-Chief."[22]

Political pressure was increasing on McClellan from outside the executive and the cabinet. On Friday December 20, 1861, the Joint Committee on the Conduct of the War held a meeting. The next day it sent McClellan a letter asking for an interview with the general in his office at the Capitol at a time that would suit him.[23] McClellan responded that he would meet the committee on Monday, December 23.[24] McClellan, however, did not attend the meeting. He sent his aid, Colonel Thomas Key, with an apology: "General McClellan is so unwell that he will be unable to perform his engagement with you today. I do not think he will leave his house at all."[25] McClellan was sick with a potentially fatal case of typhoid. On Tuesday, December 24, 1861, the committee opened for its first testimony. It provided a forum for many opponents of McClellan and the opportunity to push for a more vigorous prosecution of the war.

The committee's questions focused on McClellan's plans for military operations. The intention here was to apply as much pressure as possible to get the Army of the Potomac to fight. One of its first witnesses was General Heintzelman, a commander of a division in the Army of the Potomac. He testified that he had never been consulted about a movement of the army, and when asked what he knew of McClellan's plans, he replied, "No, sir. I have not the slightest idea—not the slightest."[26] Another division commander in the Army of the Potomac, General McDowell, was asked if he was in "possession of any plans of movement now?" He replied, "No, sir."[27] Fitz John Porter, also a commander of a division in the Army of the Potomac, could not enlighten the committee on McClellan's plans: "What these plans are it is not for me to say—that is, I think it better for you to get them from him [McClellan]."[28]

McClellan's illness had far-reaching consequences for his relationship with the president. They had initially worked well together, but the relationship had slowly become strained. The importance of McClellan's illness, which lasted three weeks, is recognized by a number of historians.[29] On December 31, 1861, Lincoln held a cabinet meeting to discuss the consequences of McClellan's illness on the military situation. The implication was clear. With McClellan incapacitated, the armies could not move. Attorney General Edward Bates urged the president to assume direct and active command of the military.[30] Lincoln resisted the idea of the war's being run by an amateur such as himself. That evening, he met for an hour and a half with members of the Joint Committee on the Conduct of the War. Senator Wade, the chairman of the committee, criticized the administration over military inactivity and the lack of a policy regarding slavery and he was highly critical of McClellan.[31] Lincoln tried to ease McClellan's concerns over the committee's purpose when he wrote him the next day and euphemistically summed up the committee's intentions: "You may be entirely relieved on this point. The gentlemen of the Committee were with me an hour and a half last night; and I found them in a perfectly good mood."[32] What he did not reveal is that the committee members must have told Lincoln of their failure to find any general who knew of McClellan's plans for the operation of the Army of the Potomac.

Lincoln could not have been certain if McClellan would recover from his illness. Even if he did recover, Lincoln could not know when. With the pressure for a military campaign, Lincoln decided to use his powers as commander in chief to perform, to a limited extent, the role of general in chief. On December 31, 1861, Lincoln sent a telegram to General Halleck in St. Louis asking, "General McClellan is sick. Are General Buell and yourself in concert? When he moves on Bowling Green, what hinders it being re-enforced from Columbus? A simultaneous movement by you on Columbus might prevent it."[33] A similar dispatch was sent to General Buell. On January 1, 1862, General Buell informed Lincoln that there was no arrangement between General Halleck and himself.[34] On the same day, Buell telegraphed Halleck to organize a coordinated movement.[35] However, Halleck replied that he could not be ready to move for another two weeks.[36] Lincoln's request for information had begun a series of correspondence that revealed the confusion and lack of direction. By placing himself between his general in chief and the two principal Union commanders in the West, Lincoln had interfered in the chain of command and had undermined McClellan's authority.

The lack of military action in the West and the lack of coordination between Buell and Halleck must have been a cause of concern for Lincoln. Lincoln could have blamed McClellan as general in chief for the lack of progress, but it was more symptomatic of the lack of clearly defined powers for the role of general in chief as it was of the rivalry between Halleck and McClellan. Halleck did not share McClellan's view that the war could be quickly won by a victory in the East, and the division of the West between himself and Buell violated the rule of the concentration of force on a single line of operation.[37] Both Buell and Halleck had lost time trying to reorganize their commands so that they would be ready for operations. This was something McClellan could understand and support. However, Halleck's experience with Missouri guerrillas had weakened his support for McClellan's conciliatory strategy and instead he began to favor a more pragmatic policy.[38]

On January 2 and 6, 1862, Lincoln visited McClellan and found his health had improved, but he was still not well enough for active command.[39] Political pressure was now mounting to have McClellan removed. In January, Confederate troops seized a new section of railroad near Hancock, West Virginia, northwest of Harpers Ferry, and Union forces in this area had fallen back to the Maryland side of the Potomac River. This event coincided with Senator Chandler's visit to Chase to discuss the idea of General McDowell's being put in command of the Army of the Potomac and military affairs generally.[40] McDowell had strong supporters on the Joint Committee on the Conduct of the War.

On Monday, January 6, the cabinet met in the evening with Chandler, Wade, Johnson, Odell and Convode, who were members of the Joint Committee on the Conduct of the War. They urged the administration to be more vigorous in the prosecution of the war and recommended that McDowell replace McClellan as commander of the Army of the Potomac.[41] The meeting was requested by the committee because it believed it had enough evidence of McClellan's incompetence to appeal to the president. The evidence they had was testimony before the committee that showed the army was strong, the weather conditions were favorable, and the roads ideal for an advance into Virginia. Also, Confederate troop strength was inferior. They demanded that the president order McClellan to advance. The chairman of the committee, Senator Wade, asked the president if he knew of McClellan's plans. Lincoln replied that he had no knowledge of McClellan's plans and he did not intend to interfere with him. Seward also supported McClellan.[42] Chase supported the committee to the extent that he believed no one person could effectively carry out the duties of commander of the Army of the Potomac and general in chief. The meeting concluded with the president announcing he would discuss this issue with McClellan.[43]

The pressure from the committee had its effect. The next day, Lincoln wrote to General Buell requesting that he "name as early a day as you safely can on or before which you can be ready to move southward in concert with Major-General Halleck. Delay is ruining us, and it is indispensable for me to have something definite. I send a like dispatch to Major-General Halleck."[44] He also put in a loan request for a copy of General Halleck's book, *Elements of Military Art and Science,* which indicated that he may have considered not only the need to know more about military art but also that he might have considered taking direct control of the army.[45] Attorney General Edward Bates had advised the president to act as the constitutional "commander in chief." Bates wanted Lincoln, as president, to command the operations of the Union military forces. He saw no reason to have a professional soldier as general in chief. He reasoned that as commander in chief Lincoln must command. Added to this constitutional argument was the necessity to know the overall military situation and plans. While some advised forming a council of generals to advise the president, Bates argued it was not "his privilege but his duty to command; and that implied the necessity to know the true condition of things."[46]

On January 10 Lincoln was advised by Halleck that he could not support Buell's advance into East Tennessee. Lincoln complained: "It is exceedingly discouraging. As everywhere else, nothing can be done."[47] The president's work to try to coordinate Halleck and Buell's operations had resulted in more frustration. Distressed, the president visited Quartermaster-General Montgomery

C. Meigs in his office. Lincoln sat down and asked, "General, what shall I do? The people are impatient; Chase has no money and tells me he can raise no more; the General of the Army has typhoid fever. The bottom is out of the tub. What shall I do?" Meigs advised that if McClellan had typhoid fever it would be at least six weeks before he could resume command of the army. Lincoln could not wait another six weeks for the Army of the Potomac or the western armies to move. Meigs reminded Lincoln of McClellan's assessment that the Confederate forces near Washington were strong and might attack on any day. He suggested meeting with "those upon whom in such case, or in case any forward movement becomes necessary, the control must fall."[48] This suggestion did have some merit. If McClellan did not recover, a replacement would have to be appointed and the new general in chief could not be expected to act immediately. An expectation for earlier action would be more probable if the potential replacements for McClellan were active in forming their plans and advising the president of them.

Lincoln acted swiftly on this idea. He summoned Generals McDowell and Franklin, Secretary of State Seward, Secretary of the Treasury Chase, and the Assistant Secretary of War Scott to the first of a series of "councils of war" in the White House at 8:00 that evening. According to McDowell, the president was "greatly disturbed" and spoke of the concerns he had related to Meigs earlier that day. He also revealed the pressure he was under from the Radical Republicans in Congress and the delicate condition of foreign relations. The president had been to McClellan's home and the general did not see him. Lincoln said he could do nothing with the western armies because they were out of his reach, but he could, in a short time, do something with the Army of the Potomac.[49] Consequently, he wanted to talk to Franklin and McDowell about the possibility of "soon commencing active operations with the Army of the Potomac." As Lincoln explained it, "If something was not soon done, the bottom would be out of the whole affair; and if General McClellan did not want to use the army, he would like to borrow it, provided he could see how it could be made to do something."[50]

McDowell responded to the president's question with a plan of action. He would reorganize the Army of the Potomac into four army corps. He suggested leaving five divisions to protect Washington and the four corps to be deployed on a line of operations similar to the one he had used in July 1861, except this time he intended to threaten the Confederate left and then outflank them on their right. This was similar to the plan Lincoln had proposed to McClellan. General Franklin was far less detailed with his response. He proposed that the army "should be taken, what could be spared from the duty of protecting the capital, to York River to operate on Richmond."[51] Franklin's proposal indicated he knew of McClellan's plan for a change of base to the York Peninsula. The discussion then turned to the ability to transport a large part of the army by water and the lack of knowledge of the condition of the army. The president decided that they would meet again the next night at 8:00 and that Franklin and McDowell should meet and obtain information from the staff of the Army of the Potomac.[52]

McDowell had known that his proposal to reorganize the army into army corps would have support within the cabinet and the Republican Party. This issue of command and control was important owing to the strong influence of the French on the U.S. professional military tradition. *Corps d'armée*, or army corps, were used during the Napoleonic Wars by the French army and had a decisive impact on battlefield operations. Army corps were small armies comprising infantry, cavalry and artillery that ensured all three arms could be used in a more effective and coordinated manner. This made command and control much easier. Corps had never existed in the U.S. Army. McClellan's delay in forming army corps had been a cause of criticism of his command.

The next day, Saturday, January 11, 1862, the Lincoln administration changed dramatically. Lincoln accepted the resignation of Secretary of War Cameron and officially appointed Edwin M. Stanton to succeed Cameron on January 13. Stanton immediately set out to make his cabinet position the most powerful in Lincoln's administration. The president was convinced Stanton would provide stronger direction and leadership at the War Department. The president must also have expected a better working relationship between the new secretary of war and McClellan. Interestingly, it was Stanton who had warned McClellan about the "councils of war" being held in the White House.[53] However, Stanton shared many of the popular views of the time about warfare. The American tradition had emphasized courage and motivation as the key to battlefield success. On January 13 Stanton told Don Piatt, a personal friend, of his plans for the War Department. Stanton wanted to accomplish three things: "I will make Abe Lincoln President of the United States. I will force this man McClellan to fight or throw up; and last but not least, I will pick Lorenzo Thomas up with a pair of tongs and drop him from the nearest window."[54]

In his first "War Bulletin" on January 22, 1862, Stanton had praised Union troops for their victory at Mill Spring, Kentucky, because of their "military and personal valor displayed in battle." He insisted, "The purpose of this war is to attack, pursue, and destroy a rebellious enemy."[55] These views were the basis of the criticism directed at McClellan and other professional, West Point–trained generals who emphasized strategy and logistics. Stanton shared the frustration of many who wanted the Army of the Potomac to advance, and immediately after his appointment to secretary of war he put pressure on McClellan to force him to order a forward movement.[56] Although Stanton had initially supported McClellan, eventually he became a strong opponent of him.[57]

As ordered, Franklin and McDowell met in the morning at the Treasury Building. McDowell identified, as a priority, the removal of the Confederate army from the vicinity of Washington because it was "beleaguering our capital, blockading the river, and covering us day by day with the reproach of impotence, and lowering us in the eyes of foreign nations, and our people both North and South."[58] Franklin suggested asking Chase about the details of General Burnside's expedition. McDowell asked him and was informed that its objective was Newbern, North Carolina. What was more important, he revealed that McClellan, by direction of the president, had advised him of the plan to move a large force of the Army of the Potomac to Urbanna or Tappahannock on the Rappahannock and then to Richmond. McDowell informed Franklin and they agreed to continue to make inquiries about the Army of the Potomac's operating by both land and water. Franklin asked whether they should inform McClellan of their actions. McDowell argued that since the orders were marked private and confidential and as the orders came from the president, the commander in chief, it should be the president who would inform McClellan.[59] McDowell wanted to be certain, so he sought the advice of Chase. Chase believed the matter lay entirely with the president.[60]

The evening of January 11 Generals McDowell and Franklin attended a meeting at the White House with the president's cabinet members, Seward, Chase and Postmaster General Montgomery Blair. Franklin and McDowell had met with the Army of the Potomac's supply officers that afternoon.[61] McDowell read from a paper that presented his and Franklin's views on the military situation. Both agreed that "in view of time, etc., required to take this army to another base that operations could best now be undertaken from the present base, substantially as proposed."[62] They also agreed that if the army was to be moved "at once," the best line of operation was to march into Virginia and not transport the troops by water. What they disagreed on was the timing. McDowell was in favor of an immediate advance into Virginia. Franklin was not.[63] An immediate advance could not be made with the seriously ill McClellan in command, so most likely McDowell would take McClellan's place.

On Sunday, January 12, 1862, Franklin and McDowell had visited Quartermaster General Meigs. Meigs believed it would take a month to six weeks to collect enough water transportation to move the army by water. They intended to pass this information on at the scheduled 3:00 p.m. meeting but Seward had rushed in and claimed to have seen McClellan and he was well.[64] Lincoln informed those present that the meeting had been called as a consequence of McClellan's illness but now he had heard that morning from him that he was feeling better. McClellan had in fact unexpectedly visited Lincoln Sunday morning. McClellan stated that his presence had the effect of "a shell in a powder magazine" and he concluded "there was something of which they were ashamed." Lincoln invited McClellan to attend a meeting on Monday.[65] Lincoln adjourned the meeting for one o'clock on Monday. Privately the president was still concerned about the lack of action. That evening he confided in his personal and political friend, the senator from Illinois Oliver Hickman Browning, that he was "thinking of taking the field himself." He also outlined a plan for simultaneous advances by all Union armies to gain the advantage of superior numbers and exterior lines.[66]

The next day, the meeting resumed, but this time with General McClellan present.[67] McClellan was still sick but he was motivated to attend because Stanton had told him, "They are counting on your death, and are already dividing among themselves your military goods and chattels."[68] The "they" he referred to was not explained but he believed McDowell was somehow behind the "affair" because he thought McDowell hoped to replace him as commander of the Army of the Potomac. The meeting provided the opportunity for McDowell to present himself in the most favorable way, but there is no evidence to suggest Lincoln intended to replace McClellan. While McClellan doubted the loyalty of McDowell, he had no doubts about the loyalty of his old friend General Franklin.[69] The president invited McDowell to describe his plan on a map and explained to McClellan why he had sought the advice of the two generals.[70] All looked to McClellan, expecting him to speak. Quartermaster General Montgomery Meigs tried to encourage McClellan to respond: "The President evidently expects you to speak; can you promise some movement towards Manassas?" Secretary of the Treasury Chase asked McClellan what he intended doing with the army and when he intended doing it.[71] McClellan was reluctant to speak though he did tell Meigs the reason why: "If I tell him (Lincoln) my plans they will be in the *New York Herald* tomorrow morning. He can't keep a secret, he will tell them to Tadd."[72] Meigs reminded McClellan that Lincoln was "the President,—the Commander-in-Chief; he has a right to know; it is not respectful to sit mute when he so clearly requires you to speak. He is superior to all."[73]

McDowell described the work Franklin and he had done under the president's order. In particular, he outlined their findings that a movement on land on the front the army currently occupied would take three weeks, and a change of base by transporting part of the army further south could take a month to six weeks. McDowell concluded by offering an apologetic explanation about the position in which the two generals had been placed. McClellan replied, "You are entitled to have any opinion you please!"[74] Franklin added that when he gave his view to operate on the York River he did it knowing that it was in the same direction as General McClellan's plan. McDowell said he "had acted entirely in the dark."[75]

General McClellan declined to provide his plans in detail but thought the best option was for Buell's army to advance in the center of the Western Theater of operations. After a pause, McClellan stated he did not want to provide the details of his plans because "in military matters the fewer persons who were knowing to them the better" and "he would tell them if he was ordered to do so."[76] The situation was tense because it was now clear that General Franklin was aware of McClellan's operational plan but the president was not. Lincoln asked McClellan if he had a plan of action for the Army of the Potomac. McClellan replied that he had. Franklin recalled that after a silence the president replied that he would not order him to reveal his plan.[77] When McClellan did not reveal his plan, Franklin remembered he overheard either Chase or Blair quietly comment, "Well, if that is Mac's decision, he is a ruined man."[78] McClellan reminded the president that he and the Secretary of the Treasury Chase were aware in general terms of his plans. McClellan refused to reveal any detail of his plans unless the president ordered it in writing.[79] Lincoln could not have been entirely satisfied but concluded the meeting because McClellan would press an advance into Kentucky.[80] McClellan had managed to hold onto his authority as general in chief but his reputation and credibility had been eroded. After the meeting, he approached the president and begged him not to be influenced by "improper influences" but to trust him and that if Lincoln left military affairs to him, he would be responsible and bring matters to a successful conclusion, thus freeing the president of his troubles.[81] In effect, McClellan wanted military matters left to the military professionals without any interference from civilians.

A farcical situation ensued as a result of this meeting when both Lincoln and McClellan sent telegrams to the commanders of the western armies, Buell and Halleck. McClellan's letter to Buell revealed the level of political pressure on the general for a military advance: "You have no idea of the pressure brought to bear here upon the Government for a forward movement. It is so strong that it seems absolutely necessary to make the advance on Eastern Tennessee at once." In a sense of desperation, McClellan advised Buell if he could not request enough wagons because people would not give them freely then he should seize them because it "is no time to stand on trifles."[82] Lincoln's letters urged action but only on the basis of acting to counter the Confederates' use of interior lines: "I state my general idea of this war to be that we have the greater numbers, and the enemy has the greater facility of concentrating forces upon points of collision; that we must fail, unless we can find some way of making our advantage an over-match for his; and that this can only be done by menacing him with superior forces at different points, at the same time."[83] Lincoln had learned from Halleck's *Elements of Military Art and Science*, because simultaneous advances were the textbook solution to nullify the advantages of interior lines.

Lincoln's more active role in military matters continued and in a manner which directly interfered with the general in chief. The president's General War Order No. 1 on January 27, 1862, set February 22, 1862, for "a general movement of the Land and Naval forces of the United States against the insurgent forces." It held all those in the higher echelons of the high command, including the general in chief, responsible for the prompt execution of the order.[84] The date was selected for no military reason, but it was the sentimental anniversary of Washington's birthday. The idea of an order to force McClellan into action had been suggested before by the Navy Department and had the support of Stanton. Both the navy and Stanton were frustrated by McClellan's lack of urgency to remove Confederate batteries from the Potomac River.[85]

There was no indication of what "a general movement" involved. The order was not directed to any military organization; instead it referred to "the Army at & about, Fortress Monroe," "the Army near Munfordsville [sic], Ky.," and "the Army and Flotilla at Cairo." Lincoln gave no details as to the objectives of any of the Union's military forces but, he warned, "[T]he Heads of Departments, and especially the Secretaries of War and of the Navy, with all their subordinates; and the General in chief, with all other commanders and subordinates, of Land and Naval forces, will severally be held to their strict and full responsibilities, for the prompt execution of this order."[86] Geoffrey Perret described it as "less an order, then, than a distress signal, one that suggested a man flailing the air."[87]

Perhaps the president realized the "General War Order" was not going to achieve anything because it was followed by the "President's Special War Order No. 1," issued on January 31, 1862. This order, directed at McClellan and the Army of the Potomac, set the line of operation for the army. It ordered "all the disposable force of the Army of the Potomac, after providing safely for the defense of Washington, be formed into an expedition, for the immediate object of seizing and occupying a point upon the rail road south westward of what is known as Manassas Junction, all details to be in the discretion of the general in chief, and the expedition to move before, or on, the 22nd. day of February next."[88] Unlike the general order, this was a plan of action, but it did not have any strategic objective beyond occupying Manassas. What was the army to do after it achieved this limited objective?

This was not an operational plan aimed at achieving the Union's war aim. These orders indicated the president's anxiety about the need for the Union's military forces to advance as soon as possible and also the president's lack of trust in McClellan to leave military matters entirely to him. Significantly, Stanton had encouraged McClellan to discuss his plan to move the Army of the Potomac to attack Richmond by the Lower Chesapeake. Lincoln had rejected McClellan's plan in favor of his own.[89] Lincoln's orders proved difficult to execute, particularly in Virginia, where bad weather in late January and February 1862 made movement by the armies almost impossible.

Lincoln's resolve to try to push the military to advance was shared by the new secretary of war, Stanton. At Stanton's first reception, he simply stated his philosophy about how the war should be fought to some Union officers: "Now, gentlemen, we will, if you please, have some fighting. It is my business to furnish the means; it is yours to use them. I leave the fighting to you, but the fighting we must have."[90] Stanton saw the success of the Union would be based upon a well-run War Department. He wanted it to be the most powerful and the most important of all the federal departments. One way in which he intended to ensure this was to adhere strictly to the chain of command. He moved the Telegraph Department from McClellan's office to the War Department. He sought advice from Dennis Hart Mahan on January 20, 1862, on two issues of interest to both the president and Radical Republicans—army corps and the duties of a chief of staff. The interest by the civilians in army corps is interesting because the army corps belonged to the regular, professional soldier's tradition and not the tradition of the amateur army. This interest also reflected Stanton's political alliance with the Radical Republicans in the Joint Committee on the Conduct of the War. He knew he could use the committee's powers to obtain information that was not available to him. Significantly, on Stanton's first day as secretary of war he had met with the whole committee and afterward became an invited guest to many of the committee's meetings. This alliance helped remove obstructions by Congress to Stanton's initiatives, but Stanton must have been influenced by the committee members' resolve to continue to push for the Union to fight a much more earnest war.[91]

Stanton was disillusioned with McClellan because he believed McClellan did not have the will to fight for the Union: "This man has no heart in the cause, he is fighting for a boundary if he fights at all; our great difficulty is to make him fight at all."[92] Stanton believed that West Point–trained officers had been taught "everything but patriotism and the art of war" and of more concern was the fact that the school had been filled by pro-slavery Democrats. The school was more of a social group that fostered a horror of abolitionism.[93] His mistrust of professional soldiers and the officer class was also shared by his political allies, the Radical Republicans.

McClellan knew he had to respond to this new political pressure. He had managed to maintain his duties as general in chief and commander of the Army of the Potomac only because his illness had ended. He needed support, so he sought the advice of trusted senior officers in the army. He discussed his plans with Generals Franklin, Fitz John Porter and William Farrar Smith— who was known to his friends as "Baldy"—at his house. McClellan outlined the strategic situation in the West and the East and the need for the western armies to begin operations first so that they would draw the attention of the Confederates from the Eastern Theater. He probably outlined his thinking on a change of base to Urbanna.[94] In response to pressure from Stanton, McClellan planned to attack and remove the Confederate batteries on the western bank of the Potomac and to open the Baltimore and Ohio Railroad by occupying Harper's Ferry. Strategically, these operations were minor, but McClellan had recognized their political importance.[95]

However, McClellan had to deal with the problem of Lincoln's war orders. McClellan disagreed with the date for the advance and, more important, the line of operations for the Army of the Potomac. He probably did not intend to follow the order because he did not follow orders he did not like and perhaps he reasoned Lincoln never intended to enforce the order because he inconsistently applied military protocol. The issue is not as clean-cut as the historical record might suggest. The two must have met many times and discussed this issue. McClellan had asked the president if the order was to be regarded as final or whether he could be permitted to put his objections in writing. Permission was granted and McClellan wrote a twenty-two page letter to the secretary of war.[96] Another indication that Lincoln did not intend to enforce this order is seen in a letter he wrote McClellan on February 3, 1862. Lincoln stated he would change his mind about the line of operation of the Army of the Potomac if he could be convinced by McClellan's answers to five questions: "You and I have distinct, and different plans for a movement of the Army of the Potomac—yours to be down the Chesapeake, up the Rappahannock to Urbana, and across land to the terminus of the Railroad on the York River—, mine to move directly to a point on the Railroad South West of Manassas. If you will give me satisfactory answers to the following questions,

I shall gladly yield my plan to yours."[97] So the president did not require the execution of his war orders but neither were they formally revoked.

This lack of effective and decisive decision making left an opportunity open for McClellan to continue to push for his movement of the army to the Lower Chesapeake. Lincoln's nonenforcement of Special War Order No. 1 could have been interpreted by McClellan to mean that Lincoln had accepted his plan. McClellan had pressed preparations for moving the army by water. To the political pressure for an advance in the East was added pressure from military victories in the West. On February 6, 1862, General Ulysses S. Grant, in Halleck's command, had captured Fort Henry on the Tennessee River. Grant then marched his army twelve miles to Fort Donelson on the Cumberland River. The fort surrendered on February 16. General Grant was made famous in the Northern press when he replied to the Confederate general Simon Bolivar Buckner's offer to negotiate surrender terms: "No terms except unconditional and immediate surrender can be accepted. I propose to move immediately upon your works."[98] Grant's decisiveness had opened the Confederate defensive line in the West and forced them to retreat towards Corinth in Mississippi.

Halleck was emboldened by Grant's victory. Even before Grant's victories at Fort Henry and Fort Donelson, Halleck had plans to combine the departments in the West into a single "Western Division," which he would command in order to "avoid any clashing of interests or difference of plans and policy."[99] McClellan would have preferred that Halleck move to Union City and then to Columbus and Buell to take the line of the Tennessee and move on Nashville.[100] Halleck, however, planned to march on Nashville with any surplus troops from Buell, whom Halleck believed should hold the Green River.[101] McClellan wanted to support Halleck by having Buell advance from Bowling Green, Kentucky, to Nashville, the capital of Tennessee.[102] This made sense because Grant was still in front of Fort Donelson. Although the thought of Buell taking Nashville did not sit well with Halleck's ego, this changed when Fort Donelson fell unexpectedly quickly to Grant.

Halleck pushed McClellan on February 20: "I must have command of the armies in the West. Hesitation and delay are losing us the golden opportunity. Lay this before the President and Secretary of War. May I assume the command? Answer quickly."[103] McClellan replied the next day, dismissing Halleck's proposal: "I do not yet see that Buell cannot control his own line. I shall not lay your request before the Secretary until I hear definitely from Buell."[104] McClellan's lack of control over his armies in the West was a concern, particularly if the military situation there caused a delay in his plans for the Army of the Potomac. He wrote to Buell, whom he believed had his confidence:

"Telegraph me at least once every day the position of your own troops, that of the rebels, and the state of affairs. Unless I have this detailed information I cannot tell whether it is necessary or not to suspend or abandon my own plans here. Neither Halleck nor yourself give me as much detailed information as is necessary for me. This is the critical period, and I must be constantly informed of the condition of your affairs."[105]

Grant's victories were examples of what the Radical Republicans and the Union public, in general, were seeking. They shared the popular perception that wars were won by battles fought by courageous soldiers and inspirational leaders and not by the application of strategy and logistics. Hand in hand with this view was the traditional distrust of trained professional officers. The attack upon these officers was based on the militia tradition of the United States. The *New York Tribune* had exposed the virtues of the citizen soldier: "However imperfect the civil appreciation may be as to military science, common sense is an attribute which buttons and bullion do not alone confer; and common sense is quite as competent as tactical profundity to decide the questions of hastening or deferring operations against the rebels."[106] Others believed that any great man in wartime "must be born with the genius of war in his breast" similar to great artists and poets.[107]

However, the supporters of these popular representations of war failed to understand that General Halleck and General Grant, both professionally trained officers, had used the sound application of military principles, in this case turning movements against Fort Henry and Fort Donelson. The Confederates had retreated from Fort Henry when their lines of communication were threatened, while at Fort Donelson Confederate communications had been cut, which forced them to attack Union forces in an attempt to reopen them. This gave Grant's forces the advantage of fighting a tactical defensive battle. The victories turned the Confederate defensive line in the West and forced them to retreat from their main positions at Bowling Green and Columbus in Kentucky. Also, the Confederate armies were separated. One retreated towards Chattanooga near the Georgia state boundary and the second to Memphis on the Mississippi. As a result, most of Tennessee was opened up to Union forces.

The contrast between the activity in the West and the lack of it in the East provided the Radical Republicans with more ammunition to criticize McClellan. The issue of slavery and whether its abolition should be a Union war aim was always closely attached to their criticism of McClellan's lack of enthusiasm to fight. Members of Lincoln's cabinet had noted the changed perceptions towards slavery. Gradually, more people in the North had identified a link between the Union war effort and the abolition of slavery. Secretary of State William H. Seward had observed that even after seven months of hostilities the nature of the war was evolving, particularly when Union troops entered Confederate territory: "We have entered Virginia, and already five thousand slaves, emancipated simply by the appearance of our forces, are upon the hands of the Federal government there." Seward astutely concluded, "Although the war has not been waged against slavery, yet the army acts immediately as an emancipating crusade."[108]

A turning movement, such as Halleck and Grant had used in the West, was also the theoretical basis of McClellan's plan of operation for the Army of the Potomac. McClellan had planned to use a strategic turning movement linked to a tactical defense. He knew it would take more than patriotic spirit to capture Richmond and defeat the Confederacy. Plans to outflank the Confederate position at Manassas were sound but the problem was that the plan assumed the enemy would fight there. If the Confederates withdrew to another defensive position nothing would have been gained. Even if the Union army eventually reached the vicinity of Richmond the supply lines would be too long, so a shorter supply line using the rivers east and south of the city would then have to be used. The logic suggested adopting a shorter supply line at the start rather than the end of the campaign. McClellan planned to land his army at Urbanna on the Rappahannock River and move through West Point to occupy Richmond before the Confederates had the time to reinforce their capital. Even if the Confederates could reinforce Richmond, McClellan could take up a position to the south of the capital. This threat to the Confederate capital would force General Johnston to abandon his prepared defensive position to try to force the Union army as far from the capital as possible. If this occurred, McClellan would have the advantage of fighting on the tactical defensive on the ground of his own choosing. The advantage was clear. With a secure line of supply by water, McClellan could keep his army fighting in this area as long as was needed. The Confederates would be disadvantaged because they would be fighting to protect or reopen their line of supply.

McClellan was also aware of the delicate problem of protecting Washington, a situation that arose after the army had moved from in front of it. Since the Army of the Potomac would be supplied by water, the turning movement would become a penetration.[109] Any attempt by the Confederates to attack and take Washington would be a raid because the Confederate line of supply would be cut by McClellan's turning movement. Even if the Confederates took Washington, they could not stay long because they would need to reopen their line of supply by moving south towards Richmond. While this made military sense, politically Lincoln could not afford the embarrassment and loss of prestige that the loss of the capital would mean domestically and abroad.[110]

Lincoln was not convinced that McClellan's proposed line of operation was the better one for the Army of the Potomac to advance upon than the one favored by he himself. He was also concerned by rumors that McClellan intended to leave Washington defenseless by moving the entire Army of the Potomac by water to Urbanna. On Saturday, March 8, Lincoln summoned McClellan to a 7:30 a.m. meeting in his office to discuss a "very ugly matter."[111] Nor was Lincoln pleased by the results of the movement to Harpers Ferry and the delay in raising the blockade of the lower Potomac River. Lincoln told McClellan that his plan had been represented as "conceived with the traitorous intent of removing its defenders from Washington, and thus giving over to the enemy the capital and the government." Lincoln did not intend to accuse McClellan of treason but the general was insulted by the suggestion of it and invited Lincoln to a meeting of division generals of the Army of the Potomac that afternoon.[112]

The generals assembled at McClellan's headquarters later that morning. McClellan presented his plan for the movement of the army and then left the meeting. The generals voted, according to General Franklin, nine in approval and three against, though it was later reported the vote was eight to four in favor of McClellan's plan. Opposed to this plan were John G. Barnard, S.P. Hientzelman, Irvin McDowell and E.V. Sumner.[113] Keyes had approved the plan provided the Confederate batteries on the lower Potomac were cleared, so, as a consequence, the meeting also voted in favor of an attack on the Confederate Potomac River batteries.[114] Immediately after the meeting, the generals went to see the president in the White House. At the meeting with the president was also the secretary of war. They had already been informed of the result of the vote taken by the generals. Stanton observed that Lincoln was surprised by the support for McClellan's plan.[115] The secretary of war asked each general his opinion of the "Urbanna" plan and finally the generals' views on the issue of whether the army should be organized into army corps. The generals unanimously agreed the army should be organized into army corps.[116]

Although Lincoln and Stanton would have preferred the generals to have voted for an overland line of advance and not have supported McClellan's Urbana plan, they finally had a strong commitment for an offensive to begin in a month's time. Lincoln also had strong support for army corps, which would please the radical elements in his political party. Nevertheless, a vote by division commanders after a presentation by their commanding general was a peculiar way for the Union high command to come to a decision.

McClellan was not on firm ground with his opposition to army corps. He was well aware that one of the reasons for Napoleon's success was his use of army corps. Army corps were in effect small armies that provided the army with greater maneuverability. McClellan had used the "council of war" to successfully outflank political opposition to his planned change of base but he was not able to defeat the push to form army corps. However, his sense of achievement that day was short lived.

When McClellan reached his office in Jackson Square, he discovered an order that reorganized the Army of the Potomac. The president's General War Order, No. 2, ordered "the Major-General commanding the Army of the Potomac proceed forthwith to organize that part of said army destined to enter upon active operations, (including the reserve, but excluding the troops to be left in the fortifications about Washington,) into four army corps." Each of the corps comprised three divisions except the First, which had four. Furthermore, according to seniority, Lincoln had appointed as corps commanders McDowell, Edwin V. Sumner, Samuel P. Heintzelman and Erasmus D. Keyes. But also important was that McDowell, Sumner and Heintzelman had opposed McClellan's change of base plan and Keyes gave it only conditional support.

The appointment of these four corps commanders represented Lincoln's lack of confidence in McClellan's plan. Edwin Sumner was born in Boston and entered the army in 1819. He had experience in Mexico and along the frontier. He was promoted when the conflict began as a result of his friendship with General Scott and the president. However, he had no experience of commanding large formations of troops. Samuel Heintzelman was an old soldier with a great deal of experience on the frontier. Brave and competent, he had been wounded at Manassas and his promotion was based on seniority. Erasmus Keyes had little experience on the frontier and had missed the Mexican War. His rise through the U.S, Army ranks was based on his relationship with General Scott. He had commanded a brigade at Manassas. A well-known Republican, he was unpopular with McClellan. Also, these generals were regarded, as John Hay described them, as "fighting generals."[117] McClellan would have preferred to have appointed Franklin, Fitz John Porter, Smith and Andrew Porter. The forces left to defend Washington were placed in the command of General James S. Wadsworth, who was also the military governor of the District of Columbia. Wadsworth was a Republican and he disliked McClellan. Lincoln did not want to leave the security of the capital entirely to McClellan. Divisions west of Washington were reorganized into the Fifth Army Corps, under General N.P. Banks, which comprised his own and General Shields' and the late General Lander's divisions.[118]

Four—"Now is the winter of our discontent"

McClellan must have recognized his powers as general in chief were being intruded upon by the president. He would have been disappointed that the corps commanders had been appointed by the president and without the president consulting him. This was not the first time, however, this had occurred. On March 3, 1862, Lincoln had ordered Secretary of War Stanton to appoint nine major generals and nine brigadier generals.[119] McClellan's power to appoint had declined from the time he had gained it through a memorandum on July 29, 1861. McDowell, a senior officer in the Army of the Potomac, was the only promotion to major general in McClelland's army, but it was an indication that Lincoln was acting more independently on military matters.

Radical Republicans had urged the creation of corps because doing so would place the senior generals, who were also Republicans, in command. T. Harry Williams contends that the Army of the Potomac's officer corps were divided into two factions, the senior officers and their followers and the younger officers, who were strongly committed to McClellan. The senior officers were also Republicans and supported wartime emancipation.[120] They were also older than McClellan and disliked his rise to a position that they regarded should have been theirs.[121] Also, they felt McClellan had treated them unjustly by favoring others.[122] The Radical Republicans saw in the corps structure an opportunity to restrict the authority and influence of McClellan because the corps commands would go to the senior officers. On the other hand, Lincoln supported the concept because it was militarily sound. It would reduce the amount of administration McClellan was doing because he would be communicating with four corps commanders and not twelve division commanders. McClellan did not want to support the formation of corps until the movement of the army gave him the opportunity to select the best officers on merit. McClellan's argument was logical but, like that of the Radical Republicans, it was political in that he did not want the interference of the Republican generals.[123]

Lincoln's second order, on March 8, 1862, General War Order, No. 3, revealed his concerns about his general in chief. It set conditions upon the movement of the Army of the Potomac to Urbanna. To make sure there would be no more delays, Lincoln ordered the movement to start on March 18, 1862. Reflecting the political doubts about the safety of Washington from such a movement, Lincoln ordered that "no change of the base of operations of the Army of the Potomac shall be made without leaving in, and about Washington, such a force as, in the opinion of the General-in-Chief, and the commanders of all the Army corps, shall leave said City entirely secure." By adding the commanders of the corps to this decision, Lincoln was telling McClellan that he still harbored doubts about the effectiveness of the plan. Also, in a move designed to rid Lincoln of the political embarrassment of the blockade of the lower Potomac, McClellan was permitted to move only two army corps until the Potomac was freed from Confederate batteries.[124]

South of the Potomac River, General Joseph E. Johnston, the commander of the Confederate troops at Manassas, was reassessing his military position. He was concerned that with the growth of the Army of the Potomac he was, in his current position, too exposed to a flanking movement. On March 9, 1862, he ordered his army to fall back to a defensive position on the Rappahannock River near Fredericksburg. He also abandoned the blockade of the Potomac River. On the evening of March 9, McClellan responded to intelligence of Johnston's withdrawal by ordering the whole army forward, hoping that Johnston might have made a mistake and be forced to battle, and also to give his troops the experience of marching and bivouacking as preparation for the transportation by water.[125] McClellan intended to move the army forward in divisions and not in corps as he had been ordered. It was not until March 13 that he executed the order to form corps.[126] When the army reached Manassas, the troops discovered Confederate defensive positions with "Quaker guns," or wooden logs painted to resemble artillery.[127] Newspaper reporters who accompanied the army noted that the Confederate army could not have been as large as McClellan had consistently estimated.[128] McClellan defended his delay to advance his army because of the large number of Confederate troops at Manassas. Apart from the public humiliation, his plan to land at Urbanna was nullified by the Confederate retreat. Yet McClellan was still determined to move the army by water. He now needed to move it further south in order for it to be successful.

Pressure on Lincoln from within the cabinet to remove McClellan as general in chief reached its crisis point at a cabinet meeting on March 11, 1862. Secretary of War Stanton complained that reports were going to McClellan but he was not reporting anything in return. Also, he accused McClellan of having "no plans but is fumbling and plunging in confusion and darkness." This was in response to McClellan's superfluous advance to Centreville and Manassas. Attorney General Bates again pressed the president to act as commander in chief without a general in chief. He argued that if the president must have a general in chief then he should not command an army.[129] The result was the president's War Order, No. 3, of March 11, 1862. Lincoln ordered McClellan removed from his position as general in chief: "Major General McClellan having personally taken the field at the head of the Army of the Potomac, until otherwise ordered, he is relieved from the command of the other Military departments, he retaining command of the Department of the

Potomac." The order also reorganized Union forces in the West into the Department of the Mississippi commanded by Major General Halleck.[130]

Halleck was a wise choice. He had been successful in the West and he had been recommended by General Winfield Scott.[131] Scott had admired Halleck ever since, as a young lieutenant, he had written a paper on defense of the seacoast for him.[132] Interestingly, the order recognized McClellan's command as the Department of the Potomac and not an army. This was the traditional U.S. military structure of departments and reversed an order by McClellan in August 1861, which created the Army of the Potomac as an army and not a geographic command. Lincoln informed the cabinet he had displayed great kindness in permitting McClellan to retain command of the Army of the Potomac and giving him an opportunity to correct his errors.[133] McClellan had learned of his displacement as general in chief in the press. He responded, at the time, graciously to the order, but in reflection he perceived the order to be "one of the steps taken to tie my hands in order to secure failure of the approaching campaign."[134] Lincoln had removed McClellan from the position of general in chief but he did not appoint another general in his place. Lincoln would now fill this void.

Only one thing could cause McClellan to be reinstated as general in chief: a successful campaign. A meeting of the Army of the Potomac's corps commanders and McClellan at Fairfax Court House on March 13, 1862, considered the options to continue the plan to move the army by water in a strategic turning movement. McClellan referred to a February 3 letter to Stanton. The letter was his response to Lincoln's call for a general advance. In his response, he proposed using Fort Monroe as a base of operations for an advance up the York-James peninsula to Richmond.[135] The meeting agreed to proceed to the York-James peninsula, provided the Confederate ironclad naval vessel, the *Merrimac*, could be neutralized, sufficient transportation was available for an immediate transfer of the army and a naval force was provided to support the landing of the army.[136] Lincoln approved the plan the same day provided that a large enough Union force was left at Manassas Junction to prevent its falling to the Confederates and Washington was left secure. The remaining troops could be sent to the new base at Fortress Monroe.[137] On March 17, 1862, troops had begun to embark for Fortress Monroe. A few weeks later, on April 1, General McClellan left to join his army for what would become known as the "Peninsula Campaign."

For many in the North, the Eastern Theater of operations during the winter of 1861–1862 was a "winter of discontent" because of inaction of the Army of the Potomac. The expectation that General McClellan would fight and win a decisive battle and capture Richmond was never realized. Of importance, the professional relationship between the president and the general in chief deteriorated. Lincoln had deferred to McClellan but this became increasingly difficult when the army had not moved and McClellan had not divulged his plan for the army to fight. Ironically, McClellan had been caught up in his own pronouncements of winning the war with his main army of operations and his belief in careful campaign planning. His sickness with typhoid increased the strains within the Union high command. The "councils of war" convened by Lincoln's order were interpreted by McClellan as an attempt to replace him with General McDowell, and Lincoln was under pressure to make such a move. Lincoln began to take a more active role in the organization of the army and its operations, a move supported by the cabinet and, in particular, by Secretary of War Stanton, who was keen to push for a more vigorous military policy. Lincoln's orders for simultaneous advances showed his understanding of the strategic situation but also his lack of knowledge about the operational reality. The reality was that the Union armies could not make a coordinated move by that date. This order therefore proved to be unsuccessful because it was ignored.

Lincoln's increasing desperation to get the Army of the Potomac to fight was exacerbated by McClellan's change of base plan. Lincoln accepted the plan only with assurances of the safety of Washington and the formation of army corps. His sacking of McClellan as general in chief may have been motivated by the reality that McClellan could not hold the two posts while on active command away from Washington. It also reflected Lincoln's lack of confidence in the plan and the fact that he intended to take a more direct role in the military and to seek military advice from elsewhere. This does not detract from the fact that the president and his general in chief managed to work together. The reason for this is that Lincoln and McClellan shared the same conciliatory approach to the war. Lincoln did not want to use overwhelming force to crush the Confederacy, nor did McClellan. By capturing Richmond, McClellan would achieve the limited aim of demonstrating that the Confederacy could not succeed.

FIVE

"Walking on in the dark": McClellan's Attempt to Win the War with a Victory in the East

The assumption that many in the Union high command held in early 1862 was that most of its strategic problems would disappear when the Army of the Potomac began to move towards Richmond. This was as optimistic as it was simplistic. The battles fought so far had demonstrated how difficult it was to destroy a civil war army. Yet the amateur tradition that viewed wars as a series of battles—and McClellan's own belief that he could fight and win a decisive battle—worked toward the conclusion that this war could be won in a single campaign. The focus of this chapter is three consecutive military campaigns: the Peninsula Campaign, the Second Battle of Manassas and the Battle of Antietam. The purpose is to examine how the structure and personal conflicts within the Union high command affected the outcomes of these campaigns and the success of the Union in the Eastern Theater of war to the end of 1862. The dominant Unionist interpretation of why the North was eventually successful is ultimately examined.

The Union high command had to deal with the problem of having no general in chief for the first time in the conflict. Without a general in chief with which to discuss the progress of the war, Lincoln needed a military advisor. On March 7, 1862, retired Major General Ethan Allen Hitchcock received a telegram from Secretary of War Stanton for a meeting in Washington. Hitchcock had the military pedigree. He was the grandson of a famous War of Independence leader, Ethan Allen. He had graduated from West Point in 1817 and had served in the U.S. Army until his retirement in 1855. On the morning of March 15, 1862, Hitchcock met Stanton. Stanton asked him if he would take McClellan's place as commander of the Army of the Potomac. This offer was beyond Stanton's authority. Hitchcock declined the offer and Stanton went on to explain the pressure the president and he had been under, resisting demands that McClellan be removed.[1] Stanton then took Hitchcock to meet the president. Lincoln took a letter out of his pocket and read it to Hitchcock. The anonymous letter urged Lincoln to "remove the traitor McClellan." This, Lincoln stated, was an example of the nature and weight of the pressure he was under. Lincoln asked Hitchcock if he could have the benefit of his experience.[2] Finally, to reinforce his concerns over McClellan's effectiveness, Stanton recounted anecdotes of McClellan's incompetence, which had a significant impact on Hitchcock, as evidenced by his recording in his diary how these stories had made him "positively sick."[3]

Hitchcock promptly agreed to be appointed as a staff officer under Stanton. Hitchcock wrote the order himself and Stanton signed it.[4] In fact, what he had accepted was more than just a position as military advisor to the president and the secretary of war; he was also head of the War Board, Stanton's solution to the organization problem of unity of command. Hitchcock's first advice to Stanton was to reorganize the Union command structure in the West by extending General Halleck's command to include the whole of the Mississippi Valley.[5] The United States had never possessed a general staff in the modern sense. The War Department's staff was more meager than the staff of field armies. The army's staff comprised special staff who reported to the secretary of war. There was a general in chief, a position not provided for by law, but there was no general staff. Since the special staff did not report to the general in chief, he could not effectively command the army, because it needed logistical support and he did not control these key areas. Constitutionally, operational control of the army was placed in the hands of the secretary of war, to maintain the civilian control over the military.[6] However, as has been well documented, the United States had not faced a military conflict of this scale before. The U.S. amateur military tradition Stanton supported did not offer solutions to the command and control problems in 1862. Stanton quickly became aware that the major problem, to "work an army of five hundred thousand with machinery adapted to a peace establishment of twelve thousand, is no easy task."[7]

To create the War Board, Stanton put the heads of several bureaus of the army into a formal structure that became a basic form of general staff. Ironically, Stanton, a strong supporter of the U.S. militia tradition and someone who therefore was suspicious of professional soldiers, had created a body that regular, trained officers in the U.S. Army had sought but had viewed as impossible to obtain. But to work effectively as secretary of war, Stanton needed the military professionals' understanding and knowledge of the complexities of waging a war on this scale. The board included Lorenzo Thomas, the adjutant general, Montgomery C. Meigs, the quartermaster general, James W. Ripely, the chief of ordinance, Joseph G. Totten, the chief engineer, Colonel Joseph P. Taylor, commissary general and, later, E.R.S. Canby, Stanton's "military aide."[8] The board met with Stanton several times each week. Hitchcock did not join the board until its third meeting, and although he served as its head he took little part in its discussions.[9]

A pressing issue for the Union's civilian leaders and General Hitchcock was the defense of Washington. It became more pressing with McClellan's change of base strategy. Unfortunately for McClellan, this issue had an impact on his operations on the peninsula. The capital was a symbol of the Union, and after the Union defeat at Manassas it became obvious that elaborate defenses needed to be constructed to protect the city. In August 1861 McClellan had placed Major John Gross Barnard of the Corps of Engineers in charge of the construction of forty-eight forts and other field works along the circumference of the city. By the end of 1861 the formal defenses of Washington comprised an impressive forty-eight defensive works.[10] Major Barnard, in a report to the assistant adjutant general, General Williams, on October 22, 1861, had determined that 33,795 troops were required to garrison the defenses of Washington.[11]

To render the capital entirely secure, the president's War Order No. 3 of March 3, 1862, had instructed General McClellan to leave a force "in and about" Washington large enough to meet this objective. A meeting of the Army of the Potomac's corps commanders on March 13 had determined that 40,000 troops would be required to defend the city.[12] Lincoln accepted this advice. Another order to McClellan on the same day reflected the president's persistent concern about the safety of Washington when so many troops would be on the peninsula. He ordered McClellan to leave a force at Manassas Junction, leave Washington "entirely" secure and move only what remained of the army down to Fortress Monroe.[13] McClellan had ordered all corps except General Banks's corps to embark for the peninsula and reported to the secretary of war that, in total, 55,456 troops were deployed to defend the capital plus 18,000 for its garrison. General Banks was expected to entrench his troops at Manassas, but the actions of General "Stonewall" Jackson's Confederate division in the Shenandoah Valley forced Banks to move into the valley. The Shenandoah Valley did not provide a strategic opportunity for the Union to threaten Richmond, but it did offer the Confederates a line of advance that could threaten Washington. Consequently, Lincoln was always concerned with Confederate military activity in the Shenandoah Valley. The movement of Banks highlighted that McClellan's 55,456 troops designated to defend the capital were deployed over a vast area. It comprised 35,467 troops under General Banks in the Shenandoah Valley and a rough estimate of 10,859 troops at Manassas.[14]

Stanton sought advice from Generals Wadsworth and Hitchcock, as head of the War Board, to determine if the president's order to leave the capital secure had been followed. With General Banks in the Shenandoah Valley, it was left to General James Wadsworth, commander of the Military District of Washington, to protect the capital. Wadsworth discovered he had only 19,022 "'new and imperfectly disciplined men' and he concluded, 'I deem it my duty to state that, looking at the numerical strength and character of the force under my command, it is my judgment entirely inadequate to and unfit for the important duty to which it is assigned.'" Furthermore, Wadsworth had no knowledge of the position General Banks would take if Washington was threatened.[15] This was far too short of the almost 34,000 troops Major Barnard had advised and the 40,000 the corps commanders had recommended.

Washington's defenses were not a continuous line that encircled the city but a series of fortified strong points. These strong points were designed to assist a field army to defend the city. In his 2007 work, *Army of the Potomac: McClellan's First Campaign, March-May 1862*, Russel H. Beatie has compared Washington's defenses to the Duke of Wellington's "Lines of Torres Vedas," which enabled his British and Portuguese army to hold off a larger French army and prevent it from taking the Portuguese capital of Lisbon in 1810 during the Napoleonic War.[16] But Wellington designed these fortifications so that the garrison was supported by his army behind the lines. This was different from 1862 with the main field army away from the defenses. Washington was not a fortress that could be defended by its garrison alone. General Hitchcock replied to Wadsworth's report and concluded the president's requirement that the city shall be left "entirely secure" had, in the opinion of the general in chief and also that of the commanders of the army corps, not been fully complied with.[17] The War Board had thus confirmed Lincoln's view that McClellan had not left the capital secure. This conclusion did not mean McClellan had been deliberately neglectful or deceptive. His view of defending Washington was based on a defense-in-depth principle rather than on defending just one geographic point. Also, McClellan had argued that his turning movement would force Confederate forces in northern Virginia to move towards Richmond to protect their line of supply. Nevertheless, McClellan's opponents used this as an example of his deceitfulness and lack of trust and respect for the civilian administration.

In the middle of March 1862 the Army of the Potomac began its change of base to Fortress Monroe on the tip of the peninsula. It was the largest amphibious military operation to date in United States military history. It took three weeks and four hundred vessels to transport 121,000 troops from Alexandria to Fortress Monroe. McClellan's plan was simple enough. With its flanks protected by the U.S. Navy, the Army of the Potomac would march quickly the seventy miles to Richmond and avoid any costly battles, because Confederate forces would not have enough time to redeploy with numbers sufficient to delay or prevent the Union advance. Once he was outside Richmond, McClellan planned to conduct a siege, take the Confederate capital and end the war. Any attempt by the Confederate army to delay Union forces on the peninsula would be thwarted by landing General McDowell's corps, nearly thirty thousand troops, on the southern side of the York River in a position to turn Yorktown. This plan required that McDowell's corps move last.[18] The successful execution of the plan depended on the quick movement of the army. General Fitz John Porter explained this plan to Edmund Clarence Stedman: "The quicker it gets there the better for the country. The quickest plan is McClellan's to take the lower Chesapeake for a basis of operations with this army. Richmond in our possession and the rebellion is broken. That object and aim is McClellan's and if sustained he will accomplish it in the shortest time and least loss of life on our side."[19]

However, McClellan's plan of operation was complicated by the view of Lincoln, Stanton and the War Board: that he had not left the capital secure. On April 3, 1862, Lincoln acted on McClellan's failure to provide enough troops to secure the capital and ordered McClellan to "leave one or the other of the corps of General McDowell and General Sumner remain in front of Washington until further orders from the Department, to operate at or in the direction of Manassas Junction, or otherwise, as occasion may require; that the other corps not so ordered to remain go forward to General McClellan as speedily as possible; that General McClellan commence his forward movements from his new base at once, and that such incidental modifications as the foregoing may render proper be also made."[20]

On the same day Lincoln had ordered McDowell's corps to remain in Washington, the United States Senate voted to abolish slavery in the District of Columbia by a vote of twenty-nine to fourteen. In a further step, on April 7 Lincoln signed a treaty with Great Britain for suppression of the African slave trade.[21] It was a small step for the Radicals in the Republican Party but it was a significant indicator of the increased political support abolition had gained almost a year into the conflict

The next day Lincoln ordered the Army of the Potomac's largest corps, McDowell's corps of 38,500 troops, to be detached to provide a field army to protect the capital.[22] McClellan vehemently complained: "It is the most infamous thing that history has recorded. I have made such representations as will probably induce a revocation of the order, or at least save Franklin to me. The idea of depriving a general of 35,000 troops when actually under fire!"[23] In a further blow to McClellan's command of Union forces in the East, Lincoln reorganized the Union forces near Washington. Two new departments were created, the Department of the Shenandoah under the command of Major General Banks and the Department of the Rappahannock under the command of Major General McDowell.[24] This decision reflected Lincoln's concern about Confederate movements in the Shenandoah Valley. Ironically, the fracturing of Union command would hinder more than it would help Union efforts to defeat General Jackson's army in May and June. The order also meant that McClellan's bases of supply, Washington and Fortress Monroe, were not under his control. Fortress Monroe had been placed under McClellan's command, but on April 3 this order was reversed and Major General Wool, the commander of the Department of Virginia, was again in command of Fortress Monroe and the troops assigned to his Department.[25] McClellan was also concerned that McDowell's command offered an alternative line of operation against Richmond and the one favored by the president. McClellan protested that this provided the Confederates with the opportunity to use interior lines to defeat one of the two armies.[26]

In Washington, General Franklin, a division commander in McDowell's corps, was ordered to a meeting at the War Department. There he found General McDowell and General Wadsworth. According to Franklin's recollection of the meeting, McDowell recounted a meeting an hour before with Stanton. Stanton had told him McClellan intended to achieve victory on the peninsula by maneuvering and not by fighting battles. This revelation was not new to Stanton, because to outmaneuver the Confederates had always been central to the plan for the change of base. But Stanton saw wars as a series of battles. Consequently, he would not send McClellan anymore troops if he did not intend to suffer casualties by fighting battles. He accused the general of political aspirations and also of disobeying the president's order to leave the capital secure by not leaving enough troops to defend Washington. McDowell argued against detaching his corps from the Army of the Potomac but without success. Stanton ordered his corps to Catlett's Station, on the Orange and Alexandria Railroad, to guard the direct line of advance on Washington from Richmond.[27] However, McDowell's protests were not enough to convince McClellan that he had not acted to undermine the campaign.

After the war, Franklin described this order as "the first great crime of the war."[28] He justified his view because Lincoln had taken from McClellan his largest corps—commanded by his second in command—which contained more than one-fourth of his army, only forty-eight hours after he had left for the peninsula. This corps was vital to the success of the campaign. Furthermore, Lincoln had taken this action without consulting McClellan and without even informing him of the intended action prior to issuing the order.[29] Alexander Stuart Webb also strongly criticized the decision: "The greatest military error that could possibly have been committed was that which removed so important a corps from an army already in motion to carry out what was a well-digested plan."[30]

The president's decision had a serious effect on McClellan and his staff's attitude toward their civilian superiors. On April 9 Major General Oliver Howard was disturbed to learn from McClellan's aide-de-camp, Colonel Colburn, of the differences between McClellan and the president. Colburn complained bitterly "of the action of the President in taking away over 50,000 troops which had been promised to McClellan."[31] Even General Keyes—commander of the Fourth Corps—whom McClellan may have liked least, wrote to Senator Ira Harris of New York complaining of Lincoln's order.[32] Harris forwarded the letter to Lincoln and Keyes sent a copy to McClellan. Keyes explained that the removal of one of the Army of the Potomac's four corps meant "the plan of campaign I voted for, if carried out with the means proposed, will certainly succeed. If any part of the means proposed are withheld or diverted, I deem it due to myself to say that our success will be uncertain."[33] McClellan might have been buoyed by support from this unexpected quarter, but he should also have been concerned that Keyes had breached the chain of command.

On April 4 the Army of the Potomac commenced its advance up the peninsula with 121,500 men. To his surprise, McClellan found the Confederates had prepared a defensive line across the peninsula that was anchored on the old American War of Independence battlefield at Yorktown. General Magruder had only fifteen thousand troops to man the twenty-kilometer defensive line and resist the Union advance.[34] McClellan's strategy was based on the need to surprise the enemy and a quick advance to Richmond. He had achieved the surprise he had needed but by April 6 he had begun to doubt that he could quickly advance to Richmond: "I will take Yorktown, but it may be a slow process." The reason for this was "the diminution of [his] forces."[35] Already McClellan was blaming Lincoln for delays in his campaign timetable by keeping McDowell's corps in front of Washington.[36] He also blamed the U.S. Navy for not being able to quickly reduce the Confederate batteries at Yorktown and Gloucester and failure to cut their land communications for delaying his advance up the Peninsula.[37] However, the navy had doubts that it could reduce these batteries by naval fire and it also believed it was not expected to take them.[38]

McClellan was still critical of the corps structure and the corps commanders who had been forced upon him. He probably believed that McDowell had been behind the decision to keep his First Corps near Washington. He no doubt reasoned that McDowell was still scheming to regain control of the Union's main army and that the failure of the Peninsula Campaign might provide the opportunity McDowell needed. On April 5 McClellan first asked Lincoln directly, not through the secretary of war, to reconsider detaching the First Corps from McDowell's command. He also asked that, since he could not have all the First Corps, if he could have only a part of it, in particular General Franklin—who was a strong supporter of McClellan's—and Franklin's division.[39] A determined McClellan repeated the request the next day.[40]

The slow progress of McClellan's advance up the peninsula was bound to increase Lincoln and the secretary of war's fear that the campaign would not be successful. One of the main sources of tension between Lincoln and McClellan had been the long period of inactivity of the Army of the Potomac. Now McClellan was conducting the campaign too cautiously to achieve a quick, decisive victory. McClellan decided not to breach the Confederate defensive line but to besiege Yorktown instead. This meant he had to wait until his siege artillery could be transported into position. This was contrary to the basis of McClellan's strategy, which required a quick advance to Richmond. Lincoln was not alone in his impatience. John Hay, the assistant to his friend and private secretary to Lincoln, John Nicolay, expressed the thoughts of many in the Lincoln administration with the delay of the army at Yorktown: "It is disgraceful to think how the little squad at Yorktown keeps him at bay."[41]

Criticism of McClellan was again given more weight with the military action in the Western Theater. John Hay believed that McClellan lacked the resolve to fight: "Grant is fighting the overwhelming legions of Buckner at Pittsburg, the Little Napoleon sits trembling before the handful of men at Yorktown, afraid either to fight or run. Stanton feels devilish about it. He would like to remove him, if he thought it would do."[42] At Shiloh on the Tennessee River, Confederate forces under Albert Sidney Johnston had struck on April 6, 1862, at the advancing Union Army of the Tennessee under General Grant before another Union army under General Don Carlos Buell could unite with it. The Confederates had initial success on April 6, but on April 7 Grant renewed the battle with Buell's reinforcements and soundly defeated the Confederates. Union losses were 13,000 out of 60,000, while the Confederates lost proportionally more, a quarter of their 40,000 troops. This was the type of fighting that fitted the public's perception of war. Lincoln acknowledged this when he defended Grant over allegations of drunkenness: "I can't spare this man: he fights."[43]

Lincoln tried to force McClellan into action. On April 6 he advised him, "You now have over one hundred thousand troops, with you independent of Gen. Wool's command. I think you better break the enemies' line from Yorktown to Warwick River, at once. They will probably use time, as advantageously as you can."[44] Privately Lincoln was impatient and dissatisfied with McClellan's slow progress.[45] In reply to a request from McClellan for more troops, he reminded him on April 9 that he was not in favor of the line of operation and the "country will not fail to note—is noting now—that the present hesitation to move upon an entrenched position is but the story of Manassas repeated." He reassured the general that he had the support of the president but also reminded him of the need to take action: *"But you must act."*[46]

McClellan prepared to take Yorktown by siege. The prospect of a long, drawn-out siege made Lincoln even more impatient. On April 13, 1862, Hitchcock arrived at McClellan's camp near Yorktown and remained there for one day. There could be no doubt that Lincoln had sent the head of the War Board to evaluate the military situation. When he returned to Washington, Hitchcock reported to Lincoln and Stanton. Hitchcock did not record any details of the meeting.[47] He had found it difficult to work with Stanton because Stanton was impatient toward him. He had often noticed him in a similar mood with other members of the War Board and he had determined not to accept it towards himself. Consequently, on April 29 he had handed in his resignation of his commission of major general of volunteers.[48] Also adding to Lincoln's frustration over the McClellan's lack of progress was the news of more success in the West. On April 25, New Orleans had been captured by Union forces.

McClellan's careful preparations for the artillery bombardment of Yorktown were almost ready when on May 4, Confederate General Joseph Johnston withdrew his Confederate army from the defensive line and moved towards Richmond. McClellan won a victory with only a few casualties, but it had taken a month of valuable time. The army set out in pursuit of the Confederates and forced a battle at Williamsburg. While he claimed a victory, reports from his trusted division commander General William "Baldy" Smith were critical of corps commander Sumner. McClellan saw an opportunity to remove not only the corps structure but the corps commanders whom he distrusted. He telegraphed Stanton on May 9 and asked "permission to reorganize the army corps. I am not willing to be held responsible for the present arrangement, experience having proved it to be very bad, and it having very nearly resulted in a most disastrous defeat. I wish either to return to the organization by division or else be authorized to relieve incompetent commanders of army corps."[49]

Stanton's quick reply indicated his anxiety about the outcome of the campaign. He advised McClellan, "The President is unwilling to have the army corps organization broken up, but also unwilling that the commanding general shall be trammeled and embarrassed in actual skirmishing, collision with the enemy, and on the eve of an expected great battle. You, therefore, may temporarily suspend that organization in the army now under your immediate command, and adopt any you see fit until farther order."[50] This was a major reversal of policy by Lincoln who, with the support of the Republican Party "Radicals," had promoted and formed army corps. Lincoln also wrote privately to McClellan on the same subject and reminded him that the decision to form corps was supported by all twelve division commanders. Furthermore, he was aware that McClellan did not consult with his corps commanders but instead with General Fitz John Porter and General Franklin. Lincoln reminded McClellan of the complex reality of a democracy at war. He asked McClellan to consider the political backlash from such a move against generals with strong support from the Republican Party: "Are you strong enough—are you strong enough, even with my help—to set your foot upon the necks of Sumner, Heintzelman, and Keyes all at once?"[51]

McClellan accepted Lincoln's pragmatic advice. He did not dissolve the corps structure. But he seized the chance on May 17 when he created two new "provisional" corps, the Fifth and the Sixth, to be commanded by officers he could trust, Generals Fitz John Porter and William Franklin.[52] These corps, made permanent on July 22, 1862, were created by weakening the other three under McClellan's command.[53] While he now had almost half of the army under men he could trust, his decision weakened the fighting capability of each corps and was another example of favoritism that increased the ill feeling of some officers towards McClellan. Franklin noted the tension within the army's officers with the organization of the new corps and as a result he had "purposely kept away from HdQrs for days together in order to silence slanderous tongues."[54] Privately, McClellan was disenchanted with the interference of his political leaders in his command: "I am heartily tired of this life I am leading always some little absurd thing being done by those gentry in Washington. I am every day more and more tired of public life, and earnestly pray that I may soon be able to throw down my sword and live once more as a private gentleman."[55] A few days later he described them as "those hounds in Washington [who] are after me again. Stanton is without exception the vilest man I ever knew or heard of."[56]

McClellan continued his advance up the peninsula and by the end of May he was close to Richmond. He preferred to approach the city from the south of the Chickahominy River but was forced to place three corps north of the river. His pleas for reinforcements had made Lincoln consider sending McDowell's corps overland to link up with the Army of the Potomac.[57] On May 18 McDowell was ordered to march by land to help McClellan with his attack on Richmond, but he was ordered to take a line of operation that would place him in a position to prevent an attack on Washington. To ensure this, Lincoln ordered that McDowell's command, the Department of the Rappahannock, remain separate from the Army of the Potomac.[58] McClellan pushed this issue with Lincoln. McClellan wanted McDowell's troops to become part of the Army of the Potomac. The president correctly informed him on May 24 that when McDowell's corps joined him he would have command of that force.[59] However, the action of General Jackson in the Shenandoah Valley had put General Banks's Union forces in such a difficult position that Harpers Ferry could be taken. About an hour later Lincoln informed McClellan that as a result McDowell's corps would now be moving to the "Valley."[60] McClellan was still convinced that Lincoln's decision not to provide reinforcements jeopardized his chances of victory because he believed he was outnumbered by the enemy. He felt Lincoln had "deliberately placed me in this position. If I win, the greater the glory. If I lose, they will be damned forever, by both God and men."[61]

Unfortunately for McClellan, the Chickahominy had become a considerable obstacle because spring rains had caused it to flood. The Confederate commander Joseph Johnston decided to take advantage of the divided Union army and defeat it in detail. He concentrated his attacks on Heintzelman's and Keyes's corps south of the river on May 31. Some initial Confederate gains were reversed by the arrival of Sumner's Second Corps. The Battle of Fair Oaks was a Union victory. One of the 6,314 Confederate casualties was General Johnston. He was replaced as commander of the Confederate army by Robert E. Lee.

Lincoln was concerned enough about the lack of progress of the Army of the Potomac to consult the retired General Winfield Scott at West Point on June 23. Scott considered the positions and numbers of Frémont and Banks adequate to protect Washington from the Shenandoah Valley and the troops at Manassas together with the forts on the Potomac, and Washington would protect the capital from the south. Scott reassured Lincoln optimistically that the objective of the campaign was correct: "The defeat of the rebels, at Richmond, or their forced retreat, thence, combined with our previous victories, would be a virtual end of the rebellion, & soon restore entire Virginia to the Union." Scott considered sending McDowell's corps to McClellan by water to help achieve a victory there.[62] Scott's assessment reassured Lincoln that the capital was safe but it also vindicated McClellan's requests for McDowell's corps to reinforce him. Two days later, on June 26, Lincoln reorganized the armies defending Washington into the Army of Virginia comprising Major Generals Frémont, Banks, and McDowell, and including the troops now under Brigadier General Sturgis at Washington. The Army of Virginia was placed under the command of Major General John Pope.[63]

Pope, like McClellan, was a graduate of West Point and a veteran of the Mexican War. He came East after successfully campaigning in the West, where he had captured Island Number 10 on the Mississippi River. In his address to his army on July 14, Pope revealed that he had come from the "West, where we have always seen the backs of our enemies, from an army whose business it has been to seek the adversary, and to beat him when found, whose policy has been attack, and not defense." He concluded, "I hear constantly of taking strong positions and holding them—of lines of retreat and of bases, of supplies. Let us discard such ideas. The strongest position a soldier should desire to occupy is one from which he can most easily advance against the enemy."[64] Such pronouncements were seen as pompous and did little to endear him to the officers in his new command. General Alphesus S. Williams, who commanded the First Division, Second Corp, in Pope's Army of Virginia, wrote "that more insolence, superciliousness, ignorance, and pretentiousness were combined in one man. It can with truth be said of him that he had not a friend in his command from the smallest drummer boy to the highest general officer."[65] Pope's confidence aside, this was a strong criticism of the handling of the Army of the Potomac under McClellan.

Still concerned by the slow progress of the Army of the Potomac, Lincoln reassessed the Union's strategy for winning the war. McClellan's strategy had been simple: take Richmond and the Confederacy would crumble. Now Lincoln disagreed that the war could be won with a decisive battle in the East. He believed the concentration of enemy troops at Richmond was now too large for McClellan to achieve success. Sending additional troops from the West to reinforce McClellan would only provide an opportunity for the Confederates to regain lost territory. Lincoln thought in terms of an offensive strategy in the West and a defensive strategy in the East and only after significant territorial gains were made in the West would the offensive be taken in the East: "What should be done is to hold what we have in the West, open the Mississippi, and, take Chatanooga & East Tennessee, without more—a reasonable force should, in every event, be kept about Washington for its protection. Then let the country give us a hundred thousand new troops in the shortest possible time, which added to McClellan, directly or indirectly, will take Richmond, without endangering any other place which we now hold—and will substantially end the war."[66] This was similar to General Scott's strategy outlined in 1861. Yet, the near proximity of the two capitals and having the Union's main army of operations near Washington would always force military attention to this theater of the war.

General Robert E. Lee had no intention of fighting a defensive battle to protect Richmond. Instead he decided to recall General Jackson from the Shenandoah Valley and to cut off, attack and destroy the Army of the Potomac. Lee hit the Union army before McClellan had time to resume his advance on Richmond. Indeed, the opportunity for the Confederates to attack had been created by McClellan. The right flank of the Union army was exposed. Furthermore, this part of the army was about one-third of McClellan's force and it was separated from the rest of the army by the Chickahominy River. This provided the Confederates with the chance to defeat the Army of the Potomac in detail by concentrating against this smaller, isolated corps.[67] On June 26 he struck north of the Chickahominy against General Fitz John Porter's Fifth Corps. The Battle of Mechanicsville was the first of the Seven Days' Battle, during which McClellan surrendered the initiative to Lee. Lee fought to stop McClellan falling back and establish a new base on the James River. McClellan had little direct involvement in the battles, which were in fact a series of encounter battles as the Confederates tried to disrupt the Union army's withdrawal. Lee never achieved any tactical success but his forces held the battlefield at the end of the fighting, a sign in many people's eyes of victory on the battlefield. The success of the Army of the Potomac was due largely to the corps structure and commanders of whom McClellan had been so critical. On June 30 McClellan telegraphed Stanton again asking for more troops. Already he was talking in terms of defeat and believed the reinforcements were critical because the safety of the army depended upon it: "Another day of desperate fighting. We are hard pressed by superior numbers. I fear I shall be forced to abandon my material to save my men under cover of the gunboats. You must send us very large re-enforcements by way of Fort Monroe, and they must come very promptly. My army has behaved superbly, and have done all that men could do. If none of us escape, we shall at least have done honor to the country. I shall do my best to save the army. Send more gunboats."[68] Lincoln responded that it was "impossible to reinforce" him but he should "save the Army at all events, even if you fall back to Fortress-Monroe."[69]

On July 1 McClellan concentrated the Army of the Potomac on Malvern Hill, a strong defensive position on the James River. He inspected his army and boarded the ship *Galena* at nine 'clock in the morning to examine Harrison's Landing. For a third time in this campaign McClellan had left his army prior to a major battle. Jeffrey D. Wert, in *The Sword of Lincoln*, has described it as a "dereliction of duty."[70] A poorly coordinated Confederate assault failed to dislodge the Army of the Potomac from its strong position. McClellan pressed Lincoln for an additional fifty thousand troops so that he could regain the initiative and the offensive.[71] But McClellan withdrew another eight kilometers to Harrison's Landing and entrenched his army. Lincoln was concerned for the safety of the army, particularly since it had been driven back from the outskirts of Richmond. He ordered 5,000 troops from McDowell's corps and another 25,000-member corps from General Halleck to strengthen McClellan.[72]

Halleck still viewed the Western Theater as more important than the battles in Virginia and the request for reinforcements to be sent to McClellan, which could affect Halleck's move towards Chattanooga, once more revealed the hostility between these two senior Union generals. Halleck refused to send troops as requested and advised Lincoln to look for the required reinforcements from other commands:

> I submitted the question of sending troops to Richmond to the principal officers of my command. They are unanimous in opinion that if this army is seriously diminished the Chattanooga expedition must be revoked or the hope of holding Southwest Tennessee abandoned. I must earnestly protest against surrendering what has cost us so much blood and treasure, and which, in a military point of view, is worth three Richmonds. It will be infinitely better to withdraw troops from the Shenandoah Valley, which at this time has no strategic importance. I am doing everything in my power to strengthen our position, and a week or two may change the aspect of affairs here.[73]

Nevertheless, McClellan had already planned to withdraw to Harrison's Landing and to fortify the position, convinced that he had "failed to win only because overpowered by superior numbers."[74] Lee correctly recognized the Union position was too strong and moved his army back to Richmond. While no one could have known it at the time, the Peninsula Campaign had ended. It had cost the Army of the Potomac 15,849 men killed, wounded, and missing. The Confederates, who fought mostly on the tactical offensive, lost 20,614.[75]

So concerned was Lincoln about the military situation on the peninsula that he decided to visit McClellan and assess the situation firsthand. He left Washington on July 7 aboard the USS *Ariel*. When he arrived at Fortress Monroe on July 8, Lincoln held a meeting with General Burnside. It may have been at this meeting that Lincoln for the first time offered command of the Army of the Potomac to Burnside.[76] Burnside's opinion was that he "did not think there was any one who could do as much with that army as General McClellan."[77] The same day, McClellan came aboard the president's ship and presented him with what has become known as the "Harrison's Landing Letter."[78] This letter was not a report on the current campaign of the Army of the Potomac but a criticism of Lincoln's handling of the war. McClellan argued that the war needed to be fought according to "the highest principles known to Christian civilization. It should not be a war looking to the subjugation of the people of any State in any event. It should not be at all a war upon population, but against armed forces and political organizations." He went further, arguing that the forcible abolition of slavery should not even be contemplated because taking these "radical views" could destroy the Union armies. Instead, the military forces of the Union should be concentrated against the Confederate armies. Once the Confederate armies were defeated the political structures that supported them would collapse. McClellan also urged the appointment of a general in chief.[79] Lincoln made no comment to McClellan concerning the contents of the letter but it would have been clear that his views about the type of war needed to win this conflict were diverging even further from McClellan's.

That night Lincoln inspected the Army of the Potomac, but the most important part of his visit began the next day when he requested that all corps commanders come onboard the *Ariel* to be interviewed individually. Lincoln was acting as both commander in chief and general in chief. The president wanted to know if the army should be withdrawn to Washington or if it could remain on the peninsula. When General Keyes arrived on the ship Lincoln asked if he would go for a walk. The president abruptly asked Keyes, "What's to be done with this army?" Keyes responded that it should be taken back to Washington. Keyes' reasoning was that the army was in retreat and the opportunity to take Richmond had passed. He also believed that the onset of the malaria season would inflict large losses on the army and if it remained any longer the Confederates would march on Washington.[80]

The evidence from the five corps commanders was certainly convincing. All except Fitz John Porter, a strong supporter of McClellan, believed the army could be moved safely from the peninsula; but Heitzelman and Porter felt it would "ruin the country" and Sumner believed such a move would signal that the Union had "given up the cause." All generals believed the army was safe in its present location but in contrast to McClellan, who believed the enemy was five miles away, they concluded the Confederates had withdrawn, with Keyes' assessment being that the Confederate army was near Richmond.[81] Two days later Keyes put his thoughts in writing to the president, ignoring the chain of command. He reinforced his concerns about operating from the peninsula and argued, furthermore, that the Army of the Potomac would need to be reinforced by one hundred thousand troops before it could march on Richmond.[82]

Lincoln must have considered the idea of returning McClellan to general in chief if his campaign was successful. But the president's doubts about the prospects of success for the Army of the Potomac on the current line of operations had forced him to appoint a new person as general in chief. Lincoln may also have been motivated to appoint a general superior to McClellan and Pope to force some cooperation between the two main Union armies in the East.[83] On July 11, 1862, Lincoln finally filled the gap in the Union high command when he ordered General Henry W. Halleck from Corinth to be "assigned to command the whole land forces of the United States as General-in-Chief, and that he repair to this capital so soon as he can...."[84] Halleck was a regular officer in the army who was held in high regard by his peers and had a recent record of success in the Western Theater of the war. He had the advantage of the informal structure of the now dispensed with War Board.[85] His first task was to determine the exact number of troops in the Army of the Potomac. Lincoln had discovered a gap of forty-five thousand troops between McClellan's estimate of his troop numbers and the number of troops actually sent to him. Lincoln needed an explanation.[86] The president sent Halleck, Meigs and General Burnside to Harrison's Landing to assess the prospect for further military action for the Army of the Potomac.[87]

Politically and militarily the tide was turning against McClellan. On Monday evening, July 21, Secretary of the Treasury Salmon P. Chase had dined with General Pope, the commander of the Army of Virginia, the army that guarded the direct line of advance from Richmond to Washington. Pope argued for "the most vigorous measures in the prosecution of the war" out of the conviction that "slavery must perish." He argued "there should be a change in command of the Army of the Potomac." Pope also believed "McClellan's incompetency and indisposition to active movements were so great, that if, in his operations, he should need assistance, he could not expect it from him." Furthermore, Pope had urged the president to remove McClellan before Halleck had arrived in Washington.[88]

The next day Chase visited Lincoln in the morning, before the scheduled cabinet meeting. Chase urged the immediate change of command of the Army of the Potomac. At the cabinet meeting the issue of arming the slaves was discussed but it did not have the president's support.[89] Lincoln read the first draft of the Emancipation Proclamation, which would become effective on January 1, 1863. McClellan's attempt to keep the Union's war aims limited through the "Harrison's Landing Letter" had, ironically, been undermined by his own failure to achieve his promised quick victory on the peninsula. Seward suggested withholding the announcement until a military victory was obtained.[90] This was not the limited war aims that McClellan had for so long advocated. Lincoln was taking control of Radical and abolitionist sentiments rather than letting the sentiments control him. The president met with General in Chief Halleck and General Burnside on Monday, July 28, to discuss General Keyes' recommendation that the Army of the Potomac withdraw from its James River base.[91] In the cabinet, both Chase and Stanton had pressed Lincoln to withdraw the army.[92] Eventually, Lincoln acted on Halleck's and Keyes's advice. Halleck ordered the Army of the Potomac to withdraw from Harrison's Landing on August 3, 1862.[93]

McClellan protested to Halleck over this decision. He complained "that it has caused me the greatest pain I ever experienced, for I am convinced that the order to withdraw this army to Aquia Creek will prove disastrous to our cause." Militarily, McClellan again argued the reason for his change of base to the peninsula: "Here is the true defense of Washington. It is here, on the banks of the James, that the fate of the Union should be decided."[94] However, McClellan's lack of success on this line of operation did not help his argument. Halleck's rebuttal was based on McClellan's own arguments about the large numbers of Confederate troops he faced. McClellan had estimated two hundred thousand Confederate troops at Richmond. Since Pope had only forty thousand troops covering Washington and the Army of the Potomac had ninety thousand at Harrison's Landing, the Confederates, who were between the two Union armies, could easily attack one or the other with superior numbers. Also, the location of the two Union armies meant that they could not reinforce each other.[95]

Despite Halleck's order to move the Army of the Potomac back to a base near Washington, McClellan appeared to have some empathy for Halleck in his new role as general in chief. He advised Halleck: "My own experience enables me to appreciate most fully the difficulties and unpleasant features of your position. I have passed through it all and most cordially sympathize with you, for I regard your place, under present circumstances as one of the most unpleasant under the Government. Of one thing, however, you may be sure, and that is of my full and cordial support in all things." The balance of the letter criticized the government for changing policy towards slavery. In particular he was critical of General Pope, who had articulated the government's changed policy regarding slavery in a series of orders to the Army of Virginia. He counseled Halleck regarding his view that the Union should be fighting a conciliatory war and that the government "should avoid any proclamations of general emancipation." He then added, "The people of the South should understand that we are not making war upon the institution of slavery, but that if they submit to the Constitution and laws of the Union they will be protected in their constitutional rights of every nature."[96]

The personal tensions within the Union high command had now existed far too long to remain secret to the general public. On August 6 Lincoln addressed a Union meeting outside the capitol building to support Secretary of War Stanton's order to draft 300,000 militia. This order, issued on August 4, was based on the firm belief that the Confederates would be defeated by the application of crushing weight. This implied a long war of attrition that would eventually destroy the South and not a negotiated settlement that would bring it quickly back into the Union. Lincoln spoke to the crowd about the reported rift between McClellan and Stanton. Lincoln explained he was in a position to observe both men better than anyone else. He argued that both men wanted to be successful and the reported dispute was about the different number of troops each had claimed was the strength of the Army of the Potomac. Lincoln explained that the difference was due to variation in the reports of the number of troops fit for duty compared to those on the rolls. Also, accusations that Stanton had hindered McClellan by denying various requests from McClellan had been taken out of context. Lincoln concluded: "I have no accusation against him.... I believe he ... is a brave and able man."[97]

Lincoln's public support for McClellan concealed a series of decisions that would in fact remove McClellan from the command of the Army of the Potomac. At the meeting with General in Chief Halleck on Monday, July 28, McClellan had asked for reinforcements so that he could renew the offensive by crossing the James River and attacking Petersburg. Halleck believed this line of operation was too risky and that he should unite with General Pope's army in front of Washington.[98] But in accepting Halleck's advice on this strategy Lincoln was acting cautiously. He had always believed the line of operation for the Army of the Potomac should be from Manassas to Richmond. McClellan's idea of threatening the Confederate line of supply to Richmond by attacking Petersburg made sense and was similar to General Grant's successful strategy in 1865. The mistrust of McClellan was underlined by General Halleck's decision to send Burnside to the James River to "act as a second in command—or as adviser of McClellan." In fact Halleck was hoping to assert some control over McClellan, even though he was pessimistic about his prospects in this regard.[99] Nevertheless, on August 18, 1862, the Army of the Potomac prepared to move back to Alexandria.

Lincoln would have been concerned that the Confederates could attack the reduced Army of the Potomac as it carried out the slow task of evacuating nearly one hundred thousand troops from the James River to Alexandria. However, General Robert E. Lee looked north to General John Pope's Army of Virginia as the target for his next attack. Lee sent General Jackson behind Pope's army, which was on the Rappahannock, to Manassas. On August 26, Jackson turned Pope's army, captured Manassas and looted the Union army's warehouses. Pope saw the opportunity to turn on Jackson and defeat him before the Confederates could be reinforced. At Alexandria, only a few hours away from Manassas by train, was General Fitz John Porter's Fifth Corps of the Army of the Potomac, which numbered twenty-five thousand troops. Once the Fifth Corps linked up with the Army of Virginia, Pope would have enough troops to crush Jackson. However, Pope was unaware that while he was trying to trap Jackson, General Lee's army was moving into position on Pope's left flank.[100]

Also on August 26, McClellan landed at Alexandria. His Third and Fifth corps were marching towards Pope. His Sixth Corps was already at Alexandria and it would soon be joined by the Second Corps on August 28. The Fourth Corps would temporarily remain at Fortress Monroe. McClellan knew that once his troops moved into the geographic department commanded by Pope, he would lose command of these forces. Two corps had already been ordered to assist Pope but McClellan debated with Halleck the use of the two corps at Alexandria. McClellan was aware that he had a command but increasingly he was losing his army. Chase had doubts, which he had expressed to the president, that McClellan would cooperate with Pope. Chase believed McClellan was loyal to the country but not to the government, which implied disloyalty to the president.[101] This situation was exacerbated by McClellan's loyal subordinate Fitz John Porter, who commanded the Fifth Corps. Porter had to send his reports to Burnside, who in turn passed them on to Washington. Porter commented on Pope's handling of his army: "The strategy is magnificent, and tactics in the inverse proportion.... I wish myself away from it, with all our old Army of the Potomac, and so do our companions."[102] On August 29 Fitz Porter was more cynical: "Pope went to Centreville with the last two (Heintzelman and Reno) as a body guard, at the time not knowing where was the enemy, and where Sigel was fighting—within 8 miles of him and in sight. Comment is unnecessary."[103]

On August 29 Pope made contact with General Lee's army at Manassas. He sent troops in frontal attacks on the Confederate lines without any success. Fitz John Porter's Fifth Corps arrived in the afternoon to reinforce Pope, but so did James Longstreet's Confederate corps of twenty-four thousand troops. Porter was ordered by Pope to attack Jackson's right. Porter noted a large number of Confederate troops that could out-flank his left if he were to advance and he also concluded it was too late in the day to order an attack. His failure to obey this order and his well-known hatred of Pope provided the basis for his court-martial. On August 30, Lee attacked and drove the Union army back towards Washington. Pope's campaign had cost the Union 14,500 casualties and the Confederates only 9,000.[104]

The psychological impact of the second defeat of a major Union army on the same battlefield so close to Washington was considerable. The defeat at the Second Battle of Manassas, or Bull Run, as it is also known, forced the treasury to begin to ship money to New York in case the capital fell.[105] Lincoln confided to John Hay his concerns over McClellan's conduct. He believed McClellan had wanted Pope defeated[106] and referred to a dispatch from McClellan in which he proposed "to concentrate all our available forces to open communication with Pope" and "to leave Pope to get out of his scrape & at once use all our means to make the capital perfectly safe."[107] General Pope agreed. He also pointed the blame at Franklin. He believed there was "open exultation" from Franklin and other officers in his corps because "their comrades had been worsted in battle."[108] Also, McClellan had panicked at the news of Pope's defeat and had ordered Chain Bridge, which connected Washington to the south bank of the Potomac River, to be blown up. This order had to be countermanded. What was "incomprehensible" was McClellan's interference with Franklin's corps, which he had recalled once and then when it had been ordered towards Pope by Halleck he had begged permission to recall it again. McClellan finally ceased his requests when Halleck told him to "push them ahead till they get whipped, or got whipped themselves." McClellan was also constantly asking both the president and Halleck what was his position and command. Lincoln added that he thought McClellan seemed to "him a little crazy." John Hay attributed McClellan's action to envy, jealousy and spite.[109] These concerns were not restricted to the president. General McDowell confided to Secretary of the Treasury Chase that the Union defeat was the result of McClellan's not forwarding reinforcements and especially the conduct of Porter.[110] Wallace J. Schutz and Walter N. Trenerry have also blamed Pope's defeat on the "McClellanism" in the army. In particular they blame General Fitz John Porter's inactivity during a crucial phase of the battle. Unfortunately for the historian, Pope has left little in the way of personal records, so their conclusions are based on Pope's own findings in the Official Records. However, while Porter's inaction is a source of debate it is hard to explain why he did not know of the presence of General Longstreet's Confederate corps on August 30.[111]

The president needed to secure the capital and consolidate Union forces near Washington. With Halleck, he had visited McClellan on the morning of September 2, 1862, and offered him the command of the defenses of Washington.[112] These verbal orders by the president were confirmed by General Orders, No. 122, from General Halleck, which directed McClellan to "command of the fortifications of Washington, and of all the troops for the defense of the capital."[113] This must have been a difficult decision for Lincoln. He had already begun preparations for the evacuation of the government from the capital if it was threatened by Lee and he knew the cabinet would be hostile to the decision.[114] In effect, the army of the Potomac was taken away from Pope and with the Army of Virginia was handed over to McClellan. Lincoln also knew of the opposition from within the cabinet, particularly from Stanton. Halleck, probably without consulting Stanton, supported Lincoln's decision.[115] However, Halleck was also aware of the concerns of some senior officers in Pope's army over General Pope's handling of the battle. Lieutenant Henry Stoddard, the young brother of Lincoln's secretary, William Stoddard, had been petitioned on September 2 by some of Pope's senior officers to raise their concerns with the president. The next day Harry Stoddard was in the president's office. Stoddard recounted the "informal coming together of a number of angry critics, leaders of a defeated army," and how he had "sat and listened, his pale face glowing with excitement or growing paler with grief as he learned the sad extent of the disasters, the details of which were unfolded."[116] This was not the first time, nor would it be the last, that the president ignored the chain of command. But the commander in chief had always found it difficult to gain exact information, so "that he felt at times as if he was walking on in the dark."[117] This meeting would be the first of a series of similar meetings that would destabilize the Union high command. So concerned was Lincoln with Stoddard's verbal report that he immediately had his brother take him to Stanton. Stanton in turn had Stoddard report to General Halleck.[118]

At the cabinet meeting on September 2, the military situation in the East was the center of the discussion. The general belief was that Pope had failed but that McClellan, Franklin, Fitz John Porter, and perhaps some others, had not adequately supported him. Lincoln informed the cabinet that he had placed McClellan in command of Union forces in Washington and that Halleck had agreed with the decision. The discussion must have been tense because Gideon Welles, the secretary of the navy noted, "There was a more disturbed and desponding feeling than I have ever witnessed in council; the President was greatly distressed."[119] Lincoln confirmed the influence of Halleck and Pope, together with Chase and Stanton, in the decision to withdraw the Army of the Potomac from the peninsula. Indeed, Welles believed that installing Halleck as general in chief and Pope as commander of Union forces near Washington was part of a plan by Stanton and Chase to remove McClellan. Pope's defeat at the second battle at Bull Run and the placing of McClellan in command of Union forces in Washington had interrupted, but not ended, this intrigue.[120]

Taking advantage of the defeat of General Pope, General Robert E. Lee raided into Maryland. This began a month of anxiety for the Union high command. Lee might have contemplated a move on Washington, but the strength of its fortifications and its large garrison meant he would have little chance of success. He intended to abandon the defensive strategy in the East and raid into Maryland based on the erroneous belief in the strong "Southern" support among the Maryland population and the military advantages a victory would achieve in uncovering Washington, Baltimore, and Philadelphia. Also, if Lee could keep the Union forces occupied north and west of Washington, Richmond would be safe from attack until the spring of 1863. There was also a more pressing logistical problem. If Lee could remain in Maryland his army could live off the country and not be dependent on food supplies from Richmond. On September 4, the Army of Northern Virginia moved northwest after the Second Battle of Manassas, crossed the Potomac and moved towards Frederick, Maryland.[121]

McClellan was pleased he was commanding all the forces in Washington and Pope had been pushed into the background. Immediately after receiving the order to take command of the defense of Washington on September 2, he wrote to Pope: "General Halleck has instructed to repeat to you the order he sent this morning to withdraw your army to Washington without unnecessary delay." McClellan then detailed the positions that elements of the Army of Virginia must take up in Washington's defenses.[122] McClellan would have felt a small victory when on September 5 Pope was relieved of his command. But his trusted supporter Fitz John Porter was also relieved of his command until charges against him and General Franklin could be examined.[123] In response to the threat from Lee, on September 3 Lincoln had ordered Halleck to "immediately commence, and proceed with all possible dispatch, to organize an army for active operations, from all the material within and coming within his control, independent of the forces he may deem necessary for the defense of Washington, when such active army shall take the field."[124] On the same day, Halleck had asked McClellan to "report the approximate force of each corps of the three armies now in the vicinity of Washington."[125] It seems Halleck had been offered command of the field force to take on Lee. The General in chief would not do this. Two days later, Halleck decided to order McClellan into motion. General Lee had crossed the Potomac and he wanted McClellan to "move immediately" and follow him.[126]

McClellan was in command of the Union army but he still did not have the full confidence of the President. At a brief cabinet meeting on September 12, Lincoln reminded the meeting of his reasons for appointing McClellan as commander of the defense of Washington and this decision was driven by necessity. He also reminded them how he had challenged McClellan's command of the Army of the Potomac when he had organized the army corps and appointed the generals to lead them. As if to calm Chase and Stanton, Lincoln recounted how he had offered command of the Army of the Potomac to Burnside but Burnside declined and declared himself unequal to the position.[127] Lincoln was also trying to distance himself from the politically sensitive issue of McClellan's reinstatement. On September 8 he had told Welles it was Halleck's idea that McClellan should command the army to oppose the Maryland invasion. Two days later he told Welles that McClellan's reinstatement was Halleck's doing.[128]

Complicating matters, however, was the fact that McClellan had been ordered to take command of the defenses of Washington. Since the Army of the Potomac had moved into the city's defenses, as well as the Army of Virginia, it was assumed that McClellan commanded these forces. But what would happen if these troops left Washington? The Army of Virginia was never formally dissolved. When the President and Halleck visited McClellan on the morning of September 2, the President had explained to McClellan that "Pope is ordered to fall back upon Washn & as he reenters everything is to come under my command again!"[129] The only official record that this occurred is correspondence from Pope to Halleck on September 5 where he questioned if he should take orders from McClellan. Halleck replied: "The armies of the Potomac and Virginia being consolidated, you will report for orders to the Secretary of War."[130] It appears from this correspondence that the Army of Virginia ceased to exist on September 2 when McClellan was appointed to command the defenses of the capital. Interestingly, Lincoln and Halleck had applied the traditional military department structure for McClellan's command of the defenses of Washington, but once McClellan's army began to move towards Lee's Confederates on September 7 it acted more like an army independent of the department structure McClellan had advocated with his move to the peninsula. McClellan also got his way by suspending the order to remove General Franklin and Fitz John Porter. These were two of his most trusted generals and he wanted them with him. Halleck and Lincoln agreed, probably because they did not want to interfere with McClellan and the success of the campaign at this critical time.[131]

In the back of Lincoln's mind, though, must have been McClellan's assurances in April that Washington was secure, as he planned to move his army to the peninsula. Just to be safe, Lincoln on September 9 ordered Major General Heintzelman to command of all the troops for the defense of Washington south of the Potomac.[132] When McClellan heard of the order, he responded in a manner that was, at the least, insubordination. He wrote to General Banks: "I prefer not to have this done.... Please recollect that I am still responsible for the defense of Washington, and that no change can be made in my arrangements without consulting me." He then ordered Heintzelman to "suspend the operation of the order until you hear from me."[133]

The Army of the Potomac, positioned northwest of Washington, held a flank position to the Confederate army as it moved northward. This meant that Lee could not move too far north or it would provide the opportunity for the Army of the Potomac to cut his tenuous supply line that ran through Harpers Ferry. Advancing too far north would also allow the Union army to take a position on Lee's rear. This is what Lincoln understood when he instructed Stanton to write to Major-General Wool, in Baltimore, to divert any troops bound for Washington to Harrisburg. The true defense of Harrisburg was the strength of McClellan's army.[134]

On September 13, 1862, a copy of General Lee's plans was discovered by Union troops. The orders, wrapped around a few cigars, were Lee's Secret Order No. 191, which revealed the movements of the Confederate army for the next four days. McClellan moved his army towards the Confederate army while they prepared to fight a battle on the tactical defensive. McClellan attacked Lee's army on September 17. The Battle of Antietam was the single, bloodiest day of the war. McClellan launched a series of poorly coordinated attacks while Lee failed to properly entrench his troops. The Confederates lost 13,724 to the Union's 12,469. Lee had been tactically successful, but he could not remain on the field because he was outnumbered, immobile and in a position where he could not feed his army by foraging or by rail. He had no option but to end the raid and withdraw to Virginia. The withdrawal from the battlefield gave victory to the Army of the Potomac. This was the first major victory by Union forces in the East.[135] But Lincoln was disappointed that McClellan had not followed his advice to "destroy the rebel army, if possible."[136] Lincoln saw the opportunity to trap Lee north of the Potomac or to destroy him with a vigorous pursuit. Gideon Welles probably had similar thoughts to the president on September 19: "Nothing from the army, except that instead of following up the victory, attacking and capturing the Rebels, they, after a day's armistice, are rapidly escaping over the river. McClellan says they are crossing and that Pleasanton is after them. Oh dear!"[137] In a meeting with Allan Pinkerton of the Pinkerton Detective Agency on September 22, Lincoln did not discover any evidence or suggestion that McClellan had let Lee escape, but Lincoln was convinced by Pinkerton's answers that Antietam was a lost opportunity to destroy Lee's army.[138]

Lincoln had been waiting for a victory since July when he promised to issue a preliminary Emancipation Proclamation but only after such a decisive victory had been achieved. On September 22, Lincoln warned the South:

McClellan, second from the left and Lincoln on the right with a group of officers at Antietam battlefield, September 1862 (Library of Congress).

> That on the first day of January in the year of our Lord, one thousand eight hundred and sixty-three, all persons held as slaves within any state, or designated part of a state, the people whereof shall then be in rebellion against the United States shall be then, thenceforward, and forever free; and the executive government of the United States, including the military and naval authority thereof, will recognize and maintain the freedom of such persons, and will do no act or acts to repress such persons, or any of them, in any efforts they may make for their actual freedom.[139]

Lincoln had used his powers as commander in chief to push through the Emancipation Proclamation. The proclamation did not abolish slavery as a legal institution. This did not occur until the Thirteenth Amendment took effect in December 1865.[140] It simply was intended to free slaves from their owners in Confederate territory. Lincoln would have been influenced by the arguments of William Whiting. Whiting, an abolitionist from Massachusetts and a solicitor at the War Department, had in 1862 published *War Powers of the President, and the Legislative Powers on Congress in Relation to Rebellion, Treason and Slavery*.[141] The book had reached its forty-third edition by 1871. Whiting drew a distinction between an offensive war that only Congress had the power to sanction and a defensive war, where the president could not wait for Congress to declare war before he called out the armed forces.[142] Whiting argued that the Constitution did not leave the nation powerless to defend itself. The president could mobilize the armed forces without the authority of Congress and therefore no declaration of war was necessary. Since a small group of slave owners had broken up the Union, overthrown justice and destroyed domestic tranquility, the Union was fighting a defensive war. The object of the war was not the destruction of property or to interfere with domestic institutions, but "*as a means of carrying on the contest,* it had become necessary and lawful to lay waste, burn, sink, destroy, blockade, wound, kill" and "in further prosecuting hostilities, the liberating, employing, or arming of slaves shall be deemed convenient for the more certain, speedy, and effectual overthrow of the enemy."[143]

The Union had now included the emancipation of slaves as one of its strategies to win the war. It was not yet one of the Union's war aims and would not be until the presidential election in 1864. Lincoln made this point in a letter to his friend Horace Greely on August 22, 1862. The president stressed that his "paramount object in this struggle is to save the Union, and is not either to save or to destroy slavery. If I could save the Union without freeing any slave I would do it, and if I could save it by freeing all the slaves I would do it; and if I could save it by freeing some and leaving others alone I would also do that. What I do about slavery, and the colored race, I do because I believe it helps to save the Union."[144] But emancipation was limited to those areas in rebellion and those who supported the rebellion. While it was not emancipation for all slaves, this was a victory for the Radical Republicans and the growing number of war pragmatists who understood the strategic importance of slavery to the Confederate war effort. It was a defeat for General McClellan and his supporters who had argued for a conciliatory, civilized war that sought to restore the Union and not to remold it.[145]

The military purpose of the preliminary Emancipation Proclamation was underlined on September 24, 1863, when Lincoln issued General Order No. 139 to the United States Army. Writing as president and commander in chief to underline that this was a military order, he reminded his soldiers that the aim of the war was the restoration of constitutional relations between the United States and each of the states that were in rebellion. But Lincoln ordered the army to "recognize and maintain the freedom of such persons, and ... do no act or acts to repress such persons, or any of them, in any efforts they may make for their actual freedom." The army was now ordered to act as an agent of emancipation.[146] Writing to General Ulysses S. Grant six months after Lincoln had issued the order, General Halleck reflected the reality of the fighting and the fact that the military policy of the Union high command had changed: "The character of the war has very much changed within the last year. There is now no possible hope of reconciliation with the rebels. The Union party in the South is virtually destroyed. There can be no peace but that which is forced by the sword. We must conquer the rebels or be conquered by them. The North must conquer the slave oligarchy or become slaves themselves—the manufacturers mere 'hewers of wood and drawers of water' to Southern aristocrats."[147]

However, Lincoln's concern at the end of September 1862 was focused on how McClellan and his supporters of a conciliatory war aim would react to the change of military policy. Early on October 1 General William F. Smith had received a note from McClellan that said he would like to see Smith at his headquarters later that afternoon. When he arrived, he found McClellan with the other generals. McClellan handed General Smith a draft of a letter that responded to the preliminary Emancipation Proclamation. While Smith could not recall the wording of the letter he could remember "the ideas conveyed were that the army had not enlisted to put down slavery which was guaranteed [by the Constitution] to be, with a pretty strong dissent from the terms of the Proclamation."[148] Smith quietly urged McClellan not to send the letter because it would ruin him with the country and it was Smith's opinion that most "military men" believed it was a military necessity.[149] Yet another general, Franklin, had lost confidence in the president over this matter. Franklin noted the reaction of the troops in his Sixth Corps when Lincoln reviewed them: "I understand that all of the other Corps cheered except mine. They were entirely silent much to my pleasure."[150]

Lincoln's sensitivity to this issue was highlighted by an incident that involved one of McClellan's staff, Major John J. Key. Major Key had a conversation with Major Levi C. Turner shortly after the Battle of Antietam. Turner had asked Major Key, "Why was not the rebel army bagged immediately after the battle near Sharpsburg?" It was alleged that Key had replied, "That is not the game. The object is that neither army shall get much advantage of the other; that both shall be kept in the field till they are exhausted, when we will make a compromise and save slavery."[151] When Lincoln learned of Key's assertions he demanded an explanation in person. Key admitted to the comments and Lincoln immediately dismissed him from the army. Lincoln dismissed Key because he feared there was a "class of officers in the army" who were playing a game not to beat the enemy when they could and he needed to send a warning to that "supposed class."[152] Lincoln was therefore concerned that McClellan and some of his senior officers might be trying to "manage things to suit themselves." This is what John Hay described as the "McClellan Conspiracy."[153]

Lincoln was forced to order McClellan to get his army moving after Lee's retreating army. On October 6 Lincoln directed McClellan to "cross the Potomac and give battle to the enemy or drive him south." Lincoln advised the use of the interior line between Washington and Lee's army but did not order it because his main concern was that McClellan move his army "as soon as possible." To add weight to the order, Halleck was directed to add that the secretary of war and the general in chief fully agreed with the president.[154] McClellan replied that logistical problems were hindering any movement by his army. This forced Lincoln to question McClellan's ability as a commander and Lincoln asked him, "You remember my speaking to you of what I called your over-cautiousness. Are you not over-cautious when you assume that you cannot do what the enemy is constantly doing? Should you not claim to be at least his equal in prowess, and act upon the claim?" Lincoln lectured McClellan on the line of operation McClellan should take: "Again, one of the standard maxims of war, as you know, is to operate upon the enemy's communications as much as possible without exposing your own." He also reminded McClellan that by using interior lines he was closer to Richmond than Lee was and that by all reason the Army of the Potomac must reach Richmond before Lee could. Lincoln urged McClellan to "try," because "if we never try, we shall never succeed." Finally, Lincoln concluded, "It is all easy if our troops march as well as the enemy; and it is unmanly to say they can not do it."[155]

McClellan had always used the numerical inferiority of the Army of the Potomac, compared to Confederate forces, as a reason for his cautious behavior. On October 20 Lincoln had written the "Memorandum on Army of the Potomac and Memorandum on Confederate Army," which showed that Union forces had 144,662 troops fit for duty and the Confederates 89,563.[156] With such a numerical advantage, Lincoln could not understand McClellan's inactivity except that McClellan might be "playing false—that is he did not want to hurt the enemy."[157] It could also be, as Joseph T. Glatthaar has argued that, despite the support of the president, McClellan was "paralyzed by his personality disorders" to the extent that he "lacked the capacity to utilize" his army effectively.[158]

While McClellan explained his inactivity to the president, the actions of the Confederate cavalry, commanded by J.E.B. Stuart was a source of further embarrassment for the Union high command. He crossed the Potomac River and raided Chambersburg, Pennsylvania, and then moved around McClellan's army before recrossing the Potomac. *Harper's Weekly* reported the impotent Union response to Stuart's raid: "The rebels went on their way with their plunder, no doubt surprised as well as rejoicing at having escaped so easily. There was, in fact, nothing which could be called even a skirmish, and but for the artillery practice obtained our troops might as well have been at Harper's Ferry." Also included were sketches depicting the Confederates' burning of the engine house and machine shops in the town and Confederate troops looting U.S. Army stores.[159]

Yet, McClellan still had significant support within the officer corps of the Army of the Potomac. Brigadier General John Cochrane was a political general. He was elected as a Democrat to Congress in 1857 and 1861 and was noted as a defender of Southern rights. When hostilities commenced he recruited the 65th New York and entered the U.S. Army as its colonel. He became a brigadier general in July 1862 and commanded a brigade in General Newton's division.[160] Cochrane believed that most people in the North ignorantly misunderstood McClellan. In particular, Cochrane cited the times he had heard McClellan condemn slavery.[161] Like others in the officers corps Cochrane believed that the conduct of the war should be left to the professional military. He believed that politicians were treating McClellan insincerely and this was a danger to the country. Therefore, what was needed was a change in the administration of the army, with enlarged powers and increased responsibilities to General McClellan. Replacing Halleck with McClellan would also provide "unanimity of support" for the prosecution of the war.[162] What followed was an interesting example of a general lobbying the civilian administration and his commander in chief.

On October 20, General John Cochrane visited both Secretary of the Treasury Chase and Lincoln in Washington and discussed the military situation. In particular he urged a change in the Union high command, namely the replacement of General Halleck with McClellan as general in chief.[163] He did this with the approval of General McClellan: "I accordingly broached the subject, and soon after left the headquarters of the army for Washington, with permission to repeat General McClellan's views to those to whom I might address the project of a change in the chief military command."[164] Cochrane visited Chase first. He talked with Chase about the army, the approaching New York and Pennsylvania elections and the lack of confidence in the administration. He also put to Chase the proposal to replace Halleck with McClellan and he recounted McClellan's critical views on slavery. Chase, while he admitted to some personal animosity toward McClellan, agreed to "co-operate with his friends in the effort to reinstate him at the head of the armies." Cochrane left Chase and told him he intended to speak with the president.[165]

Cochrane found Lincoln at the Soldiers Home with his family. Cochrane described him as "depressed." Cochrane put his proposal to replace Halleck with McClellan to the president. Lincoln listened patiently and, according to Cochrane, "expressed a willingness to try it." Despite these assurances, McClellan was not promoted to general in chief. Cochrane, while he could not be certain, blamed the secretary of war.[166] But the political mood had turned against McClellan to the extent that he would be removed from command of the Army of the Potomac. Lincoln had set a test for McClellan and he had failed it. The president could see how McClellan could intercept Lee as he moved towards Richmond and told John Hay the following:

> After the battle of Antietam, I went up to the field to try to get him to move & came back thinking he would move at once. But when I got home he began to argue why he ought not to move. I peremptorily ordered him to advance. It was 19 days before he put a man over the [Potomac] river. It was 9 days longer before he got his army across and then he stopped again, delaying on little pretexts of wanting this and that. I began to fear he was playing false—that he did not want to hurt the enemy. I saw how he could intercept the enemy on the way to Richmond. I determined to make that the test. If he let them get away I would remove him. He did so & I relieved him.[167]

On November 6 General Buckingham received two envelopes from Secretary of War Stanton. Buckingham was asked to read the orders and then seal them. He was "thunderstruck" to learn the contents of the letters and in particular the letter from the president relieving McClellan of command of the Army of the Potomac. Buckingham took the unusual step of visiting the secretary of war at his home the next morning. What Buckingham heard from Stanton must have disturbed him. Stanton told him he "had not only no confidence in McClellan's military skill, but he very much doubted his patriotism, and even loyalty, and he expressed to me some fear that McClellan would not give up the command, and he wished, therefore, that the order should be presented by an officer of high rank, direct from the War Department, so as to carry the full weight of the President's authority."[168]

On November 7, 1862, General Buckingham arrived at McClellan's headquarters at Rectortown. He handed McClellan General Orders, No. 182: "By direction of the President of the United States, it is ordered that Major-General McClellan be relieved from the command of the Army of the Potomac, and that Major-General Burnside take the command of that army." Halleck's order to McClellan did not include Lincoln's direction that General Hunter should take command of Burnside's corps and General Fitz John Porter should be relieved of the command of his corps and be replaced by General Hooker.[169] Burnside was put into a position where he could only accept Lincoln's third offer to command the Army of the Potomac. Buckingham had said to him that if he did not accept the command, it would be offered to Hooker. Burnside could not allow Hooker to command and reluctantly accepted.[170]

The sacking caused unease in the army because it appeared to have been a political decision and not a military one. George Meade concluded that if Lincoln had acted on military grounds he would have sacked McClellan immediately after Antietam. He also noticed that McClellan was sacked after the New York election: "This removal now proves conclusively that the cause is political, and the date of the order, November 5 confirms it."[171] McClellan remembered that the news of his dismissal from the Army of the Potomac "created an immense deal of deep feeling in the army so much so that many were in favor of my refusing to obey the order and of marching upon Washington to take possession of the government." What rumblings existed were soon calmed by regimental officers. If there was any threat of mutiny or the army's dissolving it soon "dissipated, leaving only grumbling."[172] McLellan believed he was able to calm these intense emotions because he remained with the army long after his dismissal. His emotional farewell to the army is reflected in his final official address:

> Officers and Soldiers of the Army of the Potomac: An order of the President devolves upon Maj.-Gen. Burnside the command of this army. In parting from you I cannot express the love and gratitude I bear to you. As an army you have grown up under my care. In you I have never found doubt or coldness. The battles you have fought under my command will proudly live in our nation's history. The glory you have achieved, our mutual perils and fatigues, the graves of our comrades fallen in battle and by disease, the broken forms of those whom wounds and sickness have disabled the strongest associations which can exist among men unite us still by an indissoluble tie. We shall ever be comrades in supporting the Constitution of our country and the nationality of its people.[173]

The problem of unity of command had plagued the Union military effort in the Eastern Theater during 1862. This was complicated because no one had yet defined the role of commander in chief or general in chief and there was no precedent, particularly because of the size and complexity of the Civil War. Lincoln may have thought he had solved this with the appointment of McClellan to general in chief, but the relationship between the two had deteriorated to the extent that Lincoln felt compelled to remove him from this position when the Army of the Potomac began to move towards the peninsula. Lincoln and Secretary of War Stanton took on the duties of general in chief. The creation of the War Board, while it has been viewed as an embryonic General Staff, was only a means for direct civilian control of the war. Its failure was as much a result of the disinterest of its head, General Hitchcock, as to the realization that administration of the country and trying to coordinate the unprecedented scope of the Union war effort were far beyond direct civilian control. On the recommendation of the retired General Scott, Lincoln on July 10, 1862, appointed General Halleck, who was known for his success in the Western Theater, to fill the vacant position. Halleck's most pressing problem was McClellan's loss of the strategic initiative on the peninsula. If anything, the failure of McClellan's Peninsula Campaign had demonstrated that the Union's strategy to fight offensively in the East was flawed. Lincoln created another problem when he established a second Union army in Virginia, commanded by General Pope. The friction and lack of cooperation between Halleck's two commanders in the Eastern Theater, McClellan and Pope, proved disastrous for the Union high command. Indeed, the Union defeat at Second Bull Run can be directly linked to the dysfunctional Union chain of command and also Halleck's, and to a lesser extent, Lincoln's inability to make the two commanders operate in concert. The Union defeat at Second Bull Run earned a reprieve for McClellan, as he was controversially entrusted with the defense of Washington and finally with the mission to defeat Lee's raid across the Potomac. The Battle of Antietam was tactically a draw but strategically it was a victory for the Union. This victory was used by Lincoln to announce a major change in the Union's strategy to include the emancipation of slaves in defined areas. The irony must have been bitter for McClellan, who had urged Lincoln not to make abolition of slavery any part of the Union's war aims or strategy. The preliminary Emancipation Proclamation was issued by the president in his capacity as commander in chief and was based on the principle of military necessity. Swinton has argued that McClellan was "sacrificed to the nation's ignorance of war."[174] However, this change of strategy, the long list of the president's concerns over McClellan, the strong political pressure to remove him and the perception that McClellan had let

Lee escape over the Potomac River led finally to the sacking of McClellan. Ironically, McClellan failed because he fed the illusion of an early Union victory by the application of the "On to Richmond" strategy. He was, as Rowland has argued, "the greatest failure and the greatest victim of the early part of the war."[175]

Six
McClellan's Shadow

It is easy to view Burnside's appointment to command the Army of the Potomac through the lens of the Battle of Fredericksburg and ask why Lincoln might have promoted him. At the time, however, the decision did make sense. Burnside had led successful campaigns to the North Carolina coast that resulted in the capture of Roanoke Island and New Bern. No one else in the Army of the Potomac officer corps had held such large independent commands. Also, Burnside was a friend of McClellan and it seemed that McClellan's supporters were more likely to support a friend rather than an outsider. Yet, only one month after McClellan had been removed from command of the Army of the Potomac a revolt occurred within the ranks of its senior officers aimed at removing Burnside and returning McClellan to command.

Complicating this intrigue was General Joe Hooker's ambitions to command the army. He was convinced he was the best qualified officer to command and to this end he had been actively undermining McClellan since the Peninsula Campaign. In his testimony to the Joint Committee on the Conduct of the War on March 11, 1863, Hooker placed the failure of the Peninsula Campaign "to the want of generalship on the part of our commander."[1] In particular Hooker made the bold assertion that the Army of the Potomac could have marched into Richmond "without another gun being fired" after the Confederate troops abandoned Yorktown if the pursuit of the Confederate forces was pressed. He also claimed that the Confederates had given up on defending Richmond until they "saw the lassitude and inefficiency of our army [and] they concluded to make a stand there."[2] Hooker went on to argue that the Army of the Potomac could have marched into Richmond after its victory at Malvern Hill. As an example of his own determination, compared to McClellan's hesitation, Hooker recounted how McClellan had received orders to evacuate Harrison's Landing. Hooker had visited him and suggested that the orders to evacuate not be obeyed and instead the army should march on

Richmond. When Hooker returned to his camp, he found an order from McClellan to prepare to march the next day and he believed the order meant to march on Richmond. Before the order could be executed, however, it was countermanded.³ Hooker retold the story of the countermanded order in a conversation with Salmon P. Chase five months later. Hooker stated to Chase that if he had been in the command of the Army of the Potomac at that time, "Richmond would have been ours."⁴ This account was also reported to The Committee on The Conduct of the War but was not confirmed in McClellan's story.⁵

General Burnside (Library of Congress).

Hooker had positioned himself well as a possible replacement as commander of the Army of the Potomac. General Meade recognized that Hooker had support within the army's officer corps. General Meade, in a letter to his son, John Sergeant Meade, revealed the following: "We have many rumors in regard to the changes in the commanding general of this army, and it seems to be generally conceded that if McClellan is removed, Hooker will succeed him." Meade believed that if fighting was the only criterion by which to judge whether an officer made general, then Hooker would distinguish himself; but Meade doubted Hooker's qualifications to command a large army.⁶ Meade and Hooker had first met at West Point and they had served together in Mexico. Like McClellan, he was a Democrat and was not an abolitionist, but Meade believed Hooker would change his political views if offered command of the army.⁷

Hooker recognized the need for political support. Consequently, he had launched what had been referred to as his "Washington campaign," a political campaign aimed at gaining support for his military ambitions. Hooker was wounded in the foot at Antietam and was sent to the Washington Insane Asylum to recover. He received many high-ranking members of the Union high command, including the president and cabinet members. This provided the ideal forum for Hooker to promote his views on the war. The visits of Secretary of the Treasury Chase must have seemed significant to Hooker. Chase still had political ambitions. He was courting the Radical Republicans for support towards a campaign for president at the next presidential election.[8] Even the popular press was convinced of Hooker's credentials to replace McClellan and he had even released to the press a statement supporting emancipation as a way of gaining more support from the Radical Republicans.[9] Despite Hooker's political lobbying, Lincoln appointed Burnside to command the army. The reason was simple enough. If Lincoln had wanted to appoint Hooker, he would have to do it at the expense of Hooker's seniors, the corps commanders Burnside, Sumner and Franklin. Lincoln was not prepared to do this.[10] He did not want to repeat the same mistake he had made when he had promoted General Pope to command the Army of Virginia over generals who were superior in age, experience and qualifications.[11]

Burnside's promotion to commander of the Army of the Potomac did not end the disquiet in the army's officer corps that the action was intended to have. In particular, Hooker did not see Burnside's promotion as a serious obstacle to his ambition because he believed it would only be a matter of time before he replaced him. Hooker had revealed this to Meade on November 23, 1862. Meade had visited Hooker while on his way to Burnside's headquarters as he wanted to make Hooker aware that Burnside had promoted General Daniel Butterfield to command the V Corps in Hooker's Central Grand Division while he himself had been given command only of the Third Division, I Corps, also in Hooker's Grand Division, even though Meade outranked Butterfield. It may have been Meade's criticism of Burnside that prompted Hooker to reveal his thoughts about command of the army. Hooker thought McClellan had treated Meade poorly when he had promoted General Reynolds over him. After this criticism of McClellan, Hooker revealed his lack of respect and confidence in Burnside. The scenario, as Hooker saw it, was that he expected to have command of the Army of the Potomac and Halleck would take command in the West while McClellan returned to Washington as general in chief. Hooker hinted to Meade that it would perhaps not be long before he was in command of the army.[12]

Burnside's success as a commander would be determined by a successful campaign. On November 11, 1862, Halleck visited Burnside to discover his plans for the Army of the Potomac. The army was soundly deployed twenty miles south of Manassas at Warrenton. In this position, it could be a potential threat to Richmond while also covering Washington. Burnside proposed to move down the north bank of the Rappahannock River to Falmouth and establish a new base at Aquia Creek or Belle Plain. J.H. Stine, who wrote a history of the Army of the Potomac, believed that Burnside intended to avoid battle until spring 1863 and then move on Richmond by way of the peninsula.[13]

Certainly, Burnside's movement to Falmouth, on the north bank of the Rappahannock, could be the first stage of a change of base to the peninsula. It seems more likely, however, that from this line of operation Burnside intended to move from Falmouth then cross the Rappahannock and take Fredericksburg by assault. With Fredericksburg in his possession, he could threaten Richmond, Lee's base of operations. Swinton, whose history of the Army of the Potomac was published in 1866, concluded, however, that Burnside did not have any plans after the movement to Fredericksburg and that the maneuver was no more than a delaying action to avoid a major action until spring.[14] Halleck disapproved of Burnside's plan and, in a meeting at Warrenton, he urged him to retain his present base and to march toward Richmond along the line pointed out in the president's letter of October 13, 1862, to General McClellan.[15] In this letter, Lincoln advised McClellan to move quickly and directly on Richmond by the "inside track," that is, to give the Army of the Potomac the advantage of interior lines.[16]

Halleck was careful to distance himself from Burnside's plans. In a report to Secretary of War Stanton, Halleck noted that Burnside did not fully agree with the president's plans but he eventually modified his plan so that the army would cross the Rappahannock by the fords of the Upper Rappahannock and then move down and capture the heights south of Fredericksburg while another small force was sent north of the river to enable General Haupt to reopen the railroad and rebuild the bridges. Halleck "refused to give any official approval of this deviation from the President's instructions until his assent was obtained." When he returned to Washington on November 13, Halleck submitted Burnside's plan to Lincoln. Halleck received Lincoln's "assent, rather than approval" and on November 14 he telegraphed to Burnside the authority to adopt it.[17]

Before he moved from Warrenton, Burnside reorganized the six corps of the Army of the Potomac into three "grand divisions" of two corps each. McClellan had given him command of two corps during the Antietam campaign, and this must have been the source of his initiative.[18] This was a surprising show of confidence in Burnside so early in his command, because only Lincoln had the authority to change the command structure of the army and the officers who commanded the corps and division. Halleck had, however, on November 10, 1862, given Burnside the authority to reorganize the army as he saw fit.[19] Consequently, the Army of the Potomac comprised the following: the Right Grand Division of the Second and Ninth corps, commanded by General Sumner; the Centre Grand Division of the Third and Fifth corps, commanded by General Hooker; and, the Left Grand Division of the First and Sixth corps, commanded by General Franklin. The Eleventh

Corps, commanded by Major General F. Sigel, constituted the reserve.[20] This reorganization was completed before the army began its move towards Fredericksburg.

On November 17, Sumner's corps arrived in Falmouth, on the north bank of the Rappahannock and opposite Fredericksburg. Sumner observed that Fredericksburg was occupied only by a small force of Confederate troops. Burnside's orders did not permit Sumner to cross the river until the pontoon bridges arrived. The temptation to cross was great and Sumner had located fords to cross the river. That night, he asked permission from Burnside to cross in the morning. Burnside ordered against it until his communications were secured.[21] The pontoon bridges were, however, slow to arrive. General Franklin, a prominent officer in the pro-McClellan faction in the army, was also concerned that the delay in crossing the river could disadvantage the Union's military position. On November 23 he wrote his wife; "The pontoon train which Gens Halleck and Meigs promised should be here as soon as the Army, has not yet arrived. Had it been here we could have crossed without firing a gun. Who is to blame we cannot tell, but delay may cause great loss of life if we have an indecisive fight near Fredericksburg."[22]

The day before the Battle of Fredericksburg, Franklin had written a letter to William Swift in which he had set out "to show what mismanagement characterizes whatever emanates from Washn [sic] in the prosecution of this war." He was severely critical of Halleck, whom he described as "an exceedingly tricky man." He was scathingly critical of the Union's civilian leaders: "[T]he Administration intended that Burnside should move forward at any cost, and did not care how many lives were lost, or what good were done only so that there was a fight. In other words it was determined to pander to the radical thirst for blood which has lately been so rife." He went even further with remarks that were treasonable: "You see that I am by no means loyal to the Admin. I think it a great pity that something has not occurred to wipe them out long ago."[23]

Burnside's delay in moving had given General Lee the opportunity to position his army on the high ground behind Fredericksburg, on the western side of the river. Burnside was confident that he could defeat the Confederate army by the application of superior numbers. Lincoln was concerned by the delay so he met with Burnside at Aquia Landing on November 26 to discuss the operations of the army. Lincoln believed Burnside's plan was too risky. Lincoln asked for a flanking maneuver by landing two forces across the river, one north of Fredericksburg and one south of it. Lincoln's plan was rejected by both Burnside and Halleck because it would take too much time to put the flanking forces into position.[24] This suggested that both generals saw the need for immediate action. Lincoln could only agree with this because he had been dissatisfied with the slowness of generals such as Buell and McClellan and now it appeared that McClellan's successor had done little to ease Lincoln's fears of more inaction.[25] The need for Union military action in the form of a Union offensive into Virginia and a battle had once again dictated Union military strategy in the Eastern Theater of the war, even though it meant fighting an enemy who had carefully chosen a strong defensive position.

Fredericksburg is on the south bank of the Rappahannock River. It is 50 miles south of Washington and 58 miles north of Richmond and about 80 miles inland from the mouth of the river. The Richmond, Fredericksburg, and Potomac Railroad ran through the town and would provide the line of supply if Burnside intended to march towards Richmond on this line. The town itself was on the flat riverbank, but just behind the town was Marye's Heights, which could form a strong defensive position. General Hooker would, after the battle, describe the Confederate position as "the strongest position they had in Virginia."[26] On December 13 the Army of the Potomac crossed the Rappahannock and began advancing towards the Confederate positions. Sumner's Right Grand Division had to cross over a mile of open ground to reach Marye's Heights. Immediately to the front of Marye's Heights was a stone wall behind which were placed four ranks of Confederate troops. Union attackers managed to reach the wall but were unable to move any further. In the face of a determined enemy holding a strong position, the Union attacks were bound to fail. Lee, who observed the failed Union assaults, memorably concluded, "It is well that war is so terrible—we should grow too fond of it." The Army of the Potomac lost 1,284 killed, 9,600 wounded and 1,769 captured. This was a total of 12,653 compared to the total Confederate loss of 5,309.[27]

It was easy to blame Burnside for the disaster at Fredericksburg. Indeed, he took the honorable course by shouldering the responsibility. He explained to the president in a telegram his reasons for withdrawing across the river. Burnside offered the military reason that he "felt the positions in front could not be carried, and it was a military necessity either to attack or retire. A repulse would have been disastrous to us."[28] The next day he wrote Halleck a more detailed admission of his failure. He bravely admitted that for "the failure in the attack I am responsible." He went even further when he distanced Lincoln and the civilian administration from the decision: "[The] fact that I decided to move from Warrenton onto this line rather against the opinion of the President, Secretary, and yourself, and that you have left the whole management in my hands, without giving me orders, makes me the more responsible."[29] Yet, only one day after the battle Burnside suspected that he had not had the full support of his senior officers and that this contributed to the lack of success on the day.

According to General Smith, Burnside had considered relieving General Sumner from command of the Right Grand Division and arresting Hooker, who commanded the Centre Grand Division. Interestingly, Smith also remembered that Burnside had considered that General Franklin could be placed in command of the army.[30]

Publicly, Lincoln was more concerned about the morale of the army than attributing blame. In a published address to the Army of the Potomac, Lincoln praised the "courage with which you, in an open field, maintained the contest against an entrenched foe, and the consummate skill and success with which you crossed and re-crossed the river, in face of the enemy, show that you possess all the qualities of a great army, which will yet give victory to the cause of the country and of popular government." Lincoln assured the army that the defeat was not the result of an error but "an accident."[31] However, many of the Army of the Potomac's officers would have agreed with Burnside: he was responsible for the defeat.

Likewise, the Committee on the Conduct of the War saw the defeat as a result of military incompetence and not an accident. This provided the opportunity to once again critically examine the Union's main army of operation and the civilian administration. This began a political crisis in the Republican Party. The Joint Committee on the Conduct of the War wasted little time in interviewing members of the Union high command. Most of the questioning of Halleck focused on the delay with pontoon bridges, which indicated the committee was after evidence to attack Lincoln and his cabinet members.[32] The committee interviewed Burnside and other senior commanders on December 19.[33] Burnside told them he regretted his decision to accept command and he had no military ambitions.[34] The committee decided not to pursue him. The reason is not clear, but the political situation in late 1862 may have influenced their decision.[35]

In the House of Representatives elections that year the Republican Party lost 22 seats while their opponents, the Democratic Party, gained 28 seats. The Republicans still had more seats than the Democrats, 86 compared to the Democrats' 72, and the Republicans could count on the support of the Unionist Party's 25 seats to hold their grip in the House.[36] Many in the Republican Party attributed the party's poor results to the lack of military success in the war. There were even some in the military who blamed the administration's poor results on having too many Democrats in high military positions.[37]

The Radical Republicans targeted Secretary of State Seward for the recent political and military reversals. They reasoned simplistically that if those who did not want to fight a war in earnest were removed from the cabinet then the Union would achieve a crushing victory. Many still remembered how, during the crisis over Fort Sumter, Seward had been the voice of conciliation and had also voiced opposition to the Confiscation Acts.[38] A committee of Republicans had met on December 17 and were unanimous in their opposition to Seward. One of the senators, Preston King, a former colleague and the friend of Seward, felt it was his obligation to immediately inform Seward of what had occurred at the meeting. Seward must have felt the political pressure building. He had already written a letter of resignation before the Battle of Fredericksburg and altered the date on the letter to December 16, 1862. According to Welles' account of this incident, which was based on Lincoln's telling at a cabinet meeting on December 19, Seward had immediately written the letter and Mr. King had tendered his resignation.[39] On the night of December 17, Senator King and Frederick Seward visited the president and handed in the resignations of Secretary of State Seward and Assistant Secretary of State Frederick Seward.[40] This was a difficult situation for Lincoln because the committee of senators could have been aware of the contents of the letter.

On December 18, 1862, Lincoln met with a committee of nine Republican senators who wanted to discuss the situation concerning Seward and the cabinet in general.[41] The committee comprised Collamer, Fessenden, Grimes, Harris, Howard, Pomeroy, Sumner, Trumbull, and Wade.[42] Lincoln did not make any reference to Seward's letter of resignation.[43] The men had presented a paper to Lincoln that argued "the only way to put down the rebellion and save the nation is a vigorous prosecution of the war." While Seward was not mentioned in the document, all the senators had detected a "lukewarmness" in Seward's attitude to the war and they considered "him the real cause of [their] failures."[44]

The next day, December 19, 1862, Lincoln called a meeting of the cabinet for 10:30 a.m. to discuss the outcome of the meeting with the senators. All the cabinet was present, except for Seward.[45] Lincoln reported that the senators' views were based on the assumption that Lincoln's cabinet needed to change so that the war could be fought with much more vigor. They had recommended to the president that he restructure his cabinet to include nine members, which would comprise six radicals and three conservatives. Eight of the nine senators believed Seward was a "serious obstacle to the prosecution of the war." Furthermore, they accused Seward of undermining Lincoln's best intentions.[46] The question that must have crossed Lincoln's mind was why the senators were targeting Seward, the secretary of state and not the secretary of war, Stanton. Lincoln would also have interpreted the attack on Seward as an indirect criticism of his own handling of the war. Lincoln understood he could not cave in to the demands of the Radical Republican senators because he would lose control of the administration and the war effort.

It was decided that Lincoln and the cabinet were to meet the committee of senators at 7:30 that evening. At the meeting the senators not only criticized Seward but also Lincoln's handling of the war. In particular, they were critical of his handling of his cabinet. Lincoln admitted that he did not call a lot of cabinet meetings but this was because he was very busy. As for the unity of the cabinet, Lincoln acknowledged that members might disagree with decisions but once the decision was made they supported the policy. Also, the U.S. cabinet was not a body that made collective decisions. Its sole purpose was to advise the president.[47] He then asked the cabinet members' views. Chase was the first to be asked.

This put Chase in a difficult position. He had been courting the Radical Republicans for a possible run for the presidency. If he supported Lincoln's statement, he would lose credibility with the Radical Republican senators. Chase did not want to make his views known in this forum. Lincoln knew, however, that Chase had been critical of Seward and himself and also that Chase resented Seward's influence on Lincoln. Chase protested angrily that he had not come to the meeting to be questioned. This reaction suggested some form of guilt. Chase left the meeting before any further damage could be done. Nevertheless, Chase had lost face in front of a political faction he had been courting.[48]

The next day, December 20, 1862, Lincoln asked Chase to see him. Lincoln had indicated some action could be taken to resolve the conflict in the cabinet because he had advised Chase to "please ... not go out of town."[49] Chase had already written his resignation. When Lincoln met with Chase, he demanded the letter: "Let me have it." Lincoln remarked, "This cuts the Gordian knot!"[50] Lincoln knew he now had the upper hand: "Now I can ride; I have a pumpkin in each end of my bag." The Radical Republican senators could not remove Seward from the cabinet without Chase being removed as well. Secretary of the Navy Welles had visited Seward and discussed his letter of resignation. Welles reported to Lincoln that he would withdraw his letter of resignation. Lincoln could not afford to lose both men. In a letter to both of them, he explained: "My deliberate judgment is, that the public interest does not admit of it."[51] The president had managed what James McPherson had judged as "the greatest challenge thus far to Lincoln's leadership."[52] While the political tensions had eased, the tensions within the officers of the Army of the Potomac over Burnside's leadership remained.

The heavy Union defeat at Fredericksburg had led many of Burnside's senior officers to question privately his ability to handle the army. Major General John F. Reynolds, who commanded the 1st Corps in Franklin's Left Grand Division, wrote his sisters about some serious errors of judgment by Burnside: "The crossing at this point was a failure, from the fact that to have been successful it ought to have been a surprise, and we should have advanced at once and carried the heights as was intended. As it was, we lost one day by the failure to throw over the Bridges at the town without serious opposition and to have risked more than we did would have probably caused the loss of the whole Army in case of another repulse. You must not show this to anyone."[53]

Burnside's plan to attack the Confederate positions at Fredericksburg again on the next day after the battle would have shaken the confidence of many of his officers. Senior officers of the Right Grand Division discussed Burnside's plan to renew the attack on the evening of the battle. They concluded that "a second attack would probably end more disastrously than the first," and that Brigadier General Rush C. Hawkins should go at once to Burnside to persuade him not to renew the attack. Hawkins reached "the Phillips house" in Fredericksburg, where he found Generals Sumner, Hooker, Franklin and Hardie, and Colonel Taylor. Burnside arrived back at one o'clock in the morning and announced that plans for the attack had been made. He was greeted by a silence that suggested the other generals present were uneasy with his plan. Burnside asked the generals their views on renewing the attack and they argued that a renewed attack should not be attempted. Consequently, the plans for the attack were cancelled.[54]

Some senior officers in the Army of the Potomac saw the Union defeat at Fredericksburg as an opportunity to force the removal of Burnside and perhaps replace him with McClellan. General Franklin optimistically believed the defeat increased the prospects of McClellan returning to command. In a letter to William Swift, Franklin hoped that McClellan would be looked at more favorably: "I presume the McClellan stock is rising somewhat just now." Franklin blamed the Union high command for the defeat: "I think the whole thing ought to eventuate in the dismissal of Stanton & Halleck."[55] Franklin could only speculate on the removal of these senior members of the Union high command, but he believed he could help force the removal of Burnside.

The anti–Burnside faction within the Army of the Potomac was led by two of its senior commanders, Generals Franklin and Smith. Franklin was the commander of the Left Grand Division. The Left Grand Division comprised two army corps. One of these corps, the VI Corps, was commanded by General William F. Smith. Franklin and Smith were old friends. During Burnside's campaign, these two shared the same tent and had a common mess and there was, according to Smith, not "the slightest disagreement between us as to plans or details."[56] Both shared the view that Burnside's Fredericksburg campaign was a poor military plan. On December 20, 1862, a week after the Battle of Fredericksburg and the day Lincoln managed to end the political crisis in his cabinet, they wrote to the president with an alternative line of operations without informing Burnside of their actions.

Franklin could have been motivated in part by having been blamed for the failure at Fredericksburg by the Joint Committee on the Conduct of the War. The committee viewed Franklin's lack of action during the battle as evidence that he had failed to obey Burnside's orders.[57] Also, the two generals had learned of Burnside's plan to force the line of the Rappahannock River, this time at Skinker's Neck, downstream from Fredericksburg.[58] Writing directly to the president was inappropriate because they would be ignoring the chain of command and showing disloyalty to their direct superior, Burnside. Once again, however, the protocols of the chain of command would be ignored.

Their letter opened with a criticism of Burnside's "plan of campaign which has already been commenced cannot possibly be successful." Their main criticism of this plan was logistical. The distance to Richmond was 61 miles and the necessity of protecting the lines of communication would require large numbers of troops, which would reduce troop numbers available to push the advance. Also, the terrain provided many good defensive positions along the line of advance, which was an advantage to the Confederates. Smith and Franklin set three criteria for a successful campaign in the East: all troops in the East should be concentrated, approach as near to Richmond as possible without fighting and secure a line of communication. What they proposed was an operation on the James River similar to McClellan's Peninsula Campaign. Troops could be "brought to points within 20 miles of Richmond without the risk of an engagement." Also, the lines of communication via the James River could be maintained without the "slightest danger of interruption."

The details of the plan required 150,000 troops to be landed on the north bank and 100,000 troops on the south bank of the James River. The two forces would be lightly provisioned to provide greater mobility. Franklin and Smith could not be sure that the advance on Richmond would result in the destruction or capture of the Confederate army, but they believed it would certainly result in the capture of Richmond and "the war will be on a better footing than it is now or has any present prospect of being."[59] The implications of these words were clear. The generals believed that the army did not have much chance of success with Burnside's plans or that the army would be successful if Burnside were to lead it in a new campaign on the James River. They had not considered, however, how they intended to move the army from its present position in front of the enemy without the Confederates being presented with an opportunity to threaten Washington.

Lincoln's response, two days later, was cautious. He had only "hastily" read the letter and he would give it more "deliberate consideration, with the aid of military men." Lincoln may have meant by this that he intended to discuss the letter with Halleck, but there is no evidence he did so. For Lincoln, the proposed plan presented the "old difficulty" between the present line the army was on and the peninsula. Lincoln had never believed that McClellan's change of base plan to the York and the James rivers had any better prospect of success than the more direct line from Manassas to Richmond. Furthermore, he reminded the generals of the political importance of the capital: "A large part of the army must remain on or near the Fredericksburg line, to protect Washington."[60]

Lincoln's reply did not end the machinations by the Army of the Potomac's officer corps against Burnside. General Cochrane, a brigade commander in Smith's VI Corps, observed the growing lack of confidence in Burnside: "Discussion around every camp-fire was Burnside's qualities as a commander." In particular, the Army of the Potomac's officers had no confidence in Burnside's plan to operate on the Rappahannock River: "It soon transpired that the officers, to whose opinions the General had referred the practicability of his plan, had without exception condemned it."[61]

News that the Army of the Potomac was preparing for a movement to cross the Rappahannock set off some of the officers in Franklin's Left Grand Division in a desperate bid to overturn the order.[62] On December 29, Brigadier General John Newton and Brigadier General John Cochrane journeyed to Washington and managed to meet with Lincoln. Cochrane was familiar with Washington. He had studied law and had served two terms in Congress, representing New York. On at least two other occasions during the war, he had visited Washington and had meetings with Salmon Chase. In the first, on October 7, 1862, Cochrane and Chase had talked "freely" about McClellan and the possibility of restoring him to general in chief. Cochrane had also met Lincoln to discuss the same issue and left both meetings believing that Chase and Lincoln would seriously consider his plan.[63] On his second visit on November 9, Cochrane had breakfast with Chase and discussed the reorganization of political parties as well as the opportunity for Cochrane to be given the military governorship of Washington if the incumbent, Wadsworth, went into the field.[64]

Cochrane commanded a brigade in Newton's division. This was one of three divisions in General Smith's VI Corps, which was part of Franklin's Left Grand Division. Franklin also had connections with Chase. In May 1861 he had worked on a committee that had been established by Chase to assist with the mobilization of the Union Army. Franklin was rewarded for his work with a promotion to colonel. Brigadier General John Newton was a Virginian who had remained loyal to the Union. He had graduated from West Point in 1842 but had missed active duty in the war against Mexico. In September 1861 he was appointed Brigadier General of Volunteers and commanded a brigade in the Peninsula Campaign and at Antietam. At Fredericksburg, he was on the left of the line at Franklin's Crossing.[65]

Cochrane justified taking leave of absence for a few days in Washington because he believed Burnside's plan would result in "inevitable disaster" and, perhaps, the "irretrievable ruin of our cause."[66] He left camp on Monday, December 29, 1861, and on the journey to Washington he had met General John Newton, who was on his way to meet his family in Washington and not to visit his home and family in Delaware as Cochrane had recorded in his memoirs.[67] The granting of leave for two senior officers before a major movement by their army is extraordinary. Newton was aware of this criticism and knew that it would reflect badly on Franklin and Smith. In his testimony to the Joint Committee on the Conduct of the War, Newton carefully explained that when he came to Washington, Burnside had not formed any plan and that a movement was only "talked of."[68] If this was the case, then it does not explain their actions to prevent the army's moving. Also, what information Cochrane had of Burnside's proposed movement had come from Newton, who had inspected the possible point of crossing the Rappahannock.[69] Perhaps the answer was that Burnside had told no one of the full details of his plan and this created a sense of uneasiness among some officers in the army. All they knew was that there would be another crossing of the Rappahannock.[70] Newton also explained that it would take three or four days before the army could move, which would give him plenty of time to return to his command.[71] As if to emphasize that Franklin and Smith were not involved, he added, "This action was of my own accord, and on my own responsibility entirely."[72] Yet he had told Franklin and Smith, "in general terms," "When I was off on leave of absence I thought I should see somebody in Washington on this matter.... Perhaps I may have said that if they advised me to go to see the President I would go."[73] Franklin testified that in granting Newton's leave of absence he was aware Newton had "become very dissatisfied with the manner in which things were going" and admitted Newton intended "to see some influential people" but he had no idea he was going to see the president.[74]

Cochrane had intended to see Mr. Wilson and Mr. Odell. Mr. Henry

Wilson was a senator from Massachusetts and chairman of the Military Committee of the Senate. Moses F. Odell of New York was a Democratic member of Congress and a member of the Joint Committee on the Conduct of the War.[75] They were absent from Washington, however, because Congress was in recess, so the two generals decided to proceed directly to the president.[76] Considering Cochrane's experience in the capital, it is surprising that he did not consider the recess of Congress in his plans. Newton wanted to "lay this state of things before some prominent individual in the confidence of the government."[77] He did not mention who the prominent individual might be but he must have known that only the commander in chief had the power to overturn Burnside's order. Cochrane admitted as much in his memoirs: "It had occurred to me, that a knowledge of the situation of the army might facilitate a remedy of superior authority."[78]

Cochrane did not find any members of Congress with whom to discuss the situation of the Army of the Potomac. So he decided to go directly to the president. He went to the president's house, where he met Seward. He told Seward he wanted a meeting with the President and the purpose and asked Seward if he could arrange it. Seward arranged the meeting for later that same day.[79] Seward advised him that he should see the secretary of war or General Halleck. Cochrane replied that he would prefer to see the president "so that I might familiarly converse with him upon a subject which I did not like to present in a formal, official, or military manner, I being inclined to commit it to him from the fact that, on previous occasions, I had spoken to him on similar subjects regarding the feelings and opinions of men in the army."[80]

The meeting with the president in the executive mansion must have been tense. Newton, the senior officer, opened the meeting by referring to rumors of a new movement to cross the river and the unfavorable opinions of him and other officers who had inspected the proposed crossing sites.[81] Newton believed the president, initially, had "very naturally conceived that they had come there for the purpose of injuring General Burnside, and suggesting some other person to fill his place."[82] Cochrane believed Lincoln's interpretation of the purpose of the meeting "characterized the disclosure as an effort, in his opinion, by subordinate officers to control the action of their commander."[83]

Newton believed that the main cause of the low morale of the army was the lack of confidence in Burnside, but he believed it improper to tell the president outright. He did mention "the reports of my own and other officers and the desertions of the men; also, that the condition of the left grand division was better, as soldiers, than that of any other division, and this means of comparison was from current report."[84] Cochrane told Lincoln of the "daily canvass of the merits of its commander" and that another attempt to cross the Rappahannock "would precipitate a reverse when a reverse might be attended with ruin."[85] Both generals managed to convince the president that they did not intend to "injure" Burnside but to "hope that the President would make inquiry, and learn the true cause himself."[86] Cochrane recognized he had disregarded the "conventional barrier of supposed etiquette" but argued that to withhold the information from the president would constitute treason.[87] The president thought silently for a few minutes and said, "You have done right. Good will come from this. I will look to it."[88]

Not long after the two generals left the White House, Lincoln sent a telegram to Burnside: "I have good reason for saying you must not make a general movement of the army without letting me know."[89] Burnside could not imagine the reason the president had for sending the order. Most of the officers in the army had been told little more than that a movement would be made. The only reason he could think of was that a major operation was to occur in another part of the country that would require his cooperation.[90] Burnside sent orders to halt the movement of the army and he determined to see the president to find out the reason for the order.[91]

On December 31, 1862, Burnside met with Lincoln in the White House. The president recounted how two generals from Burnside's command, whose names he refused to disclose had been in his office the day before and had argued that the army was demoralized and that any attempt to make a movement would end in disaster. Also, Burnside recalled "that no prominent officers of my command had any faith in my proposed movement."[92] Burnside outlined the details of his plan to the president and admitted he was aware of "some misgiving" by some of his officers regarding making any movement at all and that he was satisfied a movement should be made and that he had "come to that conclusion without any consultation with the other generals." The president had misgivings about making the maneuver but was interested in the planned cavalry raid around Richmond as part of Burnside's general plan. Nevertheless, Lincoln did not want to authorize a movement of the army without first consulting Halleck and Stanton.[93]

The morning meeting on New Year's Day 1863 with Burnside, Halleck, Stanton and Lincoln did nothing to ease the conflict in the Army of the Potomac's officer corps. Before Stanton and Halleck arrived, Burnside had given his views to Lincoln on those above him in the chain of command. The secretary of war, he told Lincoln, "has not the confidence of the officers and soldiers," and "he has not the confidence of the country." Also, he said, "The same opinion applies with equal force in regard to General Halleck. It seems to be the universal opinion that the movements of the army have not been planned with view to co-operation and mutual assistance."⁹⁴ It appears that Burnside offered his resignation but also suggested that the secretary of war and the general in chief be replaced. His argument, ironically, would also be a justification for the actions of Franklin, Smith, Newton and Cochrane: "Will you allow me, Mr. President, to say that it is the utmost importance that you be surrounded and supported by men who have the confidence of the people and the army, and who will at all times give you definite and honest opinions in relation to their separate departments, and at the same time give you positive and unswerving support in your public policy, taking at all times their full share of the responsibility for that policy?"⁹⁵ Lincoln began the meeting by giving a summary of the reason he had called the meeting. Burnside again asked Lincoln for the names of the officers who had met Lincoln, and again Lincoln refused to disclose this information. Halleck and Burnside believed that the officers should have been dismissed from the army or at least arrested at once. Burnside remained in Washington for two days but no progress was made.⁹⁶

On the same day, Lincoln, acting in his role as the commander in chief, significantly and symbolically changed the Union's military strategy. About noon, he signed the Emancipation Proclamation. Lincoln had used his power as commander in chief to strike at, as he phrased it, a pillar of Confederate strength, namely slavery.⁹⁷ All slaves in states or parts of states that were in rebellion against the United States were freed. This excluded the Union border states because Lincoln believed he did not have the constitutional authority to take a similar action there and in Tennessee and also parts of Virginia and Louisiana as they were under U.S. military control at the time of the proclamation. Lincoln explained the proclamation in terms of military necessity: "a fit and necessary war measure for suppressing said rebellion." As commander in chief, he directed the army and the navy to "recognize and maintain the freedom" of the slaves, thus making the destruction of slavery the duty of every Union soldier. Lincoln recognized that freed slaves could help solve the constant need for more recruits in the army and navy by allowing them into the armed services not to fight but "to garrison forts, positions, stations, and other places, and to man vessels of all sorts in said service," thus freeing up more "white" soldiers to fight the Confederate armies.⁹⁸ The Emancipation Proclamation also signaled to the pro–McClellan faction in the Army of the Potomac that the president had effectively ended any hope they had of McClellan's being reappointed as its commander.

Burnside was also concerned by the pro–McClellan officers in his army. His determination to try to cross the Rappahannock again might have been a product of his stubbornness and the reasoning that a successful operation would restore confidence in his command.⁹⁹ Burnside blamed the cancellation of his general movement on "rebel sympathisers in Washington" who had mysteriously learned of a plan of which his own generals did not know any details. He asked for the authority from Halleck, or someone else authorized to give it, to move across the river. He stressed the importance and necessity of his plan but again admitted he did not have the support of his generals. Burnside was willing to take the responsibility of the movement and tried to reassure Lincoln that he would not risk destroying the army. He was determined to have Halleck's permission or sanction to make the movement. Halleck cautiously replied on January 7 that, while he supported a forward movement, he could "not take the responsibility of giving any directions as to how and when it should be made."¹⁰⁰

The disaffection within the army towards Burnside had virtually reached the point of revolt. The center of gravity for this revolt was the pro–McClellan faction in Franklin's Left Grand Division. Colonel Charles S. Wainwright, an artillery officer in the Army of the Potomac, observed the extent of anti-Burnside feeling on a visit to Franklin's headquarters on January 19, 1863. Both Generals Franklin and Smith's staffs were "talking outrageously, only repeating though, no doubt, the words of their generals." While Wainwright himself had no confidence in Burnside as a commander, he believed that they had no right to disclose this lack of confidence to their staffs. Franklin had talked so much about Burnside's inability that he had demoralized his whole command to the extent failure was certain. Franklin's conduct, concluded Wainwright, had "been such that he surely deserves to be broken."¹⁰¹

Burnside's determination to cross was based simply on the fact that the Army of the Potomac was on the Rappahannock and General Lee and his Confederate army were still on Marye's Heights behind Fredericksburg with Jackson guarding Lee's southern flank. Burnside proposed to cross the river about six miles north of Fredericksburg at Bank's Ford and then turn Lee's left flank. The January weather had been mild and he saw no reason why his plan would not work. The move began when General Hooker's Central Grand Division started towards Bank's Ford on January 20, 1863.¹⁰² Shortly after the movement began, a drizzle of rain started. For the next two days, heavy rain turned the roads into mud. A march that should have taken about four hours to complete became a four-day fiasco. The army was, as Swinton described it, "embargoed: it was no longer a question of how to go forward it was a question of how to get back."¹⁰³

The "Mud March," as it became known, was another opportunity to criticize Burnside's ability as a commander. One corps commander, Major General John F. Reynolds, saw that the march was evidence of Burnside's inability to command the army and of the interference from both the civilian administration and the general in chief: "[We are] on the banks of the Rappahannock with the idea of crossing near Fredericksburg. A violent storm interposed, however, and we are now 'stuck in the mud' unable to get up our artillery or supplies and Burnside goes to Washington to know what to do! If we do not get someone who can command an army without consulting 'Stanton and Halleck' at Washington, I do not know what will become of this army. No one Gen'l officer that I can find approved of the move, and yet it was made."[104] General Meade was more understanding when he wrote his wife: "I never felt so disappointed and sorry for any one in my life as I did for Burnside. He seems to have even the elements against him."[105]

Burnside had to abandon the movement not only because of the weather but also of the almost universal feeling among Burnside's officers against it. Burnside believed that he had been undermined because some officers had freely expressed their criticism of the plan to their troops.[106] One officer reported how Generals Franklin and Smith in particular had done nothing to help the situation and had been "grumbling and talking in a manner to do all the harm possible." Also, Franklin's staff had talked freely about Franklin's taking command of the army in Burnside's place.[107] Hooker took the opportunity to criticize "the absurdity of the movement" and added the civilian administration was incapable of successfully conducting the war and what the country needed was a dictator.[108] There was no doubt that Hooker saw himself as that dictator.

It is clear from the evidence that the atrocious weather was the cause for the cancellation of Burnside's plan and provided an example of the problems of winter campaigning in Virginia.[109] Yet, Burnside was convinced he saw some more sinister cause for the failure. He believed that the lack of confidence in him among the leading generals in the Army of the Potomac was the main cause of its failure. The logic of this argument dictated that any future success of the army depended on the removal of these officers, and he had become aware of the identity of the two officers who had been responsible for the cancellation of the December 30, 1862, movement. From this information, he could deduce the roles that their commanding officers had played. Burnside naturally focused his attention on some of McClellan's trusted officers and General Hooker. He revealed to Generals Franklin and Smith over lunch that "in a day or two you will hear of something that will surprise you."[110] Both generals were already aware Burnside had arrested Brigadier General William Brooks, a brigade commander in the Smith's Sixth Corps, for insubordination.[111] They were also aware that the trial of General Fitz John Porter had ended and the verdict and sentence were with the president for approval.

On December 5, 1862, the court-martial of General Fitz John Porter commenced. By January 10, 1863, the judges had found him guilty. The charges related to his conduct during the Second Battle of Manassas. The first charges accused Porter of disobeying General Pope's orders and the second charges were termed "Misbehavior in Front of the Enemy," a term many would interpret as cowardice. The proceedings were sent to the president and, on January 21, 1863, Lincoln approved and confirmed it, including the sentence that Porter be "dismissed from the service of the United States" and "disqualified from holding any office of trust or profit under the Government of the United States." Porter was determined to fight what he believed was an unjust verdict. Eventually, in 1886, President Chester Arthur reversed the sentence. The trial had a negative impact on the Army of the Potomac's officer corps because it was seen as politically motivated. It also focused attention on the pro–McClellan faction within the Army of the Potomac's officer corps and on the West Point–trained officers in general.

The West Point professional officer corps had been looked upon suspiciously by the American public in general because of its perceived aristocratic values. The *New York Times* acknowledged the widespread suspicion about West Point officers but reminded readers that seven of the court-martials of the nine judges were West Point graduates. The paper was keen, however, to support what it saw as a stand against "Disobedient and Unwilling Generals" and, in particular, the outcome of the trial, which set out to "make it clear as the noon-day sun, that the defeats which the army suffered in the last days of August, and first of September, were in reality due to the base and treasonable jealousy of MCCLELLAN and his friends, and chief among them, PORTER."[112]

Stanton believed that Porter's lack of action at the Second Battle of Manassas was, as Stephen Sears expressed it, a "highly visible representation of McClellanism, the disease the general's detractors defined as bad blood and paralysis infecting much of the officer corps of the Army of the Potomac."[113] Stanton had come to believe that motivation and political reliability were more important than military training and experience. He reasoned that generals like McClellan could never win the war because they "felt just as pleasantly toward the enemy in front of him as he would if he had been on the other side."[114]

The assertion that McClellan was the real villain behind the defeat of Pope would have been welcomed by McClellan's opponents as justification for his removal from command. Conversely, those who have argued that there was a conspiracy to convict Porter have done so because they believe the real target of the trial was McClellan and that most of the judges were prejudiced against Porter. Also, the day after Porter's conviction, four of the judges gained promotion. It would have been easy for some officers in the Army of the Potomac to conclude that this suggested Stanton and Halleck must have been so corrupt as to have selected the judges so that a guilty verdict would be certain. Yet, the promotions had actually been granted before the trial and the Senate confirmed them after the trial.[115] The truth was that Porter, like many other Civil War generals, had struggled with the reality and complexity of handling large armies in battle. The guilty verdict was a clear sign to McClellan's supporters in the Army of the Potomac that the door was shut on a return to command by McClellan.

Nevertheless, many officers in the Army of the Potomac interpreted the Fitz John Porter conviction as an attack on the officer corps in general as well as an attack on McClellan and his friends. One officer questioned what the nation's leaders were doing by "lying and swearing away the life of this great man."[116] Another officer concluded that it was necessary for the administration that Porter was found guilty because "some scapegoat had to be found for the shortcomings of their pet, Pope, and in Porter they could hit a friend of McClellan at the same time."[117]

The conviction of Porter may have emboldened Burnside to move against officers he believed did not support him. He had once already offered his resignation as commander of the Army of the Potomac on January 1, 1863. That Lincoln had not accepted it might have influenced Burnside's bold decision to remove opposition in his army's senior ranks. Burnside wrote an order on January 23, 1863, designed to remove opposition to his command from senior officers in the army. His order, which he referred to as General Order No. 8,[118] asked the president to remove eight officers from the army. Burnside's main target was Hooker. Hooker was to be removed because he had "been guilty of unjust and unnecessary criticisms of the actions of his superior officers' and therefore he should be 'dismissed from the service of the United States as a man unfit to hold an important commission.'" Burnside believed Brigadier General W.T. H. Brooks, who commanded the First Division, Sixth Army Corps, should also be dismissed for complaining of the policy of the government. Brigadier General Newton and Brigadier General Cochrane were charged with going to the president of the United States with criticisms upon the plans of their commanding officer and consequently were dismissed. Another five generals were to be relieved from duty because they "can be of no further service to this army": Brigadier General Samuel D. Sturgis, Second Division, Ninth Corps; Brigadier General Edward Ferrero, commanding Second Brigade, Second Division, Ninth Army Corps; Lieutenant Colonel J.H. Taylor, assistant adjutant general, Right Grand Division; Major General W.B.

Franklin, commanding Left Grand Division; Major General W.F. Smith, commanding Sixth Corps.[119] Cochrane was also to be relieved of his command but Burnside had already dismissed him from service in a preceding paragraph, which suggests how rushed Burnside was to write the order and remove the officers mentioned. He was keen to have this order executed as soon as possible, but he needed the president's approval. He asked to meet the president sometime after midnight so that he could be back with his army by 8:00 a.m. on January 24.[120]

When Burnside met with the president, he presented the general order for approval and also his resignation. He wanted to force Lincoln to accept one or the other. According to Burnside, Lincoln wanted to discuss the matter with his advisors before he made a decision.[121] Lincoln, however, would not remove Hooker even though he was aware of his open criticism of fellow generals. He confided to Henry J. Raymond, the editor of the *New York Times*, that Hooker was "stronger with the country today than any other man. Even if the country was told of Hooker's talk they would not believe it."[122] Also, Lincoln could see that morale was low in the army. Major General Carl Schurz in the XI Corps had written Lincoln:

> I am convinced that the spirit of the men is systematically demoralized and the confidence in their chief systematically broken by several commanding generals. I have heard generals, subordinate officers, and men say that they expect to be whipped anyhow, that "all these fatigues and hardships are for nothing, and that they might as well go home." Add to this that the immense army is closely packed together in the mud, that sickness is spreading at a frightful rate, that in consequence of all these causes of discouragement desertion increases ever day—and you will not be surprised if you see the army melt away with distressing rapidity.[123]

While General Schurz was exaggerating to emphasize his point, desertions were considerably large, estimated to be about 200 a day. Hooker reported that there were 85,123 officers and men absent from the army at this time.[124] The low morale was evidence of a lack of confidence in Burnside from the troops in the army. One incident that revealed this was a review of the 2nd Corps shortly after the Battle of Fredericksburg. Burnside was present and he received a "freezing silence" as a reception. The corps commander, General Sumner, had General Couch call for cheers from the troops but this request was answered with only "a few derisive cries."[125]

Burnside returned to Washington on the morning of January 25 for a 10:00 a.m. meeting to get the president's decision.[126] Halleck and Stanton had met Lincoln first. Lincoln recounted to them that Burnside had proposed the dismissal of several high-ranking officers of the Army of the Potomac and that if this order was not approved by the president he wished to resign. Burnside had always been the reluctant commander of the army and this may have affected the confidence of the officer corps. Meade thought this was a major factor in his troubled relations with the officer corps. He wrote his wife there "was a very general opinion among officers and men, brought by his own assertions, that the command was too much for him. This greatly weakened his position."[127] The president announced he accepted Burnside's resignation from command of the Army of the Potomac and appointed General Hooker as the new commander. Neither Halleck nor Stanton had been consulted by Lincoln, nor did he ask for their opinion about his decision. Had he done so, both Stanton and Halleck would have argued in favor of General George G. Meade, the commander of the 5th Corps.[128]

As was the situation when Lincoln had sacked McClellan, there was no obvious replacement for Burnside. McClellan was not considered despite his strong support in the army. General William Rosecrans, the commander of the Army of the Cumberland, had recently won, but only just, the Battle of Stones River, which lasted from December 31, 1862, to January 2, 1863. Lincoln must have been mindful of how General Pope had failed when he had come from the Western Theater and the lack of cooperation he had with the Army of the Potomac's officer corps. This restricted the selection pool to senior officers in the Army of the Potomac. Suggestions that Chase had exerted pressure to get Hooker the command in return for Hooker's support for Chase's presidential ambitions miss the point that Lincoln alone had made the decision.[129] Lincoln studied the four senior corps commanders, Sumner, Hooker, Meade and Franklin. Sumner was clearly too old. Franklin was under investigation for his conduct at Fredericksburg, which ruled him out. The decision between Hooker and Meade was simple. Hooker outranked Meade and had a strong reputation in the army and the public in general.[130] Moreover, Hooker was not looked upon with "suspicion of undue attachment to the fortunes of General McClellan."[131] Lincoln confided to Republican senator Orville Hickman Browning that he really did not know of any better solution. He knew Sumner and Franklin would not work with Hooker, so he intended to relieve them of their commands. Browning believed from talking to officers and men of the army that "McClellan possessed their confidence to a greater extent than any other man, and I thought they would fight under him better than under any other Genl we had." Lincoln admitted McClellan "stood very high with all educated military men, but the fact was he would not fight."[132]

Burnside was then admitted to the meeting and Lincoln informed him of his decision. Burnside wanted to resign from the U.S. Army entirely and not just as commander of the Army of the Potomac.[133] Halleck then urged him to withdraw his resignation. Burnside agreed and made the trip to the army's headquarters at Falmouth to present Hooker with the president's order.[134] Burnside's offer of resignation and his General Order No. 8 were eventually made public. This was not Lincoln's intention but more the machinations of Hooker, who had found a copy of the order at the Army of the Potomac's Falmouth headquarters and leaked it to the press.[135] Burnside went on leave and would return to the West to command the Army of the Ohio.

Lincoln's General Order Number 20, which promoted Hooker to command of the Army of the Potomac, was influenced by the need to restore confidence in the army's officer corps. To accomplish this, Lincoln must have believed he needed to do more than just replace Burnside with Hooker. He also relieved Major General E.V. Sumner, "at his own request," and Major General Franklin as well.[136] Sumner outranked Hooker, so Lincoln might have been motivated to remove a potential destabilization of Hooker's command. Sumner was appointed to command the Department of Missouri but he died in New York on March 21, 1863, before he could take up his new role. Franklin was assigned to the Nineteenth Corps in Louisiana in August 1863. He took part in Nathaniel Banks's Red River Campaign, during which he was wounded in the leg. He eventually resigned his command in May 1864 and took no further part in the war.[137]

The revolt of some high-ranking officers in the Army of the Potomac's officer corps did achieve one of its objectives: Burnside had been removed from command. However, Hooker and not McClellan had replaced him. The revolt highlighted the contradictory forces at work in an army that had achieved limited success. While the pro–McClellan faction led by Franklin and Smith was critical of the interference of the civilian administration, they still understood the importance of political support to remove Burnside. The officer corps was critical of the influence of military "amateurs" in the military decision making but at the same time, many were prepared to ignore the chain of command to seek political support for their purposes. The instability in the officer corps was as much the officers' fault as it was Lincoln's. Lincoln had selected Burnside because he had lost confidence in McClellan. Burnside was a reluctant commander. His failure at Fredericksburg was as much his own failure to modify his plan as it was that of Lincoln and Halleck, who had forced him into action. The equation for Lincoln was simple enough but it was difficult to find the solution. To remove the instability in the Army of the Potomac's officer corps and to remove the ghost of McClellan, he needed a general who could win.

Seven
"And now, beware of rashness"

The appointment of General Hooker to command the Army of the Potomac seemed to offer a simplistic solution to the Union high command problems in the East. Hooker appeared to be a general who would not only fight but also win the decisive battle most people believed would win the war. He had been part of the revolt that removed General Burnside. But while most of the generals who sought Burnside's removal wanted McClellan to replace him Hooker schemed so that he could gain the prize. Also, the problems within the Union high command—the indifference to the chain of command, an ineffective general in chief, and the interference of the president in operational and the tactical areas—would again hamper the effectiveness of the Army of the Potomac.

Joseph Hooker was born on November 13, 1814. He studied at West Point and graduated in 1827 with William Sherman. He served in the 2nd Seminole War in Florida and along the Canadian border. He then moved back to West Point in the role of adjutant of the academy. Like many West Pointers of the period, he served in the Mexican War. After the war he was moved by the army to California. In 1851 he bought 550 acres of land near Sonoma, north of San Francisco, where he planted grapes. Hooker was not successful as a farmer or in his attempt to enter political life. In 1858 he was appointed superintendent of the military roads in Oregon. A year later he was back in the military as a colonel in the California militia. Henry W. Halleck had also served in the California militia, as a brigadier general, which has led to speculation that this was the origin of the animosity between the two men. The prospect of war sent Hooker to Washington to seek a command. General Scott did not like Hooker, so his request was denied.[1] Hooker witnessed the First Battle of Manassas and was motivated to make a personal request to the president. He was introduced to Lincoln as "Captain" Hooker.[2] Hooker's reply indicated how determined he was not to lose this opportunity:

Mr. President, I am not Captain Hooker, but I once was Lieutenant Colonel Hooker in the Regular Army. I was lately a farmer in California, but since the Rebellion broke out I have been here trying to get into service, and I find that I am not wanted. I am about to return home, but before going I was anxious to pay my respects to you, and to express my wishes for your personal welfare and success in quelling this Rebellion. And I want to say one more word more. I was at Bull Run the other day, Mr. President, and it is no vanity in me to say I am a damned sight better general than any you had on that field.[3]

The president was impressed. He told Hooker: "Colonel—not Lieutenant Colonel—Hooker, stay. I have use for you and a regiment for you to command."[4] Hooker rapidly rose up the chain of command. He commanded a brigade and then a division in the Army of the Potomac. During the Peninsula Campaign, he commanded the 2nd Division of the III Corps and was eventually given command of the III Corps in Pope's Army of Virginia. At Antietam, where he was wounded in action, he commanded the I Corps of the Army of the Potomac. When he recovered, he was placed in command of Burnside's Central Grand Divisions at the Battle of Fredericksburg. During all this time, his ambition had driven him to seek to command the Army of the Potomac.

The Army of the Potomac learned Lincoln had replaced Burnside with Hooker on January 25, 1863.[5] The next day Hooker proclaimed in his General Orders Number 1 his confidence and readiness to fight the enemy: "In equipment, intelligence, and valor the enemy is our inferior; let us never hesitate to give him battle wherever we can find him." Hooker could not ignore the recent turmoil in the army's officer corps, however, and he knew that to achieve success he would "require the cheerful and zealous co-operation of every officer and soldier in this army."[6]

Also on January 26, Hooker met with Lincoln at the White House. It was at this meeting that most historians have concluded Lincoln handed Hooker his letter of appointment. The letter is often quoted because it reveals as much about Lincoln as it does about Lincoln's view of Hooker:

To Joseph Hooker
Major General Hooker: Executive Mansion,
General Washington, January 26, 1863

    I have placed you at the head of the Army of the Potomac. Of course I have done this upon what appear to me to be sufficient reasons. And yet I think it best for you to know that there are some things in regard to which, I am not quite satisfied with you. I believe you to be a brave and a skilful soldier, which, of course, I like. I also believe you do not mix politics with your profession, in which you are right. You have confidence in yourself, which is a valuable, if not an indispensable quality. You are ambitious, which, within reasonable bounds, does good rather than harm. But I think that during Gen. Burnside's command of the Army, you have taken counsel of your ambition, and thwarted him as much as you could, in which you did a great wrong to the country,

Seven—"And now, beware of rashness" 157

General Hooker (Library of Congress).

and to a most meritorious and honorable brother officer. I have heard, in such way as to believe it, of your recently saying that both the Army and the Government needed a Dictator. Of course it was not for this, but in spite of it, that I have given you the command. Only those generals who gain successes, can set up dictators. What I now ask of you is military success, and I will risk the dictatorship. The government will support you to the utmost of it's [sic] ability, which is neither more nor less than it has done and will do for all commanders. I much fear that the spirit which you have aided to infuse into the Army, of criticising their Commander, and withholding confidence from him, will now turn upon you. I shall assist you as far as I can, to put it down. Neither you, nor Napoleon, if he were alive again, could get any good out of an army, while such a spirit prevails in it.

And now, beware of rashness. Beware of rashness, but with energy, and sleepless vigilance, go forward, and give us victories.

Yours very truly A. LINCOLN[7]

We know little about what happened at the meeting or Hooker's response to the letter. But Hooker did reveal some of his own thoughts to Noah Brooks, a journalist and friend of the president, just before the Battle of Chancellorsville in late April 1863. Brooks was already aware of the contents of the letter but was happy for Hooker to read it to him. Hooker vehemently objected to Lincoln's view that he had "thwarted" Burnside. When Hooker resumed reading the letter, Brooks noticed that his tone had softened and he finished reading it almost with tears in his eyes. Hooker said, "That is just such a letter as a father might write to his son. It is a beautiful letter, and, although I think he was harder on me than I deserved, I will say that I love the man who wrote it." Hooker added, "After I have got to Richmond, I shall give that letter to you to have published."[8] Hooker thought the publication of the letter in newspapers would "be amusing." When this was told by Brooks to Lincoln, he said, with a sigh, "Poor Hooker! I am afraid he is incorrigible."[9]

Hooker did gain a major concession from Lincoln. Hooker would report directly to the president and not the General in chief, Halleck. This was, according to Hooker, the only request he made to the president. The reason for this unusual request was that, in Hooker's view, Halleck had been "identified with the army of the west and seemed to think there was no other army in the republic." Of more importance, Halleck had opposed Hooker as a possible replacement for McClellan and more recently Halleck had opposed his replacing Burnside.[10] Why Lincoln accepted the request is not clear, and he must have known he was disrupting the chain of command and undermining the position of general in chief.

Lincoln did not give any specific strategic or operational instruction to Hooker, but Halleck referred him to the general instructions regarding the army that had been sent to Burnside on January 7, 1863, and was still in effect. These instructions were operational and not strategic. Halleck had advised to "cross by the fords above Fredericksburg, then use your cavalry and light artillery upon his communications," and, of importance, "that our first object was not Richmond, but the defeat or scattering of Lee's army, which threatened Washington and the line of the Upper Potomac."[11]

One of the reasons Lincoln had removed Burnside concerned the low morale of the troops in the Army of the Potomac. Historians accept that Hooker took command of an army that was in a terrible condition. The defeat at Fredericksburg and the humiliating "Mud March" were the major factors that had affected morale but they were not the only reasons. The troops had not been paid and the camps were in an unhealthy condition. Hooker made an immediate impact. He ensured that the commissary and quartermaster services did their jobs. Paymasters got the troops' pay up to date. He removed corrupt supply officers, upgraded the troops' food by ensuring they received fresh vegetables and fruit and established clean hospitals. These measures cut the sick rate in half. He tightened discipline with measures such as a crackdown on alcohol distribution, but he also established a leave system for each company. He also raised morale through the creation of badges for each corps and division.[12] A significant indication of the improvement in morale was the return of thousands of absent troops who were encouraged by the improved conditions and Lincoln's March 10 promise of amnesty to deserters who returned by April 1, 1863.[13]

Hooker's reorganization of the army was equally impressive. On February 5, he abolished Burnside's grand divisions and replaced them with seven corps whose commanders reported directly to him. The structure was the First Corps, Major General John F. Reynolds; Second Corps, Major General D.N. Couch; Third Corps, Brigadier General D.E. Sickles; Fifth Corps, Major General George G. Meade; Sixth Corps, Major General John Sedgwick; Eleventh Corps, Major General Franz Sigel; and Twelfth Corps, Major General H.W. Slocum. He also concentrated most of the cavalry into a Cavalry Corps under the command of Brigadier General Stoneman, which provided a cavalry force large enough to threaten the flanks and rear of Lee's Confederate army.[14]

While Hooker had managed to raise the morale of the troops in his command, Lincoln needed victories to raise the morale of the Union's citizens. In the West, General Grant's attempts to turn Vicksburg and open the Mississippi had failed. Halleck reminded Grant of the following on March 20, 1863: "The eyes and hopes of the whole country are directed to your army. In my opinion, the opening of the Mississippi River will be to us of more advantage than the capture of forty Richmonds."[15] Grant's failure had been the catalyst for more rumors about his excessive drinking and calls for his sacking. On April 2 Halleck warned Grant of Lincoln's "impatience" with the Union effort to take Vicksburg. Stanton dispatched his special investigating agent, Charles A. Dana, to the West to evaluate Grant's performance. Dana soon began sending favorable reports to Stanton, which convinced Lincoln that his decision to continue to support Grant was correct. The president was soon justified. Grant abandoned the plan to operate against Vicksburg from the north for a line of operations from the south. His army moved down the west bank of the Mississippi and linked up with Admiral Porter's ships, which had run the Vicksburg batteries on the night of April 17. Grant was able to move two-thirds of his army to the east bank of the river forty miles south of Vicksburg on April 30.[16] Grant was now about to operate on the lines of communications of Vicksburg and by having his army "live off the land" he was able to increase its mobility and deny resources to the Confederate army and civilian population.

By early April Hooker had had almost two months to prepare his army for a movement in spring or summer 1863. The president decided to inspect the progress he had made with the army and to discuss Hooker's operational options in person. On April 5 Lincoln disembarked at Aquia Creek and boarded a train for Hooker's headquarters at Falmouth, about fifteen miles away. Lincoln was accompanied by Mrs. Lincoln and Tad, Noah Brooks, a Californian journalist, Dr. Henry from Washington Territory, Attorney General Edward Bates, Captain Crawford of Oregon and Mrs. Brookes of California.[17] On April 6, the party reviewed General Stoneman's ten thousand strong cavalry corps. On 8 and April 9, all the infantry were inspected. Lincoln was impressed by the spectacle and even more by the enthusiasm of the troops.[18] Lincoln must have felt some justification for his decision to appoint Hooker. The army of almost 170,000 troops was battle ready but Lincoln needed to know where and when it would fight.[19]

At some time during the visit Lincoln outlined what he believed should be the principles that underpinned Hooker's plans for the army. The basis of this discussion is probably outlined in *Memorandum on Joseph Hooker's Plan of Campaign Against Richmond*. Lincoln's advice was operational and tactical. While the president should have been directing the strategy of the war, Hooker was in an unusual position because the president was in effect his general in chief. First, Lincoln stressed that Hooker's objective was "the enemies' army in front of us, and is not with, or about, Richmond—at all, unless it be incidental to the main object." To Lincoln this was a sound strategy because it recognized that the destruction of Lee's army would have an immense psychological impact on the Confederacy and it fit the popular perception that wars were about battles and the destruction of enemy armies. This statement is also seized upon by those who see it as evidence of Lincoln's brilliance as a military commander because it was closer to Clausewitz than Jomini.[20] But it had already been demonstrated how hard it was to destroy a civil war army. But by making Lee's army the objective it confused this strategy with the more widely accepted "On to Richmond" strategy because one of the main purposes of Lee's army was to protect Richmond. If the Army of the Potomac were successful in defeating Lee in northern Virginia, then Lee would move towards Richmond because it was his base of supply. Lincoln believed the Army of the Potomac was in a stronger position than Lee's and should not be concerned by any attempt by the Confederates to raid towards Washington.

There could have been another reason why Lincoln advised Hooker to target Lee's army. Lincoln would have been aware that Hooker was a professional officer. Hooker belonged to the "supposed class" of officer he had suspected of not wanting to beat the enemy when they could. He would have remembered McClellan's lack of pursuit of Lee's army after Antietam and the revelation from Major John J. Key shortly after the battle that beating the enemy was not the game. Lincoln's advice was therefore a reminder to Hooker of his purpose: to fight and defeat Lee and if possible to pursue and destroy his army.

Finally, Lincoln advised against attacking Lee in his present position, but instead recommended that Hooker "should continually harass and menace him, so that he shall have no leisure, nor safety in sending away detachments. If he weakens himself, then pitch into him."[21] The political situation weighed on the president's mind. The shock of the unnecessary loss of life at Fredericksburg was such that probably another army could not be raised and therefore Hooker should be careful to avoid any great risk.[22] Lincoln had one further bit of tactical advice for Hooker and his second in command, General Darius Nash Couch, which reflected his concerns over McClellan's handling of the Battle of Antietam: "I want to impress upon you two gentlemen—in your next fight, put in all of your men."[23]

Hooker put his plans to Lincoln on April 11 and seemed to have taken Lincoln's advice. He intended to turn Lee's left because he reasoned this was the best way to inflict a heavy blow on the enemy. He also intended that such a movement could, if practicable, sever Lee's line of communication with Richmond. If Lee decided to fall back towards Richmond, Hooker envisioned that the Union cavalry could position themselves between Lee and Richmond so that Lee could be held up, thus allowing Hooker's infantry to attack the rear of the Confederate army. If Lee decided to move to Richmond by Culpeper and Gordonsville, Lee would be forced to operate on a longer line of operations and with his supplies cut. As a preliminary action, the Union cavalry would raid Lee's line of communications from Fredericksburg to Richmond. Union infantry near Fredericksburg would feint a crossing while the rest of the Union infantry moved around the Confederate left flank.[24] This was a bold plan because it meant dividing the Union army in the face of the enemy, but Hooker had twice the number of troops of General Lee's army.

The weather became so bad that it forced Hooker to postpone the movement. At 9:15 p.m. on April 14, Hooker was forced to advise Lincoln that, because of heavy rain, the Rappahannock had risen too high to allow Stoneman's cavalry to cross.[25] Lincoln was deeply concerned by Stoneman's lack of progress. He telegraphed Hooker one hour later. The rain and mud, he told Hooker, were to be expected, but Stoneman was not moving rapidly enough to make the movement successful. While Lincoln qualified his criticism by admitting he did not know that anything better could be done, he still greatly feared "it is another failure already." He instructed Hooker, "Write me often. I am very anxious."[26]

By April 16, the movement had been postponed and the whole of Stoneman's cavalry corps were back on the north bank of the Rappahannock.[27] On April 19, Lincoln, Halleck and Secretary of War Stanton paid a quick visit to Hooker at Aquia Creek. Stanton had been invited because he had a good relationship with Hooker. This was to balance the personal animosity that existed between Hooker and Halleck.[28] Hooker presented a new plan to crush Lee's army between two large Union infantry forces. The 11th, 12th and 5th corps were to cross the Rapidan River at Kelly's and United States' fords. This would turn Lee's position at Fredericksburg. Meanwhile, the 6th, 1st and 3rd corps would demonstrate an attack towards Fredericksburg to hold Lee's forces in position until Hooker's main force could fall on the rear of the Confederate army. The Union cavalry was expected to raid the Confederate line of communications.[29] Hooker would have his decisive battle, which would not only result in Lee's defeat but also the capture of Richmond.

On April 27, 1863, the Army of the Potomac initiated its turning movement without any delay or encountering any obstacles. Hooker confidently predicted, "My plans are perfect, and when I start to carry them out, may God have mercy on Bobby Lee; for I shall have none."[30] Most of the 70,000 Union troops allocated to the turning movement crossed the Rapidan and moved through the "Wilderness" towards a crossroads named Chancellorsville. By May 1 Hooker had this force deployed near Chancellorsville. He must have felt that he was close to success, because he had turned the Confederate position at Fredericksburg.[31] Showing signs of the arrogance Lincoln had warned him about, Hooker felt confident enough to inform his troops as follows: "It is with heartfelt satisfaction the commanding general announces to the army that the operations of the last three days have determined that our enemy must either ingloriously fly, or come out from behind his defenses and give us battle on our own ground, where certain destruction awaits him. The operations of the Fifth, Eleventh, and Twelfth Corps have been a succession of splendid achievements."[32]

Lee did not fall back towards the North Anna River, however, in the way Hooker had expected. Instead, on May 1 he moved the majority of his force from Fredericksburg to block the Army of the Potomac from advancing out of the Wilderness. Hooker decided to stand on the defensive and invite Lee to make costly frontal attacks. In a daring and brilliant move Lee turned Hooker's turning movement by sending General Thomas J. "Stonewall" Jackson around the exposed Union right flank held by the XI Corps. Jackson's Second Corps of 28,000 troops surprised the Union troops at 5:30 p.m. on

May 2 and drove them towards Chancellorsville. The Confederate success was costly, because Jackson was wounded by friendly fire and eventually died on May 10. Only darkness on May 2 stopped the complete collapse of the Union right. The next day General Stuart led Jackson's corps and captured Hazel Grove, a low hill. Confederate artillery could fire from Hazel Grove on Chancellorsville, where Hooker's headquarters was stationed. A shell struck the Chancellor house and wounded Hooker. Hooker was stunned and Major General Darius Couch directed a retreat to the United States Ford. Meanwhile, Union forces under General Sedgwick had managed to take Fredericksburg. Lee recognized the threat to his rear and attacked Sedgwick, forcing him to retire towards Bank's Ford on the Rappahannock. Around midnight on May 4, Hooker called a meeting of his corps commanders to discuss the tactical situation.

The tactical question Hooker put to his corps commanders was whether the army should retreat or fight. The five corps commanders voted three to two in favor of continuing the fight. General Reynolds was angry that Hooker had called the meeting when he intended to retreat anyhow. General Couch agreed, "It was evident from the first that the Gen. had determined to fall back across the river."[33] General Meade was surprised by Hooker's intention not to fight: "Who would have believed a few days ago that Hooker would withdraw his army, in opposition to the opinion of a majority of his corps commanders?" In a letter to his wife, Meade observed that Hooker had "disappointed all of his friends by failing to show his fighting qualities at the pinch."[34] Hooker ignored the advice and lost the respect of many of the army's senior commanders. On May 6 he had moved the whole army to the north bank of the Rappahannock.[35]

The Battle of Chancellorsville represented a major Confederate victory. The Army of the Potomac had lost 1,606 killed, 9,762 wounded and 5,919 missing, a total of 17,278 casualties from its force of 133,868. The Confederates, with an estimated strength of 60,000, had lost 1,665 killed, 9,081 wounded and 2,018 missing, a total of 12,764 casualties. The battle has been described as Lee's greatest victory, "a masterpiece of skill and audacity."[36] He had defeated a force twice as large as his own by dividing his force in the front of the enemy and thus ignoring one of the most fundamental of military principles. But in achieving this victory, the Confederates had lost a greater proportion of their army than had the Union.

The primary responsibility for the Union defeat was naturally directed at Hooker. Some have explained Hooker's failure as owing to his excessive drinking, while others have argued that his decision to abstain from alcohol was the problem.[37] Meade believed Hooker had learned that it is easy to "talk very big" when you are a subordinate and "quite a different thing, acting when you are responsible" for a large army.[38] A lot of attention has been given to the "loss of nerve" thesis to try to understand why Hooker lost the battle. Certainly, he lost the initiative to Lee when he delayed the movement of the Union right wing near Chancellorsville on May 1. Perhaps the account of his being stunned from an injury at his headquarters on May 2 is more to do with lessening the blows on Hooker than explaining the lack of leadership in the field that had already been evident. Proponents of the "loss of nerve" argument have placed much weight on Hooker's self-criticism: "For once I lost confidence in Hooker." This comment is often quoted from John Brigalow's *The Campaign of Chancellorsville*,[39] which was published in 1910 and is attributed to a conversation between General Doubleday and Hooker during the Gettysburg Campaign in July 1863. However, Stephen W. Sears has described this as a myth. Sears has discovered that Bigelow had quoted from a letter written in 1903 by an officer on General Doubleday's staff and there was also no evidence that Doubleday and Hooker actually met. Furthermore, Doubleday made no mention of the conversation in his history of the Chancellorsville battle published in 1882.[40]

Lincoln received the news that the Army of the Potomac had retreated to the north bank of the Rappahannock on May 6. The president was stunned. He took the dispatch into another room in the White House and handed it to Noah Brooks. Lincoln's face was "ashy gray in hue and his eyes streaming with tears." He exclaimed: "My God! My God! What will the country say?"[41] Within an hour, Lincoln and General in Chief Halleck were on their way from Washington to Aquia Creek and from there to Hooker's headquarters to learn the details of the defeat.

Hooker did not seem to share the president's gloomy view on the outcome of the battle. In his General Orders Number 49 Hooker congratulated the army on its achievements of the last seven days because it had "accomplished all that was expected." He explained away the retreat as the right of the army to "give or decline battle whenever its interest or honor may demand." He went on to describe the movement of the last week as an accomplishment that "may swell with pride the heart of every officer and soldier of this army. We have added new luster to its former renown" because we "have taken from the enemy 5,000 prisoners; captured and brought off seven pieces of artillery, fifteen colors; placed hors de combat 18,000 of his chosen troops; destroyed his depots filled with vast amounts of stores; deranged his communications; captured prisoners within the fortifications of his capital, and filled his country with fear and consternation."[42]

Hooker's publicly optimistic view of the outcome of the battle to his troops was not reflected in his meeting with Lincoln and Halleck on May 7. In private, Hooker blamed the defeat on cavalry commander General Stoneman and General Sedgwick, both of whom had failed to execute their orders.[43] Indeed, the Joint Committee on the Conduct of the War, which did not investigate Chancellorsville until February 25, 1864, supported Hooker's conclusions in its findings. The committee's findings, released in May 1865, seemed to be directed more at removing any notion that Hooker, who was looked upon favorably by many Radical Republicans, was responsible for the defeat of the army. The report listed four main causes for the defeat: the stampede of the 11th Corps on May 1, Hooker's injury, the failure of General Sedgwick to carry out his orders and the failure of the cavalry corps under General Stoneman.[44]

While he visited Hooker, Lincoln also talked to the corps commanders. He did not say much about the recent battle nor did he ask for the generals' opinions.[45] He did not blame anyone for the defeat but he thought the battle had been unfortunate. He also thought the result of the battle, both at home and overseas, "would be more serious and injurious than any previous act of the war."[46] Lincoln wanted this reversed. In a letter written in Washington, he reminded Hooker that the Battle of Chancellorsville had ended without the Union army's achieving its objective, contrary to what Hooker had announced to the troops. Lincoln wanted an early movement to take advantage of the disruption to the Confederate communications and to "supersede the bad moral effect of the recent one." He advised Hooker that if he had a plan he should put it into motion. If he did not, Lincoln asked that Hooker consult with him.[47] Hooker believed he had enough troops to effectively operate against Lee, even allowing for the losses incurred in the battle.[48] He did not think it was the best time to begin a new movement, but he had decided on a plan that would, this time, allow him to personally supervise the operations of all the corps.[49] This revealed Hooker's lack of faith in the abilities of his corps commanders and also, as T. Harry Williams has argued, his inability to command a large army because he could not picture in his mind the position of troops he could not see.[50]

However, Hooker's high assessment of his military abilities was now not shared by the Army of the Potomac's senior officers. Many senior officers would have agreed with Swinton's assessment that it was Hooker and not the Army of the Potomac that was defeated at Chancellorsville.[51] They blamed the defeat on Hooker and immediately canvassed the possibility that he could be removed. McClellan and, to a much lesser extent Burnside, could look to the support of loyal subordinates. Hooker could not and all the army's officers would have been aware of how his often public criticism of his predecessors had undermined their positions. Meade believed that once it became known the retreat could have been avoided Hooker would be held responsible. But Meade believed, unlike McClellan and Burnside, "Hooker has one great advantage over his predecessors in not having any intriguer among his subordinate generals, who are working like beavers to get him out and themselves in."[52] Meade's veiled criticism of Hooker was not entirely correct on the level of opposition to Hooker.

General Halleck had remained in the Army of the Potomac's headquarters after Lincoln's May 7 meeting with Hooker. Lincoln had instructed Halleck to remain in camp until he knew everything. Halleck had been ignored in the planning of the Chancellorsville campaign and he did not know that Hooker had crossed the Rappahannock to try to turn Lee until after an officer in Washington told him.[53] He had no problem in getting generals and staff officers to reveal their views about Hooker.[54] Halleck reported to Lincoln and Stanton that the defeat at Chancellorsville and the retreat were inexcusable and that Hooker could not be trusted to lead the army into another battle. Halleck also brought an interesting message from Hooker. Hooker wished to inform the president that he had never sought command and that he could resign it without embarrassment and would be happy to have command of his old division so as to remain in active service.[55] This was not the confident, ambitious general Lincoln had placed in command about three months earlier.

Senior commanders in the Army of the Potomac had begun to canvass a replacement for Hooker. This move was led by Generals Couch and Reynolds. General Meade was the focus of their attention as a possible replacement, and Meade was "gratified by the frequent expression of the opinion" that he should be placed in command. On May 10, Couch, Slocum and Sedgewick, all senior in rank to Meade, had informed him that they would be willing to serve under him. Even the press, which had so often supported Hooker, had begun to criticize him.[56]

The cabinet was also divided on its support for Hooker. Secretary of War Stanton wrote to all Union commanders and state governors that, while the "principal operation of General Hooker failed, there has been no serious disaster to the organization and efficiency of the army." Furthermore, Stoneman's cavalry operation had been a "brilliant success" and "the Army of the Potomac will speedily resume offensive operations."[57] Yet, Stanton still supported Halleck's recommendation from the May 7 meeting that Hooker could not be trusted to command the army in another battle.[58] Blair and Welles had also lost confidence in him.[59] Despite increasing doubts over Hooker's ability to command the army, Lincoln believed he should still give him one more chance.[60]

On May 13, 1863, Hooker was summoned to Washington to see the president. Lincoln had asked to see Hooker in response to Hooker's latest operational plan, which had been sent earlier that day: "I hope to be able to commence my movement to-morrow, but this must not be spoken of to anyone." Lincoln telegrammed, "Please come and see me this evening."[61] Hooker made no record of the meeting that evening, but Lincoln's letter to him the next day provides some insight. Regarding Hooker's planned movement, Lincoln recommended caution. As usual, Lincoln did not order Hooker not to move but wrote that he would "not complain if you do no more for a time than to keep the enemy at bay." However, if Hooker believed he could renew the attack successfully, Lincoln would not "restrain" him. The reason Lincoln advised caution was not that he had doubts about Hooker's plan but that he had become aware of "some painful intimations that some of your corps and division commanders are not giving you your entire confidence." What is interesting is that Lincoln asked Hooker to "ascertain the real facts beyond all possibility of doubt" before he began a major movement.[62]

Hooker immediately asked Lincoln for the names of the disaffected generals. Lincoln declined to name them but did reveal the sources of his information: Governor Curtin of Pennsylvania and another man, Barclay, from Philadelphia. Both had recently visited the army's camp. Hooker told the president that he was not aware of any corps or division commanders not supporting him and rather than wrongfully accuse any of his generals he asked that they be allowed to meet with the president so that he could learn their views. Hooker never learned the result of any of these interviews but he did learn that most of the corps commanders did visit Washington.[63]

Major General Darius Couch was the senior corps commander at the Battle of Chancellorsville and was Hooker's second in command. He had visited Lincoln on May 22 and was scathing in his criticism of Hooker. Couch told Lincoln at the meeting that Hooker was incompetent and proposed that Meade would make a good choice to replace him.[64] Furthermore, he confirmed what Lincoln already knew, that there was "great dissatisfaction among the higher officers at the management at Chancellorsville."[65] General Sumner had "an absolute want of confidence in Hooker." Most of the corps commanders in the Army of the Potomac were either against Hooker's retaining command or had a lack of confidence in his ability. Reynolds and Slocum opposed Hooker. Hooker had been directing the blame for the defeat at Chancellorsville towards Sedgwick, Howard and Stoneman, so there is no reason to believe that they would have supported him. Even Lincoln had shown a lack of confidence in Hooker's tactical ability when he had speculated that if the shot that had stunned Hooker at Chancellorsville had instead killed him, then perhaps the Union would have been successful.[66]

While Hooker had told the president he did not suspect any of his generals of a lack of support, he was aware that Curtin and Barclay were the source of the president's intelligence and that these two had visited his headquarters a few days before and spoken to Generals Meade and Stoneman.[67] He suspected that one or both could be disloyal. The next day, Hooker visited General Meade and told him Governor Curtin had been telling people that he, Hooker, had lost the confidence of the army and, in particular, of Meade and Reynolds. Meade told Hooker that he disagreed only with his decision to withdraw the army on the night of May 4. Hooker was not convinced. He accused Meade and Reynolds of having been in favor of withdrawing across the river but that they were now denying it. Meade responded by sending letters to those present in the council of war on the night of May 4 to corroborate his position.[68] Reynolds replied that Meade, like himself, had been in favor of an advance.[69] Meade would have been happy with the support from Reynolds but it added to the rift between the corps commanders and Hooker.

Every senior commander in the Army of the Potomac now knew of the level of distrust and animosity that had developed between Hooker and Meade. On May 25, General Gibbon had observed, "Gen. Hooker is seeking someone upon whose shoulders to place the responsibility of his defeat and to the astonishment of everyone has selected Gens. Meade and Reynolds, more especially the former. This has made an open issue between himself and Gen. Meade, who is known to have urged in the strongest terms an advance. His severest criticism was that, "No one whose opinion is worth anything now has any confidence in Gen. Hooker and the President has been told so...."[70] Meade believed Hooker's antagonism towards him was an effort to remove what Hooker perceived as an attempt to have himself replaced by Meade: "I suppose he has heard some of the stories flying around camp in regard to my having command, and these ... have induced him to believe that I am maneuvering to get him relieved, that I may step in his shoes."[71] This could also explain Hooker's antagonism towards Reynolds. Reynolds outranked Meade, and Hooker would have known this. No change to the command of the Army of the Potomac could occur without Reynolds also being considered.[72]

General Robert E. Lee's raid into Maryland and Pennsylvania in June and early July 1863 led to a change in the structure of the Union high command that revealed Lincoln's increasing lack of confidence in Hooker. Lee's objectives were operational and strategic. He did not want to stay in his present position because it invited Hooker to try to turn his position again. Also, by staying in Virginia the Confederates did not gain any advantage and Lee did not want to face the Army of the Potomac in set-piece battle such as had occurred in the Peninsula Campaign. Instead, he wanted to turn Hooker from the Rappahannock and move into Pennsylvania. The Union would be forced to attack in order to drive him back, which would give Lee the opportunity of fighting on the tactical defensive. The supply problem was foremost in Lee's mind. A raid north would mean his army could forage off the land and not consume resources from the south. As for strategy, he hoped the raid would weaken the resolve of the Northern public to continue to fight. On June 3 Lee's Army of Northern Virginia began to move along the south bank of the Rappahannock towards the Shenandoah Valley. By June 5, Hooker was aware that Lee was moving and interpreted it as either an attempt to cross the Upper Potomac or to move his army between the Army of the Potomac and Washington. He advised the president that he intended to attack the rear of Lee's strung-out army at Fredericksburg and sensibly asked that all Union forces that were in a position to take part in operations against the Confederates should be placed under one command.[73] A cavalry battle near Brandy Station on June 9 convinced Hooker that Lee would be forced to abandon his raid into Maryland and would have to reinforce this position with infantry. This would weaken the Confederate position opposite Hooker. Hooker hoped to then push his forces towards Richmond.[74] He was still working under the dictum that places and not the enemy's army was his objective.

Lincoln disagreed with Hooker's proposed operational plan. He advised Hooker not to move south towards Richmond while Lee's army moved north. If Richmond could be placed under siege it would take too much time, which Lee could use to interfere with Hooker's communications and eventually defeat the Union army. Lincoln reminded Hooker, "Lee's army, and not Richmond, is your sure objective point. If he comes toward the Upper Potomac, follow on his flank and on his inside track, shortening your lines while he lengthens his. Fight him, too, when opportunity offers. If he stays where he is, fret him and fret and fret him."[75] Hooker had misread the reports of the Confederate movements. By June 13 it was clear that Lee was in the Shenandoah Valley and heading north.

Also of concern to Hooker was that it appeared he was now being directed by General in Chief Halleck. On June 13 Halleck ordered the Army of the Potomac from the line of Aquia Creek to the Orange and Alexander Railroad.[76] Lincoln again interfered in operational matters by asking Hooker on June 14, "[If] the head of Lee's army is at Martinsburg and the tail of it on the Plank road between Fredericksburg and Chancellorsville, the animal must be very slim somewhere. Could you not break him?"[77] But Hooker was more interested in the situation at Harpers Ferry than in trying to cut Lee's column.

He wanted to know who was in command at Harpers Ferry and suggested to the president that a considerable Union force should be deployed there.[78]

The disruption in the Union high command was threatening to impede the Union response to Lee's movement north. Hooker had moved his headquarters to Fairfax Station, just outside Washington, by June 16. Here he was visited by General Herman Haupt, who was chief of a bureau responsible for military railroads. Haupt wanted to know Hooker's plans so that he could prepare for them. He found Hooker in "bad humour." At 11:00 a.m. that day, Hooker had written to Lincoln and reminded him, "I have not enjoyed the confidence of the major-general commanding the army, and I can assure you so long as this continues we may look in vain for success, especially as future operations will require our relations to be more dependent upon each other than heretofore." Hooker proposed to prevent a junction of A.P. Hill's corps with those of Ewell and Longstreet. Hooker asked for orders: "If so, please let instructions to that effect be given me."[79] Hooker told Haupt he did not plan to move until he got orders and then "he would obey them literally and let responsibility rest where it belonged." Hooker complained that he had made "various suggestions which had not been approved by the powers that be in Washington, and if he could not carry out his own plans, others must give orders, and if disaster ensued his skirts would be clear." Haupt was sympathetic to Hooker: "If the powers in Washington would not permit him to carry out his own plans, they must give him orders."[80]

Concerned by what he had heard, Haupt quickly returned to Washington and called on Halleck. He told Halleck that Hooker would not move until he got orders and that immediate action should be taken to get the Army of the Potomac moving to respond to Lee. Halleck replied that some of Hooker's statements were not correct and he drew a bundle of correspondence between Hooker and the president from his desk and read them. After reading the letters Halleck left his office. About half an hour later, he returned, threw his cap on the table and said, "Hooker will get his orders."[81] Haupt's account seems to suggest that his intervention helped to force the Union high command to act with some degree of unity, but this was not the case.

The disagreement between Hooker and Halleck over the importance of Harpers Ferry in the current campaign finally forced the president's hand to clarify the command structure in the East. On June 13 Hooker was interested in the situation at Harpers Ferry and wanted to know the Union strength there and who was in command. On June 16 Halleck advised him that to "follow the enemy's advance, by moving a considerable force first to Leesburg, and thence as circumstances may require, is the best one I can make. Unless your army is kept near enough to the enemy to ascertain his movements."[82] Later that day Halleck wrote Hooker that Confederates were surrounding Harpers Ferry. Halleck expected that the Union forces could not hold out very long and also that no relief was expected "excepting from your army."[83] Hooker may have jumped at this as an invitation to finally march on Harpers Ferry. He reported to Halleck at 4:00 p.m. that he intended to take "a couple of long marches from here" to reach Harpers Ferry and asked about the disposition of Union forces there.[84] At 7:30 p.m. Hooker was able to report to Halleck: "In compliance with your directions, I shall march to the relief of Harper's Ferry. I put my column again in motion at 3 a.m. tomorrow. I expect to reach there in two days, and, if possible, earlier."[85] Halleck responded about an hour later, informing Hooker that his questions about the Union troop positions at Harpers Ferry had been sent to the Union commander, Tyler, and that any troops he had sent to his relief should be in motion.

Yet, Hooker must have felt uncertainty about his movement to Harpers Ferry was the appropriate response to the current operational situation. He did not have enough information about Lee's movements. In a veiled criticism of Halleck, Hooker advised the president that "of information to the north of the Potomac I really have nothing. I wish that it might be made the duty of some person in the telegraph office in Washington to keep me informed of the enemy's movements in Maryland."[86] The president had been losing confidence in Hooker but this request must have made the president realize that the defeat of Lee was being hampered by the disjointed command structure. Previously, at 11:00 a.m. Lincoln had read a telegram from Hooker that concerned his relationship with Halleck: "I have not enjoyed the confidence of the major-general commanding the army, and I can assure you so long as this continues we may look in vain for success."[87]

Hooker might have been looking for Lincoln to remove any interference from Halleck over his command. But Hooker had misread the situation. If Lincoln could not get Hooker and Halleck to cooperate then he needed one commander to direct the operations of Union forces in and around Maryland and Pennsylvania. Ten minutes after receiving Hooker's request for more information, Lincoln ordered him to take orders directly from Halleck: "To remove all misunderstanding, I now place you in the strict military relation to General Halleck of a commander of one of the armies to the general in chief of all the armies. I have not intended differently, but as it seems to be differently understood, I shall direct him to give your orders and you to obey them."

Fifteen minutes later, Halleck used his new authority over Hooker to stop the general movement of the Army of the Potomac towards Harpers Ferry. He wrote Hooker that he was "given no directions for your army to move to Harper's Ferry." What Halleck wanted to discover was where Lee's army was and where it was heading. He advised Hooker to "push out your cavalry, to ascertain something definite about the enemy. You are in command of the Army of the Potomac, and will make the particular dispositions as you deem proper. I shall only indicate the objects to be aimed at."[88] But the conflict between the two Union commanders continued.

Lincoln felt compelled to write to Hooker about his reasons for taking the decision to place him under Halleck. The letter was hand delivered by special courier. Lincoln tried to reason Hooker out of his distrust of Halleck. Lincoln believed that Hooker had become too emotional—"you state the case much too strongly"—and that Halleck's lack of confidence in him was too small "to do you any harm." The basis of Halleck's lack of confidence was that Hooker reported directly to the president, "but I do not think he withholds any support from you on account of it." Lincoln then directed Hooker's attention to Lee's army. Lincoln believed an opportunity existed now similar to the one McClellan had "lost" in the Antietam campaign. Lincoln needed Hooker to attack while Lee was north of the Potomac. Lincoln added the following: "Quite possibly I was wrong both then and now; but, in the great responsibility resting upon me, I cannot be entirely silent. Now, all I ask is that you will be in such mood that we can get into our action the best cordial judgment of yourself and General Halleck, with my poor mite added, if indeed he and you shall think it entitled to any consideration at all."[89]

While the president had tried to reassure Hooker about his relationship with Halleck, Hooker also had concerns about the size of his command. He still believed that his command was smaller than Lee's. He complained to Halleck on June 26: "It must be borne in mind that I am here with a force inferior in numbers to that of the enemy, and must have every available man to use on the field." He also asked Halleck if Maryland Heights should be abandoned and by implication the troops there added to Hooker's command. Halleck denied this request. The next day Hooker petulantly wrote to Halleck: "That there may be no misunderstanding as to my force, I would respectfully state that, including the portions of General Heintzelman's command, and General Schenck's, now with me, my whole force of enlisted men for duty will not exceed 105,000." On June 27 Hooker tried to force Halleck to add the 10,000 Union troops at Harpers Ferry to his command because there were no strategic or tactical reasons for them to remain. What would have concerned Halleck was Hooker's implied lack of confidence in him. Hooker wanted to ignore Halleck because he wanted Halleck to present this request "to the Secretary of War and His Excellency the President." Hooker's plan was good because he wanted to use the troops from Harpers Ferry to operate on Lee's lines of communication. But the plan was also politically sensitive because he could be seen to be exposing Washington.[90]

Perhaps too hastily, Hooker sent another telegram five minutes later offering his resignation: "My original instructions require me to cover Harper's Ferry and Washington. I have now imposed upon me, in addition, an enemy in my front of more than my number. I beg to be understood, respectfully, but firmly, that I am unable to comply with this condition with the means at my disposal, and earnestly request that I may at once be relieved from the position I occupy."[91] Hooker might have tried to call Halleck's bluff with the intention also of giving himself greater autonomy over the operations of the army. It could also have been, as Stephen E. Ambrose has concluded, that Hooker did not want to fight Lee again and was looking for a way to escape from commanding the army.[92]

The next day, June 28, Lincoln's 10:00 a.m. cabinet meeting was dominated by the new crisis in the command of the Army of the Potomac. Lincoln took from his pocket Hooker's telegram asking to be relieved of command. He had observed in Hooker the same failings that he had observed in McClellan after the Battle of Antietam, a lack of eagerness to obey and a greedy call for more troops. Lincoln believed that Hooker wanted to strip Washington bare of troops and the garrison at Harpers Ferry added to his command. Hooker had been angered by the refusal and had tendered his resignation.[93] Lincoln's comparison of Hooker to McClellan would have concerned the cabinet members. This was also linked to the sensitive political issue of the defense of Washington. Cabinet members would have been alarmed by the idea of leaving Washington exposed in the current military crisis, but it would also have brought to mind McClellan's determination to leave Washington with a small garrison while he moved the army to the Peninsula in 1862. In their minds Hooker may have been, in the end, too much like McClellan. There was no discussion about whether Hooker should be retained or not. Instead, the cabinet discussed who should replace him.[94]

The cabinet discussion about a replacement for Hooker was purely academic. While the names of Sedgwick, Meade and Couch were raised, it soon became apparent to Secretary of the Navy Gideon Welles that the discussion was merely to make it appear that the cabinet had been consulted and that, in fact, Meade had already been appointed.[95] Welles was correct. Meade had received his order appointing him as commander of the Army of the Potomac on June 27, the day before the cabinet meeting.[96]

General Reynolds was not mentioned as a candidate for the command of the Army of the Potomac in Welles' recollections, but there has always been speculation on the question of whether Reynolds was actually offered command. Reynolds did outrank Meade and it would seem reasonable that he would have been considered by Lincoln. But Reynolds made no mention of it. Edward J. Nichols has made a careful analysis of the issue. There are only two letters, one by Meade and the second by Eleanor Reynolds, and much opinion.[97] Meade had written in his diary on June 13 that Reynolds had stopped to see him that day. Reynolds told Meade that a friend in Washington had informed him he was talked about as a replacement for Hooker. Reynolds had then immediately gone to see the president and told him he "did not want the command and would not take it."[98] The evidence provided by Eleanor Reynolds, the sister of General Reynolds, is far less reliable. In a piece written on August 20, 1913, at the behest of her nephew, Eleanor recalled how on the evening of June 2, 1863, her brother had told her of his meeting with the president that day. According to her story, the president had offered him command of the Army of the Potomac, which he told the president he would accept if he was not interfered with from Washington. The president would not promise this, so Reynolds declined the offer.[99]

An important factor that influenced Lincoln's decision to appoint Meade to command the Army of the Potomac was the support Meade had from the subordinate commanders. This was the decisive factor behind the decision to remove Burnside and now Hooker. Meade did have the support of the majority of the corps commanders since the Battle of Chancellorsville. Lincoln would have been aware that changing the commander of an army during the course of a major operation could be risky and this was acknowledged in the June 27 appointment order: "Considering the circumstances, no one ever received a more important command; and I cannot doubt that you will fully justify the confidence which the Government has reposed in you." Regarding the current operation of the army Halleck advised Meade, "Your army is free to act as you may deem proper under the circumstances as they arise." Halleck did instruct Meade of "the important fact that the Army of the Potomac is the covering army of Washington as well as the army of operation against the invading forces of the rebels. You will, therefore, maneuver and fight in such a manner as to cover the capital and also Baltimore, as far as circumstances will admit." Interestingly, Halleck had changed his position in relation to Harpers Ferry. Several hours before, he had written Hooker that the 10,000-man garrison could not leave the town and be added to Hooker's command. However, Meade was told, "All forces within the sphere of your operations will be held subject to your orders. Harper's Ferry and its garrison are under your direct orders." In a move designed to ensure that Meade had the support of his subordinate officers he was "authorized to remove from command, and to send from your army, any officer or other person you may deem proper, and to appoint to command as you may deem expedient."[100]

Probably no other general in the Civil War had been given a mightier task than General Meade. His June 29 operational plan was designed to cover both Washington and Baltimore and, if the opportunity arose, to fight a battle on the tactical defensive. Meade had known that Lee's army was spread over a wide area in southern Pennsylvania. He also recognized there could be the chance of attacking part of it while it was on the march. Meade brought his corps closer together so that he could concentrate quickly: "My endeavor will be in my movements to hold my force well together, with the hope of falling upon some portion of Lee's army in detail."[101] As early as June 30, 1863, Meade could feel that his dispositions were correct. Lee was falling back towards Harrisburg and appeared to be concentrating his forces near Chambersburg.[102] Meade had selected a defensive line at Pipe Creek in Maryland just near the border with Pennsylvania. This line extended from Manchester, through Winchester and to Frederick. The line covered Washington and Baltimore but also placed the Union army in a position to attack if the opportunity arose.[103] In response to Lee's concentration, Meade's dispositions at 7:00 a.m. on July 1 were one corps at Emmitsburg, two at Gettysburg, one at Taneytown, one at Two Taverns, one at Manchester, and one at Hanover.[104] By 1:00 p.m. on July 1 it was clear to Meade "Lee [was] advancing in force on Gettysburg, and I expect the battle will begin to-day."[105]

This was exactly what Lincoln wanted as well. He revealed his thoughts in a response to Governor Parker of New Jersey's June 29 appeal for General McClellan to be reappointed to command the Army of the Potomac. Parker argued that McClellan would be the best commander to drive the enemy if he could be driven out of Pennsylvania.[106] Lincoln reminded Governor Parker that no one knew more about "the difficulties and involvements of replacing Gen. McClellan in command" than the president himself. What was more important, Lincoln viewed Lee's movement into Pennsylvania as "the best opportunity we have had since the war began."[107] Lincoln was encouraged by the opportunity of fighting a decisive battle north of the Potomac. In this area Lee would have long lines of communications and would be far from his safe defensive lines behind the Rapidan and the Rappahannock. Lincoln reasoned that if Lee's army could be defeated and trapped north of the Potomac then the Confederacy would be defeated.

On July 1 the Union and Confederate armies accidently fell upon each other at the crossroads town of Gettysburg in Pennsylvania. The Army of the Potomac (93,500 troops) and the Army of Northern Virginia (75,000 troops) fought the Battle of Gettysburg from July 1 to July 3 on a battlefield that has been commonly described as a fish-hook shape. Lee was able to concentrate his forces more quickly and on July 1 was thus able to drive Union forces out of Gettysburg and onto Cemetery Hill. This was the type of encounter battle Lee had sought, where he could maneuver; as a result, he had the advantage on the first day. One of the Union fatalities on the first day of the battle was Major General John F. Reynolds. Reinforcements arrived for each side during the night. On July 2 Lee attacked the Union left at the Peach Orchard, the Devil's Den and the Round Tops. Then Ewell's divisions attacked the Union right at Culp's and East Cemetery Hills. Lee could still maneuver but all Confederate attacks failed and the day ended in a stalemate. On July 3, Lee attacked the Union center on Cemetery Ridge. The plan was to break the Union army into two parts. General Longstreet disagreed with the plan but Lee ordered the attack despite the objections. Lee committed 15,000 troops to the infantry assault comprising six brigades from A.P. Hill's Third Corps, General Pickett's three brigades and General Anderson's two brigades. The failure of this Confederate attack convinced Lee that he had lost the battle. The outcome was predictable. The Army of the Potomac was concentrated and at full strength so that it could fight a set-piece battle, on the tactical defensive, to its advantage. After three days of fighting the casualties were enormous. The Union sustained 23,049 casualties and the Confederates sustained 28,063.[108]

The Battle of Gettysburg is widely regarded as a turning point in the Civil War, but historians are divided over the military importance of the battle. McPherson has argued that Lee and his army "never again possessed the power and the reputation they carried into Pennsylvania those balmy midsummer days of 1863" and this is why "Gettysburg and Vicksburg proved to have been its crucial turning point."[109] Wert also views Gettysburg as significant, because from that point onwards the Union was in a position to win the war: "On the roads that led away from Gettysburg, the Army of the Potomac followed a different fork."[110] Stoker holds a similar view: "The Gettysburg Campaign was a disaster for the Confederacy and gained them nothing, and Lee admitted that he returned to the South far sooner than he had anticipated."[111] On the other hand, Hattaway and Jones concluded that the "strategic impact of the Battle of Gettysburg was, therefore, fairly limited."[112] Swinton agreed that the battle was not strategically decisive, but it did give the Union an important victory for the Army of the Potomac: "For once, that sorely tried, long-suffering army had the freely-given boon of a nation's gratitude."[113]

At the time, most of the people in the North would have agreed with the headline in the *Philadelphia Inquirer*, which proclaimed "Victory! Waterloo Eclipsed!"[114] This represented the commonly accepted belief that wars were about winning big, decisive battles and that as a result of winning these battles the war could also be won. Lincoln believed that as a result of the victories at Gettysburg and Vicksburg the Confederacy was on the eve of collapse.[115] But his own experience of costly defeats at Fredericksburg and Chancellorsville should have informed him how hard it is to achieve a victory decisive enough to win the war. It was common for Civil War armies to disengage from battle and recover. Meade had forced Lee to end his raid in Maryland and Pennsylvania but Lee's army was still a formidable fighting force.

Meade had won the battle but the campaign was not over. Lee was still on Northern soil. Meade, in his General Orders, Number 68 on July 4, 1863, praised the army for their "glorious result" against an "enemy, superior in numbers." He reminded his troops that the "task is not yet accomplished, and the commanding general looks to the army for greater efforts to drive from our soil every vestige of the presence of the invader."[116] The fact that Meade did not immediately begin a pursuit of Lee's army has been a source of criticism. It began to rain heavily on the night of July 4. That night Meade met with his corps commanders, who decided to move cautiously. There was no support for an attack on Lee's retreating army.[117]

Lincoln urged action. Halleck reminded Meade, on July 7, "You have given the enemy a stunning blow at Gettysburg. Follow it up, and give him another before he can reach the Potomac."[118] On the same day, Lincoln, buoyed by the news of the surrender of Vicksburg to General Grant's Union army, urged Halleck to get Meade moving: "Now, if General Meade can complete his work, so gloriously prosecuted thus far, by the literal or substantial destruction of Lee's army, the rebellion will be over."[119] The excitement of the two Union victories certainly fueled Lincoln's optimism. He was seeking the decisive battle that would win the war by destroying Lee's weakened army and hoped that this battle would be fought north of the Potomac River. Meade responded to Halleck's request for him to strike at Lee by informing Halleck that the weather had slowed his movement by making the roads "almost impassable" and that a "large portion of the men [were] barefooted." Furthermore he reminded Halleck of the reality of the operational situation: "I do not desire to imitate his example at Gettysburg, and assault a position where the chances were so greatly against success. I wish in advance to moderate the expectations of those who, in ignorance of the difficulties to be encountered, may expect too much. All that I can do under the circumstances I pledge this army to do."[120] What Meade was trying to avoid was an encounter battle, such as on the first day at Gettysburg, where Lee could maneuver. But the slowness of the pursuit must have reminded Lincoln of McClellan's actions after the Battle of Antietam. On July 13 Lincoln worried, "Nothing can save them, if Meade does his duty. I doubt him. He is an engineer."[121]

Meade was cautious. He intended to attack on July 13, 1863, but in a meeting to discuss the attack five out of six of his corps commanders were totally opposed to it. Considering the lack of support of his corps commanders and fearing the consequences of failure, Meade did not feel "authorized to attack" until he had made a more careful study of Lee's dispositions. His intelligence so far showed Lee was strongly entrenched.[122] Halleck urged an attack but without actually ordering Meade to do it: "You are strong enough to attack and defeat the enemy before he can effect a crossing. Act upon your own judgment and make your generals execute your orders. Call no council of war. It is proverbial that councils of war never fight. Re-enforcements are pushed on as rapidly as possible. Do not let the enemy escape."[123] The next day Meade's troops probed forward but found that Lee had withdrawn across the Potomac on the night of July 13.[124]

Lincoln was bitter and melancholy. On July 14 he told Welles that he blamed Meade and his corps commanders for the lack of decisive action and suspected that, like McClellan, Meade did not want to destroy Lee's army: "There is bad faith somewhere. Meade has been pressed and urged, but only one of his generals was for an immediate attack, was ready to pounce on Lee; the rest held back. What does it mean, Mr. Welles? Great God! what does it mean?" Welles recalled that he had on "only one or two occasions … ever seen the President so troubled, so dejected and discouraged." Lincoln was also concerned by Halleck's lack of leadership. Lincoln could not understand why Halleck had not visited Meade's headquarters to "advise and encourage him." Welles had also noted the "inertness, if not incapacity, of the General-in-Chief" in the current situation.[125] Halleck conveyed the president's displeasure to Meade the same day: "I need hardly say to you that the escape of Lee's army without another battle has created great dissatisfaction in the mind of the President, and it will require an active and energetic pursuit on your part to remove the impression that is has not been sufficiently active heretofore."[126] Meade felt that, "Having performed my duty conscientiously and to the best of my ability, the censure of the President conveyed in your dispatch of 1 p.m. this day, is, in my judgment, so undeserved that I feel compelled most respectfully to ask to be immediately relieved from the command of this army."[127] But Lincoln could not afford to accept the resignation of a general who had just won the largest battle of the war. Even the radical Republican members of the Joint Committee on the Conduct of the War, who would have preferred Meade sacked and Hooker reinstated, were powerless to act because of Meade's victory.[128] Halleck wrote Meade that he could not accept his resignation: "My telegram, stating the disappointment of the president at the escape of Lee's army, was not intended as a censure, but as a stimulus to an active pursuit. It is not deemed a sufficient cause for your application to be relieved."[129]

In the midst of this criticism Meade did receive support from an unexpected source, George B. McClellan:

> New York, July 11, 1863
> My dear General:
> I have abstained from writing to you simply because I hear that you have no time to read letters—but I will say a word now, anyhow.
> I wish to offer you my sincere and heartfelt congratulations upon the glorious victory you have achieved, and the splendid way in which you assumed control of our noble old army under such trying circumstances.
> You have done all that could be done and the Army of the Potomac has supported you nobly. I don't know that, situated as I am, my opinion is worth much to any of you—but I can trust saying that I feel very proud of you and my old Army. I don't flatter myself that your work is over—I believe that you have another severe battle to fight, but I am confident that you will win.
> That God may bless you and your army in its future conflicts is the prayer of
> Your sincere friend
> Geo. B. McCLELLAN.[130]

From the end of July to December 1863, both Meade and Lee looked to use maneuver to find a tactical advantage. Both of them had lost troops to aid their forces at Chattanooga in Tennessee. Lee moved north on October 9, 1863, and Meade fell back to the Rapidan and Rappahannock rivers and finally to an entrenched position along the Centreville-Chantilly ridge. With the approach of winter and his poor supply situation Lee withdrew on October 17. Meade followed him and by the end of October he was back on the Rappahannock. Lee was in a strong, entrenched position, but Meade planned to attack if he could find a weak point in the Confederate line. When he could not find a weak point in Lee's line, Meade fell back towards the Rapidan on December 1, 1863. Both sides saw no operational advantage so they went into their winter camps.[131]

The stalemate in the east contrasted to some dramatic operations in the West. After driving Branxton Bragg's Confederate army from Tullahoma in Tennessee, during June 1863, General Rosecrans' Army of the Cumberland finally began to move towards its main objective, Chattanooga on the Tennessee River, on August 16. Rosecrans' turning movement forced Bragg to withdraw from Chattanooga to protect his line of supplies and on September 9 Rosecrans could announce that he held the city. But Bragg was reinforced and concentrated his forces and in the ensuring Battle of Chickamauga on September 19 and 20, he drove the Union army back to Chattanooga. The Union army was besieged and began to run low on supplies. On October 16, the Union achieved unity of command in the West. The new Military Division of the Mississippi, combining the departments of the Ohio, the Cumberland and the Tennessee, was formed under Major General Ulysses S. Grant. The new command structure produced an immediate result. On November 23, 1863, the three-day Battle of Chattanooga began. Bragg was convincingly defeated and Union armies could now threaten Atlanta, Georgia. Grant's victory placed him as the predominant Union field commander. On March 9, 1864, Lincoln appointed Grant to the rank of lieutenant general.[132] The next day, Halleck, at his own request, was relieved from duty as general in chief and replaced by Grant.[133]

The instability within the officer corps of the Army of the Potomac continued with Hooker's tenure as its commander. Lincoln was right when he advised Hooker that the culture of criticism of the commander and the withholding of confidence could turn on him. As with Burnside, Hooker's failure on the battlefield brought these tensions to the surface. Lincoln believed that although he had a "fighting" General Hooker who would achieve much needed success in the East, the problems in the Union high command did not help the Union's military operations there. Hooker reported directly to the president, which meant that the general in chief could not operate effectively by being able to coordinate all Union armies in the East. Eventually the personal animosity between Hooker and Halleck and the concerted effort of many senior officers in the Army of the Potomac resulted in Hooker's resignation. The appointment of Meade ended the unrest in the officers' corps because Meade was the general they believed was best suited to lead them. His leadership was tested and questioned, but not because of a determined campaign from within the senior officers in the army to remove him. The supporters of General McClellan had either been removed from the army or those who remained believed Meade was a legitimate and able replacement for McClellan.

Conclusion

This book has studied the events that surrounded General George B. McClellan's tenure as commander of the Army of the Potomac and general in chief. Through the lens of McClellan it has examined the tensions within the Union's high command as it struggled to achieve a working unit to design and implement the Union's war aims and strategies to win the Civil War and the successful operations to put these strategies into action. The examination of the Union's high command through McClellan and not Lincoln provides new insights into the workings of the high command by offering some fresh understanding about this often overlooked subject. The Union did not have the high command necessary to achieve victory in the first two years of the war. The development of Union war aims and strategy in those two years was a complicated, disjointed and disrupted affair that was frustrated by a lack of cohesion and cooperation among the members of the Union high command. This helped the Confederates achieve a string of notable military victories during that time and it hindered the Union's efforts to achieve an early victory.

The Union's high command lacked cohesion and purpose because the chain of command was regularly ignored. McClellan's role as commander of the Army of the Potomac and his sacking increased the existing problems within the high command. The tensions about the Union's war aims, strategy and the nature of the war were accentuated by the lack of confidence between senior officers in the Army of the Potomac and the civilian administration and by the many times military protocol was ignored. In 1861 McClellan deliberately undermined his superior officer, General Winfield Scott, by reporting directly to President Lincoln. The president invited McClellan to provide advice on war aims and strategy, without General Scott's knowledge. Having set the scene early in the war Lincoln ignored the chain of command in many of his dealings with McClellan and other senior military officers, which destabilized the Union high command. The campaign by a group of pro-McClellan senior officers in the Army of the Potomac to replace two commanders with McClellan and to influence a major campaign was possible only because they had access to the president. It was extraordinary that Generals Franklin and Smith could contact the president with an alternate plan of operation for the army without the knowledge of their commanding officer, General Burnside. This activity continued when Generals Newton and Cochrane visited the White House to petition the president to stop the current movement by the Army of the Potomac. Hooker replaced Burnside, but after another Union defeat Generals Slocum and Couch and other senior officers worked to have Hooker replaced. Most corps commanders at some time accepted an invitation from the president to visit him and discuss Hooker's position as the Army of the Potomac's commander. This disruption to the army's chain of command encouraged intrigue among the Army of the Potomac's senior officers and a lack of cohesion in the Union's high command. This impacted negatively on the Army of the Potomac's operations.

For the first two years of the war the Union failed to plan and implement a strategy to achieve its war aims. The Union's principal war aim during this time was the restoration of the Union. General Winfield Scott had developed, in 1861, a military strategy to defeat the Confederacy that was consistent with this war aim. His plan aimed to minimize the loss of life and property by applying military and economic pressure through a naval blockade and by securing the Mississippi River. The main operations for the Union army would be in the West, while it remained on the defensive near Washington. This would also give the Union time to assemble the large forces it would need to overwhelm the rebellious states. This strategy was rejected by Lincoln in favor of the popular "On to Richmond" strategy when the decision was made to attack the Confederate army at Manassas.

The rejection of General Scott's advice so early in the conflict exposed one of the problems that the Union high command faced during the war: the divide between the amateur military tradition and professionally trained officers. The American military tradition that saw a divide between the elitist values of the professional officer corps on the one hand and the amateur, militia values on the other had contributed to a sense of caution in the minds of the Union's civilian leaders in their dealings with professional military officers that created impediments to the Union high command's working cohesively. McClellan and his supporters believed that the Union war effort should be entrusted to the nation's military professionals. Unfortunately the actions of both the civilian administration and McClellan and his supporters reinforced these stereotypes. The division between these two groups hampered the Union high command's ability to plan and implement the strategy needed to win the war in its first two years.

A lack of any clearly defined roles for the president and the general in chief also acted against the Union high command's working cohesively. Lincoln had defined the role of commander in chief as the conflict developed. He used his "war power" decisively to mobilize troops and to remove the threat in 1861 of having Washington's line of communication with the rest of the nation cut off. But there was little to guide the president and the general in chief about their respective roles. General Scott, the general in chief when the Civil War commenced, had seen his advice ignored by Lincoln on several occasions. Unfortunately this played into the hands of an ambitious General McClellan as he worked to ignore and undermine Scott.

General McClellan rose to prominence on the back of a large ego and some minor military victories. Those victories were blown out of proportion by a Northern public hungry for victory. McClellan was placed in command of the troops in and around Washington, but Lincoln treated him in a manner that was not appropriate to his command but was consistent with the public image of him. McClellan's ego and ambition helped to fuel a feud between him and his superior, General Scott, which adversely affected the Union's having a coherent military strategy.

The Union high command should have worked more cohesively when on November 1, 1861, one person, McClellan, became both general in chief and commander of the Army of the Potomac, the Union's largest army. He identified the Eastern Theater as being more important than the Western and he looked to defeat the main Confederate army there in a decisive battle somewhere near Richmond. After this victory, the South would be finally defeated when McClellan's army marched down the eastern seaboard. President Lincoln disagreed. He believed the Union strategy should be one of simultaneous advances. This would mean attacking in the west as well as the east. However, McClellan's strategy appealed to Lincoln and his cabinet because of its emphasis on capturing Richmond and on destroying the main Confederate army in one enormous battle. This was unrealistic. The reality was that a decisive battle eluded both sides. McClellan should have realized how hard it was to destroy a Civil War army in a battle.

Furthermore, the unrealistic expectations regarding the time line for McClellan to launch a major operation with the Army of the Potomac caused a lot of concern for Lincoln and many within his cabinet. McClellan forged a large army, but the president, the cabinet and the Radical Republicans were concerned that it had not been into battle. They were also concerned that he had not revealed any plans he had to carry out the eastern offensive strategy.

This resulted in a loss of confidence in McClellan that was demonstrated in Lincoln's order for simultaneous advances of all Union armies on February 22, 1862. This order is usually given as an example of the military genius of Lincoln because he understood the best way to defeat an enemy who was using interior lines. This order was problematic because it was ignored by all the commanders of Union armies and the Union's military forces were not in an operational position to do it anyway.

The order was also evidence that by this stage the relationship between Lincoln and McClellan had become dysfunctional. There had been McClellan's famous snub of the president and Lincoln's attempt to borrow the Army of the Potomac through a series of councils of war convinced McClellan that Lincoln wanted to interfere in the operations of the army and the role of general in chief. There was no doubt that McClellan found it difficult to perform the duties of general in chief and commander of the Army of the Potomac at the same time, particularly when the army was about to begin a major campaign. But Lincoln's solution to this problem was to take on the role of general in chief himself. This decision had a divisive impact on the Union's high command. McClellan and his supporters resented this further interference in military matters by amateur civilians.

McClellan's major operation on the peninsula failed as a result of his poor management of the army on the peninsula and intervention from Lincoln over the strategic importance of Washington. McClellan tempted his own fate by creating false expectations by appealing to those who wanted quick military action and a decisive result in the East. Eventually, the position of general in chief returned to another professional officer with the appointment of General Halleck to the role. Halleck's first major job was to recommend the end of McClellan's campaign on the peninsula.

The failure of the Peninsula Campaign also demonstrated that fighting offensively in the East was the wrong strategy. This demonstrated that both Lincoln and McClellan had got it wrong. It provided the Confederates with terrain that greatly assisted the tactical defense and as a result almost gave them the victories that they needed to achieve their independence. That Lee could fight in Maryland and Pennsylvania was the consequence of this flawed strategy. Ironically, the Union's concentration of so much of its military manpower in northern Virginia was also the result of Lincoln's preoccupation with keeping Washington secure as well as popular pressure to take Richmond.

Confusion over the Union's war aims added to the tension within the Union's high command. McClellan, Lincoln and Scott had in 1861 supported the aim of a limited war to return the rebellious states to the Union. This aim was supported by the assumption that there was strong Union support in the

South. This was a false and optimistic assumption. By the middle of 1862 many had come to believe that this assumption was wrong. Increasingly, the Radical Republicans' view that slavery should be made the war aim for the Union and that the war should be fought with more aggression increased the political pressure on Lincoln and McClellan. The tension between the Radical Republicans who wanted a "hard" war and McClellan and many of the Union's professional officers who sought a limited, conciliatory war adversely affected Union war aims and operations.

The preliminary Emancipation Proclamation was issued by Lincoln using his authority as commander in chief and demonstrated that the nature of the war had changed. This important and pragmatic decision was significant because it added the emancipation of slaves in defined areas as a key strategy for the Union to win the war. McClellan and many senior officers who supported him in the Army of the Potomac were convinced that it was an example of the reckless intervention by civilians in military affairs. Significantly, Lincoln had issued the proclamation after McClellan's victory at Antietam. Lincoln was concerned that McClellan's lack of a vigorous pursuit of Lee's army indicated that McClellan may have deliberately let Lee's army escape destruction so that the war would draw to a stalemate, which would allow for a negotiated settlement to the war. This was a serious lack of trust that also disrupted the effective operation of the Union's high command.

The Union's high command did not work effectively enough to be able to achieve a Union victory in the first two years of the Civil War. This rebuts the Unionist interpretation that holds the Union had the high command, in particular through Lincoln's skills as commander in chief, to achieve victory but lacked the generals who could fight and win. By looking at the Union high command from the perspective of McClellan rather than of Lincoln, we can see that the Union's war aim in the first two years of the war—the restoration of the Union—was not supported by the strategy and operations needed to achieve it. A combination of Lincoln's preoccupation with the safety of Washington and his desire to defeat General Lee's army, McClellan's ego and poorly considered strategy, and an ineffective and often disrupted high command who had determined that the Union's main army was in the East conducting offensive operations on lines that assisted the Confederate defenders. Furthermore, even after he had been sacked, McClellan's shadow still hung over the Army of the Potomac. His supporters deliberately disrupted the Union war effort in the East through their lack of support for two of McClellan's replacements and by undermining a major operation.

Chapter Notes

Introduction

1. J. David Hacker, "A Census-Based Count of the Civil War Dead," *Civil War History* 57, no. 4 (December 2011), 307–348.
2. For a general overview of the Civil War see James M. McPherson, *Battle Cry of Freedom* (New York: Oxford University Press, 1988).
3. Bryan Conrad and H.J. Eckenrode, *George B. McClellan: The Man Who Saved the Union* (Chapel Hill: University of North Carolina Press, 1941); Warren W. Hassler, Jr., *General George B. McClellan, Shield of the Union* (Baton Rouge: Louisiana State University Press, 1957); Russel Beatie, *Army of The Potomac: McClellan's First Campaign March-May 1862* (Cambridge: Da Capo, 2007). All have argued that political interference in the Peninsula Campaign was a significant reason for the failure of the campaign.
4. See Stephen W. Sears, *George McClellan: The Young Napoleon* (New York: Ticknor and Fields, 1988); also Kenneth P. Williams, *Lincoln Finds a General: A Military Study of the Civil War* (New York: Macmillan, 1949) and T. Harry Williams, *Lincoln and His Generals* (New York: Gramercy, 1952).
5. Williams, *Lincoln Finds a General*.
6. Sears, *Controversies and Commanders: Dispatches from the Army of the Potomac* (Boston: Houghton Mifflin, 1999),133.
7. Williams, *Lincoln and His Generals*, vii.
8. James M. McPherson, "Lincoln and the Strategy of Unconditional Surrender," in *Lincoln, the War President: The Gettysburg Lectures*, Gabor S. Boritt, ed. (New York: Oxford University Press, 1992), 29–63.
9. Mark E. Neely, Jr., "The Generalship of Grant and Sherman: Was the Civil War a Modern 'Total' War? A Dissenting View," in *Major Problems in American Military History: Documents and Essays*, ed. John Whiteclay Chambers II, and Kurt G. Piehler (Boston: Houghton Mifflin, 1999), 178–186.
10. Mark Grimsley, *The Hard Hand of War: Union Military Policy Towards Southern Civilians, 1861–1865* (New York: Cambridge University Press, 1995).
11. Herman Hattaway and Archer Jones, *How the North Won: A Military History of the Civil War* (Urbana: University of Illinois Press, 1983), 107–108.
12. Steven E. Woodworth, *Jefferson Davis and His Generals: The Failure of Confederate Command in the West* (Lawrence: University Press of Kansas, 1990), 305.
13. Donald Stoker, *The Grand Design: Strategy and the U.S. Civil War* (Oxford: Oxford University Press, 2010), 23.
14. Woodworth, *Jefferson Davis and His Generals*, 18.
15. Stoker, *The Grand Design*, 19, 27.
16. Woodworth, *Jefferson Davis and His Generals*, 20.
17. Ibid., 24, 34–45.

Chapter One

1. John Shy, "American Wars as Crusades for Total Victory," in *Major Problems in the Era of the American Revolution, 1769–1791* (Lexington: D.C. Heath, 1992), 113.
2. Thomas J. Goss, *The War Within the Union High Command: Politics and Generalship During the Civil War* (Lawrence: University Press of Kansas, 2003), 19.
3. Richard W. Stewart, ed., *American Military History*, vol. 1, *The United States Army and the Forging of a Nation, 1775–1917* (Washington, D.C.: Center of Military History, United States Army, 2005), 30–31.
4. Ibid., 34–35.
5. Russell F. Weigley, *Towards an American*

Army (New York: Columbia University Press, 1962), 3–4.

6. Russell F. Weigley, *The American Way of War: A History of United States Military Strategy and Policy* (Bloomington: Indiana University Press, 1973), 5–6.

7. Weigley, *Towards an American Army*, 5.

8. General Nathanael Greene, cited in Don Higginbottom, "The Strengths and Weaknesses of the Militia," in *Major Problems in the Era of the American Revolution, 1769-1791* (Lexington: D.C. Heath, 1992), 239.

9. Weigley, *Towards an American Army*, 6.

10. Washington to Congress, December 20, 1776, cited in John C. Fitzpatrick, "George Washington Himself" (Westport: Greenwood, 1933), 276.

11. John R. Galvin, *The Minute Men: The First Fight; Myths and Realities of the American Revolution* (Washington: Pergamon-Brassey's, 1989).

12. Higginbottom, "The Strengths and Weaknesses of the Militia," 240.

13. Stewart H. Holbrook, *Lost Men of American History* (New York: MacMillan, 1946), 34.

14. James Thatcher, M.D., *Military Journal 1783*, no. 1 (16 May 2006), http://www.americanrevolution.org.

15. "General Washington Calls for a Standing Army, 1783," in John Whiteclay Chambers, *Major Problems in American Military History* (Boston: Houghton Mifflin, 1999), 99.

16. Cited in Weigley, *Towards an American Army*, 1.

17. Article II of the Constitution, Militia Act of 1792, Second Congress, Session I, Chapter XXVIII, http://www.constitution.org/mil/mil_act_1792.htm (accessed 25 August 2006).

18. Weigley, *Towards an American Army*, 14.

19. Antifederalist article New York newspaper, 1787, in Chambers, *Major Problems in American Military History*, 103.

20. Stewart, *American Military History*, vol. 1, pp. 52–54.

21. Weigley, *Towards an American Army*, 12–19.

22. Militia Act of 1792, Second Congress, Session I. Chapter XXVIII, http://www.constitution.org/mil/mil_act_1792.htm, (accessed 25 August 2006).

23. Weigley, *The American Way of War*, 41.

24. Thomas Jefferson, first inaugural address, Washington D.C., Wednesday, March 4, 1801, American Presidents from Revolution to Reconstruction http://odur.let.rug.nl/~usa/P/tj3/index.htm (accessed 5 September 2006).

25. Weigley, *American Way of War*, 45.

26. James Madison first inaugural address, Saturday, 4 March 1809, American Presidents from Revolution to Reconstruction, http://odur.let.rug.nl/~usa/P/tj3/index.htm (accessed 5 September 2006).

27. "Volunteers to Arms," 1812, in John Whiteclay Chambers, *Major Problems in American Military History* (Boston: Houghton Mifflin, 1999), 106.

28. James Madison, Fourth State of Nation: American Presidents from Revolution to Reconstruction, http://odur.let.rug.nl/~usa/P/tj3/index.htm (accessed 5 September 2006).

29. Stewart, *American Military History*, vol. 1, pp. 73–74.

30. Weigley, *Towards an American Army*, 45–67.

31. William B. Skelton, "An Officer Corps Responds to an Undisciplined Society by Disciplined Professionalism," in *Major Problems in American Military History* (Boston: Houghton Mifflin, 1999), 135.

32. Stewart, *American Military History*, vol. 1, p. 74.

33. Ibid., 75.

34. Ibid.

35. Skelton, "An Officer Corps Responds to an Undisciplined Society by Disciplined Professionalism," 136.

36. Weigley, *Towards an American Army*, 54–55.

37. Ibid., 56.

38. Ibid., 56–57.

39. James L. Morrison Jr., "Educating the Civil War Generals: West Point, 1833–1861," *Military Affairs* 38, no. 3 (October 1974), 108–111.

40. Timothy D. Johnson, *Winfield Scott: The Quest for Military Glory* (Lawrence: University Press of Kansas, 1998), 234.

41. T. Harry Williams, "The Military Leadership of North and South," in David H. Donald ed., *Why the North Won the Civil War* (Baton Rouge: Louisiana State University Press, 1960), 23–47.

42. Weigley, *Towards an American Army*, 57.

43. Halleck, cited in Weigley, *Towards an American Army*, 59.

44. Weigley, *Towards an American Army*, 60–64.

45. Ibid., 62.

46. Stewart, *American Military History*, vol. 1, pp. 75–77.

47. James Monroe, Seventh State of Nation, Washington, D.C., 1823, American Presidents from Revolution to Reconstruction, http://odur.let.rug.nl/~usa/P/tj3/index.htm (accessed 5 September 2006).

48. Stewart, *American Military History*, vol. 1, p. 77.

49. Andrew Jackson, first inaugural address, Wednesday, March 4, 1829, American Presidents from Revolution to Reconstruction, http:

//odur.let.rug.nl/~usa/P/tj3/index.htm (accessed 5 September 2006).
50. Weigley, "How Americans Wage War: The Evolution of National Strategy," in Chambers, *Major Problems in American Military History*, 3.
51. Shy, "American Wars as Crusades," 111.
52. Stewart, American *Military History*, vol. 1, pp. 77-81.
53. James K. Polk, inaugural address, Tuesday, March 4, 1845, American Presidents from Revolution to Reconstruction, http://odur.let.rug.nl/~usa/P/tj3/index.htm (accessed 5 September 2006).
54. Stewart, *American Military History*, vol. 1, p. 82.
55. Stewart, *American Military History*, vol. 1, pp. 84-89.
56. William Starr Myers, ed., *The Mexican War Diary of George B. McClellan* (Princeton: Princeton University Press, 1917), 18.
57. Myers, *The Mexican War Diary of George B. McClellan*, 18, 42-43.
58. Skelton, "An Officer Corps Responds to an Undisciplined Society by Disciplined Professionalism," 141.
59. Robert E. May, "An Officer Corps Responds to Opportunities for Expansion with Images of Heroic Expeditions," in John Whiteclay Chambers, *Major Problems in American Military History* (Boston: Houghton Mifflin, 1999), 142-151.
60. May, "An Officer Corps Responds to Opportunities for Expansion with Images of Heroic Expeditions," 142-151.

Chapter Two

1. Allan Nevins, ed., *The Diary of George Templeton Strong: The Civil War Years, 1860-1865*, vol. 3 (New York: McMillan, 1952), 144.
2. Stewart, *American Military History*, vol. 1, pp. 197-198.
3. Herman Hattaway and Archer Jones, *How the North Won: A Military History of the Civil War*, 9-10.
4. Beattie, *Army of the Potomac: Birth of Command*, 74.
5. Stewart, *American Military History*, vol. 1, pp. 203- 204.
6. *Harper's Weekly*: A Journal of Civilization, 25 May 1861, p. 322, (accessed 29 November 2006), http://www.sonofthesouth.net/.
7. E.D. Keyes, *Fifty Years' Observation of Men and Events Civil and Military* (New York: Charles Scribner's Sons, 1885), 431.
8. "Notes on the War," *New York Times*, 6 June 1861.
9. Abraham Lincoln, *Life and Works of Abraham Lincoln*, vol. 6, *State Papers, 1861-1865*, Marion M. Miller, ed. (New York: Current Literature, 1907), 173-174.
10. John Keegan, *The American Civil War: A Military History* (London: Vintage, 2010), 70.
11. Stewart, *American Military History*, vol. 1, pp. 202-203.
12. Archer Jones, *Civil War Command and Strategy: The Process of Victory and Defeat* (New York: Free Press, 1992), 12-13.
13. James M. McPherson, *Battle Cry of Freedom* (New York: Oxford University Press, 1988), 328-329.
14. Goss, *The War Within the Union High Command*.
15. Roy P. Basler, Marion Dolores Pratt, and Lloyd A. Dunlap, ed., *The Collected Works of Abraham Lincoln*, 9 vols. (New Brunswick, NJ: Rutgers University Press, 1953), vol. 4, p. 316.
16. Williams, *Lincoln and His Generals*, 16.
17. Ibid., 4.
18. Hattaway and Jones, *How the North Won*, 105-106.
19. E.D. Townsend, *Anecdotes of the Civil War in the United States* (New York: Appleton, 1884), Appendix A, 249-253.
20. Townsend, *Anecdotes of the Civil War in the United States*, Appendix A, 252.
21. Ibid.
22. Ibid., 255-256.
23. Ibid.
24. A.K. McClure, *Abraham Lincoln and Men of War-Time*, 4th ed. (Lincoln: University of Nebraska Press, 1892), 67-69.
25. Wert, *The Sword of Lincoln*, 7-8.
26. Williams, *Lincoln and His Generals*, 4-5.
27. Mark A. Snell, *From First to Last: The Life of Major General William B. Franklin* (New York: Fordham University Press, 2002), 54-57.
28. Frederick William Seward, *Reminiscences of a War-time Statesman and Diplomat, 1830-1915* (New York: G.P. Putnam's Sons, 1916), 167-168.
29. Wert, *The Sword of Lincoln: The Army of The Potomac*, 8 (*Official Records*, Series 1, vol. 2, p. 2).
30. McClure, *Abraham Lincoln and Men of War-Time*, 63.
31. Horatio Nelson Taft, *The Washington Diary of Horatio Nelson Taft*, Manuscript Division, Library of Congress, Diary Entries 18 April, 19 April, 21 April 1861, http://memory.loc.gov/ammem/tafthtml/tafthome.html (accessed 3 January 2007).
32. *Official Records*, Series 1, vol. 2, p. 583.
33. McPherson, *Battle Cry of Freedom*, 285.
34. Beattie, *Army of The Potomac: Birth of Command*, 100.
35. *Official Records*, Series 1, vol. 2, General Order 3, pp. 580, 582-583, 586.

36. *Official Records*, Series 1, vol. 2, p. 584.
37. *Official Records*, Series 1, vol. 2, General Orders No. 12, p. 607.
38. *Official Records*, Series 1, vol. 2, Report of Col. Edward F. Jones, Sixth Massachusetts Militia, April 22, 1861, pp. 7-9.
39. Russell F. Weigley, *A Great Civil War: A Military and Political History, 1861-1865* (Bloomington: Indiana University Press, 2000) 38.
40. *New York Times*, 20 April, 1861.
41. *Official Records*, Series 1, vol. 2, 9-11, Office Board of Police Commissioners, Baltimore, May 3, 1861.
42. *Official Records*, Series 1, vol. 2, pp. 16-19, Report of Hon. George William Brown, Mayor of Baltimore, May 9 1861.
43. Basler, *The Collected Works of Abraham Lincoln*, vol. 8, p. 121.
44. *Official Records*, Series 1, vol. 2, p. 586.
45. Basler, *The Collected Works of Abraham Lincoln*, vol. 9, p. 107.
46. Lincoln, *Life and Works of Abraham Lincoln*, vol. 4, p. 347.
47. *Official Records*, Series 1, vol. 2, 607.
48. Ibid., 623-624.
49. Ibid., 633-634, 11 May 1861, Schuyler Hamilton, Lieutenant-Colonel and Military Secretary to Butler, where it was determined "Baltimore is within your department."
50. *Official Records*, Series 1, vol. 2, p. 638.
51. Ibid., 634, 640.
52. Ibid., 641-642.
53. Ibid., 640-641.
54. Beatie, *Army of The Potomac: Birth of Command*, 144-147.
55. "Civilians in Military Command: Views and Impressions Current in Military Circles in Washington," *New York Times*, 16 June 1861.
56. *Report of the Joint Committee on the Conduct of the War*, vol. 2 (Washington: Government Printing Office, 1863), 3.
57. *Official Records*, Series 1, vol. 2, pp. 719-721, McDowell to Townsend.
58. "Gen. Scott and the Cabinet—The Duty of the President," *New York Times*, 26 July 1861.
59. Stephen W. Sears, ed., *The Civil War Papers of George B. McClellan: Selected Correspondence, 1860-1865* (New York: Ticknor and Fields, 1989), 12-13.
60. *Official Records*, Series 1, vol. 51, part I, Serial 107, Supplements, 339.
61. Basler, *The Collected Works of Abraham Lincoln*, vol. 4, pp. 338-339, 346-347.
62. *Official Records of the Union and Confederate Navies in the War of the Rebellion* (Washington: Government Printing Office, 1894), Series 1, vol. 5, pp. 753-754, Stringham to Welles, 29 June, 1861.
63. Townsend, *Anecdotes of the Civil War in the United States*, 55-56.

64. Jones, *Civil War Command and Strategy*, 21-22.
65. Geoffrey Perret, *Lincoln's War: The Untold Story of America's Greatest President as Commander in Chief* (New York: Random House, 2004), 55-59.
66. *Official Records*, Series I, vol. 51,1, pp. 369-370, Scott to Maj. General McClellan, Union Correspondence, Orders, and Returns Relating to Operations in Maryland, Eastern North Carolina, Pennsylvania, Virginia, and West Virginia, from January 1, 1861, to June 30, 1865,
67. James M. McPherson, *Drawn With the Sword: Reflections on the American Civil War* (New York: Oxford University Press, 1996), 73.
68. "Gen. Scott and the Cabinet—The Duty of the President," *New York Times*, 26 July 1861.
69. Grimsley, *The Hard Hand of War*, 27.
70. Jones, *Civil War Command and Strategy*, 22-23.
71. Jeffrey D. Wert, *The Sword of Lincoln: The Army of the Potomac* (New York: Simon and Schuster, 2005), 13.
72. *Harper's Weekly*: A Journal of Civilization, 4 May 1861, p. 274, http://www.sonofthesouth.net/ (accessed 29 November 2006).
73. Ibid., 29 November 2006, 25 May 1861, http://www.sonofthesouth.net/.
74. Williams, *Lincoln and His Generals*, 18.
75. Gideon Welles, *Diary of Gideon Welles* (Boston and New York: Houghton, 1911), vol. 1, p. 242.
76. *Official Records*, Union Letters and Reports, Series III, vol. 1, p. 59, Galusha A. Grow to Simon Cameron, 5 May 1861.
77. "Gen. Scott's Plan," Letter to the editor, *New York Times*, 3 July 1861.
78. Grimsley, *The Hard Hand of War*, 29.
79. Michael Burlingame, ed., *With Lincoln in the White House: Letters, Memoranda, and Other Writings of John G. Nicolay, 1860-1865* (Carbondale: Southern Illinois University Press, 2000), 14.
80. *Official Records*, Series 1, Vol. 2, pp. 662, 664-665.
81. Wert, *The Sword of Lincoln*, 13.
82. William Swinton, *Campaigns of the Army of the Potomac* (New York: Charles B. Richardson, 1866), 28.
83. Basler, *The Collected Works of Abraham Lincoln*, vol. 4, pp. 438-439.
84. Ibid., pp. 421-441.
85. Basler, *The Collected Works of Abraham Lincoln*, vol. 6, pp. 29-30, 428.
86. Stewart, *American Military History*, 207-208.
87. "Affairs at the Capital: The Advance of the Army—A Grand Spectacle—Probable Duration of the War," *New York Times*, 21 July 1861.

88. Ibid.
89. McDowell had 35,000 troops of which 18,000 crossed Bull Run. Beauregard had 32,000 troops and ordered 18,000 into action.
90. Stewart, *American Military History*, vol.1, pp. 210–212.
91. Herman Hattaway, *Shades of Blue and Gray: An Introductory Military History of the Civil War* (Columbia: University of Missouri, 1997), 50.
92. *Report of the Joint Committee on the Conduct of the War*, vol. 2, p. 5.
93. Weigley, *The American Way of War*, 96.
94. The Prince De Joinville, *The Army of the Potomac: Its Organization, Its Commanders and Its Campaign* (New York: Anson D. F. Randolph, 1862), 10.
95. Edwin M. Stanton, *The Diary of a Public Man* (New Brunswick: Rutgers University Press, 1946), 127.
96. Stewart, *American Military History*, vol. 1, pp. 213–214.
97. Weigley, *A Great Civil War: A Military and Political History, 1861–1865*, 61.
98. Basler, *The Collected Works of Abraham Lincoln*, vol. 4, p. 458.
99. Burlingame, *With Lincoln in the White House*, Nicolay to Therma Bates, 23 July 1861, p. 52.
100. Stewart, *American Military History*, vol. 1, p. 213.
101. *Harper's Weekly*, August 1861, "What General Scott Said to Mr. Raymond," http://www.sonofthesouth.net/ (accessed 29 November 2006).
102. *Official Records*, Series 1, vol. 2, p. 753.
103. Ibid., 766, General Order 47, p. 763.
104. Townsend, *Anecdotes of the Civil War in the United States*, 62.
105. Stanton, *The Diary of a Public Man*, 128.

Chapter Three

1. Samuel P. Huntington, *The Soldier and the State: The Theory and Politics of the Civil-Military Relations* (Cambridge: Belknap Press, 1957), 80–85.
2. Russell F. Weigley, *The Journal of Military History* 57, no. 5, Special Issue: Proceedings of the Symposium on "The History of War as Part of General History" at the Institute for Advanced Studies, Princeton, New Jersey (October 1993): 27–58.
3. Sears, *The Young Napoleon*, 17.
4. William Roscoe Thayer, *The Life and Letters of John Hay*, 2 vols. (Boston and New York: Houghton and Mifflin, 1915), vol. 1, p. 121.
5. *Official Records*, Series 1, vol. 2, p. 766.
6. Sears, *The Civil War Papers of George B. McClellan*, 28–29, McClellan to Lincoln, May 30 1861.
7. George B. McClellan, *McClellan's Own Story: The War for the Union, the Soldiers Who Fought It, the Civilians Who Directed It, and His Relations to It and to Them* (New York: C.L. Webster, 1887), 66.
8. James G. Randall, *Lincoln, the President*, 4 vols. (New York: Dodd, Mead, 1945–55), vol. 1, p. 393.
9. McClellan, *McClellan's Own Story*, 66.
10. *Official Records*, Series 1, vol. 5, p. 11, General Reports, McClellan to Cameron.
11. McClellan, *McClellan's Own Story*, 68.
12. *Official Records*, Series 1, vol. 5, p. 13, General Reports, McClellan to Cameron.
13. Beatie, *Army of the Potomac: Birth of Command*, 426.
14. McClellan, *McClellan's Own Story*, 70.
15. *Official Records*, Series 1, vol. 5, p. 12, General Reports, McClellan to Cameron.
16. Sears, *The Civil War Papers of George B. McClellan*, 71.
17. *Official Records*, Series 3, vol. 1, 400, [PUBLIC-No.22.] AN ACT, "supplementary to an act entitled 'An act to increase the present military establishment of the United States,' approved July twenty-ninth, eighteen hundred and sixty-one."
18. Sears, *The Civil War Papers of George B. McClellan*, McClellan to Mary Ellen McClellan, July 27, 1861.
19. Sears, *The Civil War Papers of George B. McClellan*, 71–72, Memorandum to Lincoln, August 2, 1861.
20. Ibid.
21. Sears, *The Civil War Papers of George B. McClellan*, 71, Letter to Mary Ellen, July 30, 1861.
22. Williams, *Lincoln and His Generals*, 30–31.
23. Sears, *The Young Napoleon*, 98–99.
24. Williams, *Lincoln Finds a General*, 125.
25. "The Act of August 5, 1861, 12 Statutes at Large, 294, Century of Lawmaking for a New Nation: U.S. Congressional Documents and Debates, 1774–1875, Statutes at Large, 37th Congress, 1st Session," 294, http://memory.loc.gov/ammem/amlaw/lawhome.html (accessed 5 October 2007).
26. Sears, *The Civil War Papers of George B. McClellan*, 75, Letter to Mary Ellen, August 2, 1861.
27. Ibid., 78–79, Letter to Mary Ellen, August 4, 1861.
28. *Official Records*, Series 1, vol. 11, part 3, pp. 3, 8 August 1861, McClellan to Scott.
29. Ibid.
30. Sears, *The Civil War Papers of George B. McClellan*, 79–80, Letter to Scott, August 8, 1861.

31. Ibid., 80.
32. Ibid., 81.
33. Ibid.
34. Ibid., 81–82.
35. *Official Records*, Series 1, vol. 11, part 3, pp. 4, 9 August 1861, Scott to Secretary of War.
36. *Official Records*, Series 1, vol. 11, part 3, 4–5, 10 August 1861, McClellan to Lincoln.
37. Ibid., 5–6, 12 August, 1861, Scott to Secretary of War.
38. Ibid.
39. Sears, *The Civil War Papers of George B. McClellan*, 83–84, Letter to Welles, August 12, 1861.
40. Ibid., 84–85, Letter to Mary Ellen, August 15, 1861.
41. *Official Records*, Series 1, vol. 5, p. 575.
42. *Official Records*, Series 2, vol. 1, p. 679.
43. Sears, *The Civil War Papers of George B. McClellan*, 95–96, McClellan to Cameron, September 8, 1861.
44. *Official Records*, Series 2, vol. 1, 679.
45. Seward, *Reminiscences of a War-time Statesman and Diplomat*, 174–178.
46. *Official Records*, Series 2, vol. 1, p. 678.
47. Ibid., 679.
48. Ibid., 681.
49. Sears, *The Civil War Papers of George B. McClellan*, 100.
50. *Official Records*, Series 3, vol. 1, part 1, p. 519.
51. Ethan S. Rafuse, *McClellan's War: The Failure of Moderation in the Struggle for the Union* (Bloomington: Indiana University Press, 2005), 135.
52. McClellan, *McClellan's Own Story*, 91.
53. Welles, *Diary of Gideon Welles*, vol. 1, p. 241.
54. Ibid., 242.
55. McClellan, *McClellan's Own Story*, 91.
56. Rafuse, *McClellan's War*, 136.
57. Sears, *The Civil War Papers of George B. McClellan*, 106–107.
58. *Official Records*, Series 1, vol. 5, pp. 15–17.
59. Wert, *The Sword of Lincoln*, 37–38.
60. McClellan, *McClellan's Own Story*, 170.
61. Ibid.
62. McClellan, *McClellan's Own Story*, 170; Sears, *The Civil War Papers of George B. McClellan*, 109, Letter to Mary Ellen, October 19, 1861.
63. *Official Records*, Series 1, vol. 5, pp. 308–312.
64. Brian Holden Reid, "Historians and the Joint Committee on the Conduct of the War, 1861–1865," *Civil War History* 38 (December 1992): 319–341.
65. John Hay, *Lincoln and the Civil War in the Diary and Letters of John Hay* (Connecticut: Negro University Press, 1939), 31, Diary entry of October 26, 1861.
66. Hay, *Lincoln and the Civil War in the Diary and Letters of John Hay*, 32, Diary entry of October 27, 1861.
67. *Official Records*, Series 3, vol. 1, p. 611.
68. *Harper's Weekly*, http://www.sonofthesouth.net/ (accessed 29 November 2006).
69. Ibid., Saturday, November 16, 1861, pp. 1–2, http://www.sonofthesouth.net/ (accessed 29 November 2006).
70. *Official Records*, Series 1, vol. 5, p. 639.
71. *Official Records*, Series 3, vol. 1, p. 613.
72. Hay, *Lincoln and the Civil War in the Diary and Letters of John Hay*, 32–33.
73. McClellan, *McClellan's Own Story*, 199.
74. Grimsley, *The Hard Hand of War*. A discussion of the Union's conciliation policy can be found on 23–46.
75. *Official Records*, Series 1, vol. 4, p. 342, McClellan to Buell.
76. Ibid., p. 355.
77. *Official Records*, Series 1, vol. 3, pp. 466–467, 30 August 1861.
78. Ibid.
79. *Official Records*, Series 1, vol. 3, p. 553, General Orders, No. 18.
80. Wert, *The Sword of Lincoln*, 44.
81. McClellan, *McClellan's Own Story*, 202.
82. Ibid., 207–209, McClellan to Halleck 11 November, 1861.
83. Ibid.
84. Ethan S. Rafuse, "McClellan and Halleck at War: The Struggle for Control of the Union War Effort in the West, November 1861–March 1862," *Civil War History* 49, no. 1 (March 2003): 32–51.
85. McClellan, *McClellan's Own Story*, 209–210, McClellan to Buell 7 November
86. Sears, *The Civil War Papers of George B. McClellan*, 114–118.
87. Ibid., 134, McClellan to Cameron, 15 November 1861.
88. Chester G. Hearn, *The Capture of New Orleans, 1862* (Baton Rouge: Louisiana State University Press, 1995), 100.
89. David D. Porter, *Incidents and Anecdotes of the Civil War* (New York: D. Appleton, 1885), 95–96.
90. Porter, *Incidents and Anecdotes of the Civil War*, 95–96.
91. W.M.D. Kelley, *Lincoln and Stanton: A Study of the War Administration, 1861 and 1862, with Special Consideration of Some Recent Statements of Gen Geo B. McClellan* (New York: G.P. Putnam and Sons, 1885), 4.
92. Rafuse, *McClellan's War*, 157.
93. Hay, *Lincoln and the Civil War in the Diary and Letters of John Hay*, 34–35, Diary entry of November 13, 1861.

94. Rafuse, *McClellan's War*, 158.
95. Sears, *The Young Napoleon*, 425–426. Sears criticizes the theory put forward by Warren W. Hassler, Jr.

Chapter Four

1. Burlingame, *With Lincoln in the White House*, 62–63.
2. *Harper's Weekly*, 7 December 1861, http://www.sonofthesouth.net/ (accessed 29 November 2006).
3. George C. Meade, *Life and Letters of General George Gordon Meade*, 3 vols. (New York: Scribner's, 1913), vol. 1, p. 236.
4. *Official Records*, Series 3, vol. 1, p. 699.
5. Perret, *Lincoln's War*, 106.
6. *Official Records*, Series 3, vol. 1, p. 708.
7. Perret, *Lincoln's War*, 107.
8. Ibid., 108.
9. Meade, *Life and Letters of General George Gordon Meade*, vol. 1, p. 236.
10. Basler, *The Collected Works of Abraham Lincoln*, vol. 5, p. 49.
11. Ibid., 34, Memorandum to McClellan, 1 December 1861.
12. A good explanation of interior and exterior lines can be found in Hattaway and Jones, *How the North Won*, 713–715. "Defeat in detail" is a military term which refers to the tactic of bringing a large part of one's own force against a small part, or a detail, of the enemies force in sequence rather than attacking the bulk of the enemy army.
13. Basler, *The Collected Works of Abraham Lincoln*, vol. 5, p. 35, McClellan to Lincoln, 10 December 1861.
14. McClellan, *McClellan's Own Story*, 158.
15. John Niven, ed., *The Salmon P. Chase Papers* (Kent, Ohio: Kent State University, 1993), vol. 1, p. 324, Journal entry, Saturday, January 11, 1862.
16. Swinton, *Campaigns of the Army of the Potomac*, 81, McDowell's transcript of a meeting dated 10 January 1862.
17. *Official Records*, Series 1, vol. 5, p. 622, Letter dated 18 October, 1861.
18. Ibid., 624, Letter dated 22 October, 1861.
19. Beatie, *Army of The Potomac: McClellan Takes Command*, 398.
20. *Report of the Joint Committee on the Conduct of the War*, vol. 1, p. 388.
21. Ibid., 631.
22. Swinton, *Campaigns of the Army of the Potomac*, 79.
23. *Report of the Joint Committee on the Conduct of the War*, vol. 1, pp. 68–69.
24. Ibid.
25. Ibid., 70.
26. Ibid., 117.
27. Ibid., 131.
28. Ibid., 172.
29. Sears, *The Young Napoleon*, 136–137; Ethan S. Rafuse, "Typhoid and Tumult: Lincoln's Response to General McClellan's Bout with Typhoid Fever During the Winter of 1861–62," *Journal of the Abraham Lincoln Association* (Summer 1997), http://www.historycooperative.org/journals/jala/18.2/rafuse.html (accessed 5 February 2008).
30. Rafuse, "Typhoid and Tumult," 3.
31. Perret, *Lincoln's War*, 113.
32. Basler, *The Collected Works of Abraham Lincoln*, vol. 5, p. 88.
33. *Official Records*, Series 1, vol. 7, p. 524, Lincoln to Halleck, 31 December, 1861.
34. Ibid., 526, Buell to Lincoln, 1 January 1862.
35. Ibid., Buell to Lincoln, 1 January 1862, 11:00 p.m.
36. Ibid., Halleck to Lincoln, 1 January 1862.
37. Ethan S. Rafuse, "McClellan and Halleck at War: The Struggle for Control of the Union War Effort in the West, November 1861-March 1862," *Civil War History* 49, no. 1 (March 2003): 36–37.
38. Grimsley, *The Hard Hand of War*, 50–51.
39. Basler, *The Collected Works of Abraham Lincoln*, vol. 5, p. 88, Lincoln to Chase.
40. Niven, *The Salmon P. Chase Papers*, vol. 1, 321, Sunday, 5 January 1862.
41. Ibid., 322.
42. T. Harry Williams, *Lincoln and the Radicals* (Madison: University of Wisconsin Press, 1972), 83.
43. Niven, *The Salmon P. Chase Papers*, vol. 1, pp. 321–322, Monday, 6 January 1862.
44. *Official Records*, Series 1, vol. 7, p. 535, Lincoln to Buell, 7 January 1862.
45. Rafuse, "Typhoid and Tumult," 9.
46. Howard K. Beale, *The Diary of Edward Bates, 1859–1866* (Washington: United States Printing Office, 1933), 218–220.
47. *Official Records*, Series 1, vol. 7, p. 533, Lincoln to Cameron. This note is on the back of a dispatch from Halleck, 10 January 1862.
48. Montgomery C. Meigs, "General M.C. Meigs on the Conduct of the Civil War," *The American Historical Review* 26, no. 2 (January 1921): 285–303, 292.
49. William B. Franklin, "The First Great Crime of the War," in *The Annals of the War*, J.M. Harper, 72–81 (London: Musson, 1913), 76.
50. Swinton, *Campaigns of the Army of the Potomac*, 80, McDowell's transcript of the meeting.
51. Ibid., 81.
52. Ibid.

53. McClellan, *McClellan's Own Story*, 155.
54. Fletcher Pratt, *Stanton: Lincoln's Secretary of War* (Westport: Greenwood, 1970),133. Lorenzo Thomas was the adjutant general.
55. George C. Gorham, *Life and Public Services of Edwin W. Stanton*, 2 vols. (Boston and New York: Houghton, Mifflin, 1899), vol. 1, p. 253.
56. *Official Records*, Series 1, vol. 5, p. 41, McClellan's Report.
57. McClellan, *McClellan's Own Story*, 153.
58. Swinton, *Campaigns of the Army of the Potomac*, 82, McDowell's transcript of the meeting.
59. Ibid., 82–83.
60. Ibid., 83.
61. Snell, *From First to Last: The Life of Major General William B. Franklin*, 79.
62. Swinton, *Campaigns of the Army of the Potomac*, 83, McDowell's transcript of the meeting.
63. Snell, *From First to Last: The Life of Major General William B. Franklin*, 80.
64. Franklin, "The First Great Crime of the War," 78.
65. McClellan, *McClellan's Own Story*, 156.
66. Theodore Pease and James Randall, ed., *Diary of Orville Hickman Browning*, vol. 1, 1850–1864 (Springfield: Illinois State Historical Library, 1925), 523, Diary entry of 12 January 1862.
67. Meigs, "General M.C. Meigs on the Conduct of the Civil War," 292.
68. McClellan, *McClellan's Own Story*, 155.
69. Ibid., 156.
70. Swinton, *Campaigns of the Army of the Potomac*, 84, McDowell's transcript of the meeting.
71. Ibid., 85.
72. Meigs, "General M.C. Meigs on the Conduct of the Civil War," 293.
73. Ibid.
74. Swinton, *Campaigns of the Army of the Potomac*, 84, McDowell's transcript of the meeting.
75. Ibid., 85.
76. Ibid.
77. Franklin, "The First Great Crime of the War," 79.
78. Ibid.
79. McClellan, *McClellan's Own Story*, 158.
80. Meigs, "General M.C. Meigs on the Conduct of the Civil War," 293.
81. McClellan, *McClellan's Own Story*, 158–159.
82. *Official Records*, Series 1, vol. 7, p. 547, McClellan to Buell, 13 January 1862.
83. Basler, *The Collected Works of Abraham Lincoln*, vol. 5, p. 99, Lincoln to Buell, 13 January 1862.
84. Ibid., 111–112, Lincoln, General War Order No. 1, 27 January 1862.
85. Welles, *Diary of Gideon Welles*, vol. 1, 61.
86. Basler, *The Collected Works of Abraham Lincoln*, vol. 5, p. 112, Lincoln, General War Order No. 1, 27 January 1862.
87. Perret, *Lincoln's War*, 123.
88. Basler, *The Collected Works of Abraham Lincoln*, vol. 5, p. 115, Lincoln, Special War Order No. 1, 31 January 1862.
89. *Official Records*, Series 1, vol. 5, p. 41.
90. Don Piatt, *Memories of the Men Who Saved the Union* (New York and Chicago: Belford, Clarke, 1887), 61.
91. Benjamin P. Thomas and Harold M. Hyman, *Stanton: The Life and Times of Lincoln's Secretary of War* (New York: Alfred A. Knopf, 1962), 148–149.
92. Piatt, *Memories of the Men Who Saved the Union*, 75–76.
93. Ibid., 75.
94. Russel H. Beatie, *Army of The Potomac: McClellan Takes Command*, September 1861-February 1862 (Cambridge: Da Capo, 2004), 546.
95. *Official Records*, Series 1, vol. 5, p. 41.
96. McClellan, *McClellan's Own Story*, 228–229.
97. Basler, *The Collected Works of Abraham Lincoln*, vol. 5, p. 118.
98. Hattaway, *Shades of Blue and Gray*, 67.
99. *Official Records*, vol. 7, 593, Halleck to McClellan, 8 February 1862.
100. Ibid., McClellan to Buell, 7 February 1862.
101. Ibid., 593, Halleck to McClellan, 8 February 1862.
102. Ibid., 617, McClellan to Halleck, 15 February 1862.
103. Ibid., 641, Halleck to McClellan, 20 February 1862.
104. Ibid., 645, McClellan to Halleck, 21 February 1862.
105. Ibid., McClellan to Buell, 21 February 1862.
106. *New York Tribune*, 13 December 1861, cited in T. Harry. Williams, "The Attack Upon West Point During the Civil War," *Mississippi Valley Historical Review* 25, no. 4. (March 1939), 492.
107. *Harper's Weekly*, "Have We a General Among Us?," 17 January 1863, http://www.sonofthesouth.net/ (accessed November 2006).
108. George E. Baker, *The Works of William H. Seward, 1853–1884* (New York: AMS, 1972), vol. 5, p. 48, Journal entry of 10 February 1862.
109. A penetration is an advance along a line of communications capable of supplying the attacking army. A penetration that permits

a long-term occupation of territory can be distinguished from a raid that involves only temporary occupation of territory. See Hattaway and Jones, *How the North Won*, 83.

110. *Official Records,* Series 1, vol. 5, pp. 42–45, McClellan to Stanton, 3 February 1862.
111. McClellan, *McClellan's Own Story*, 195.
112. Ibid., 196.
113. Franklin, "The First Great Crime of the War," 79.
114. Pratt, *Stanton: Lincoln's Secretary of War*, 173.
115. Ibid., 172.
116. Franklin, "The First Great Crime of the War," 79.
117. Thayer, *The Life and Letters of John Hay*, vol. 1, pp. 188–189.
118. Basler, *The Collected Works of Abraham Lincoln*, vol. 5, pp. 149–150, President's General War Order No. 2, 8 March 1862.
119. Ibid., 142.
120. Williams, *Lincoln and His Generals*, 68.
121. Williams, *Lincoln and the Radicals*, 118.
122. Meade, *Life and Letters of General George Gordon Meade*, vol. 1, p. 253.
123. Williams, *Lincoln and His Generals*, 68–69.
124. Basler, *The Collected Works of Abraham Lincoln*, vol. 5, p. 151, President's General War Order No. 3, 8 March 1862.
125. McClellan, *McClellan's Own Story*, 222.
126. Ibid., 223–224.
127. Niven, *The Salmon P. Chase Papers*, vol. 1, p. 333.
128. Williams, *Lincoln and His Generals*, 70.
129. Beale, *The Diary Of Edward Bates, 1859–1866*, 239.
130. Basler, *The Collected Works of Abraham Lincoln*, vol. 5, p. 155.
131. Stephen E. Ambrose, *Halleck: Lincoln's Chief of Staff* (Baton Rouge: Louisiana State University Press, 1962), 60–61.
132. Ambrose, *Halleck: Lincoln's Chief of Staff*, 61.
133. Hay, *Letters of John Hay and Extracts from Diary*, vol. 1, p. 55.
134. McClellan, *McClellan's Own Story*, 224–225.
135. Sears, *The Civil War Papers of George B. McClellan*, 162–170.
136. *Official Records,* Series 1, vol. 5, p. 55.
137. Basler, *Collected Works of Abraham Lincoln*, vol. 5, pp. 157–158.

Chapter Five

1. Ethan Allen Hitchcock, *Fifty Years in Camp and Field: Diary of Major General Ethan Allen Hitchcock, U.S.A*, W.A. Croffut, ed. (New York: G.P. Putnam's Sons, 1909), 428–439.
2. Hitchcock, *Fifty Years in Camp and Field*, 439.
3. Ibid., 440.
4. Ibid.
5. Basler, *The Collected Works of Abraham Lincoln*, vol. 5, p. 155.
6. Hattaway and Jones, "The War Board: The Basis of the United States First General Staff," *Military Affairs* 46, no. 1 (February 1982): 1.
7. Charles A. Dana, *Recollections of the Civil War: With the Leaders at Washington and in the Field in the Sixties* (New York: D. Appleton, 1898), 6.
8. Thomas and Hyman, *Stanton: The Life and Times of Lincoln's Secretary of War*, 159.
9. Hattaway and Jones, "The War Board: The Basis of the United States First General Staff," 2.
10. Franklin B. Cooling, "Civil War Deterrent: Defenses of Washington," *Military Affairs* 29, no. 4 (Winter 1965–1966), 169.
11. *Official Records,* Series 1, vol. 5, p. 624, Report to Assistant Adjutant-General, General Williams, on 22 October, 1861 from Major Barnard.
12. *Official Records,* Series 1, vol. 11, part 3, p. 58.
13. Ibid., 58–59.
14. *Report of the Joint Committee on the Conduct of the War,* vol. 1, pp. 13–14.
15. *Official Records,* Series 1, vol. 11, part 3, pp. 60–61.
16. Beattie, *Army of The Potomac: McClellan's First Campaign*, 298.
17. *Official Records,* Series 1, vol. 11, part 3, pp. 61–62.
18. Franklin, "The First Great Crime of the War," 80; *Official Records,* Series 1, vol. 11, part 3, p. 77, McClellan to Wool, 7 April 1862.
19. Stedman, *Life and Letters of Edmund Clarence Stedman*, 270.
20. *Official Records,* Series 1, vol. 11, part 3, pp. 65–66.
21. Basler, *The Collected Works of Abraham Lincoln*, vol. 5, p. 265.
22. *Official Records,* Series 1, vol. 11, part 3, p. 66, Lincoln to McClellan, 4 April 1862.
23. McClellan, *McClellan's Own Story*, 308, Letter, 6 April 1862.
24. *Official Records,* Series 1, vol. 11, part 3, pp. 67–68, Thomas to McClellan, 4 April 1862.
25. Ibid., 3 April 1862, p. 65.
26. Ibid., 6 April 1862, p. 74.
27. Franklin, "The First Great Crime of the War," 81.
28. Ibid.
29. Ibid.

30. Alexander Stuart Webb, *The Peninsula: McClellan's Campaign of 1862* (New York: Charles Scribner's Sons, 1882), 178.
31. Oliver Otis Howard, *Autobiography of Oliver Otis Howard, Major General, United States Army* (New York: Baker and Taylor, 1907), 209.
32. Keyes, *Fifty Years' Observation of Men and Events Civil and Military*, 445. Keyes admitted in his account of the event that in regard to his command he owed much to General McDowell and nothing to General McClellan.
33. Keyes, *Fifty Years' Observation of Men and Events Civil and Military*, 444, Letter to Harris, 7 April, 1862.
34. *Official Records,* Series 1, vol. 11, part 3, p. 64, McClellan to Sumner, 3 April 1862.
35. Ibid., 74, McClellan to Thomas, 6 April 1862, 1:35 p.m., 8:00 p.m.
36. John G. Hay, *Abraham Lincoln: A History*, vol. 5 (New York: Century, 1890), 360.
37. McClellan, *McClellan's Own Story*, 264.
38. *Report of the Joint Committee on the Conduct of the War*, part 1, p. 630, Testimony of Captain G.V. Fox, Assistant Secretary of the Navy.
39. *Official Records,* Series 1, vol. 11, part 3, p. 71, McClellan to Lincoln, 5 April 1862.
40. Ibid., 6 April 1862, pp. 73–74.
41. Thayer, *The Life and Letters of John Hay*, vol. 1, p. 126, 3 April 1862.
42. Ibid.
43. Hattaway, *Shades of Blue and Gray: An Introductory Military History of the Civil War*, 68–72.
44. *Report of the Joint Committee on the Conduct of the War*, vol. 1, p. 18.
45. Pease, *Diary of Orville Hickman Browning*, vol. 1, p. 540, Diary entry of 10 April 1862.
46. Basler, *The Collected Works of Abraham Lincoln*, vol. 5, pp. 184–185, Lincoln to McClellan, 9 April 1862.
47. Hitchcock, *Fifty Years in Camp and Field*, 441.
48. Ibid.
49. *Official Records,* Series 1, vol. 11, part 3, pp. 153–154, McClellan to Stanton, 9 May 1862.
50. *Official Records,* Series 1, vol. 11, part 3, p. 154, 9 May 1862, Stanton to McClellan.
51. Ibid., 154–155, 9 May 1862, Lincoln to McClellan.
52. McClellan, *McClellan's Own Story*, 342.
53. *Official Records,* Series 1, vol.11, Part 3, p. 333, General Order 84, 22 July 1862.
54. Snell, *From First to Last: The Life of Major General William B. Franklin*, 106–109.
55. McClellan, *McClellan's Own Story*, 357, Diary entry of 15 May 1862.
56. Sears, *The Civil War Papers of George B. McClellan*, 269, to Mary Ellen McClellan, 18 May 1862.
57. McClellan, *McClellan's Own Story*, 345.
58. Ibid., 345–346, Stanton to McClellan, 18 May 1862.
59. Ibid., 350–351, Lincoln to McClellan, 24 May 1862.
60. McClellan, *McClellan's Own Story*, 351, Lincoln to McClellan, 24 May 1862.
61. Sears, *The Civil War Papers of George B. McClellan*, 270, McClellan to Burnside, 21 May 1862.
62. Basler, *The Collected Works of Abraham Lincoln*, vol. 5, p. 284.
63. Ibid., 287.
64. *Harper's Weekly:* A Journal of Civilization, 13 September 1862, pp. 577, 29, http://www.sonofthesouth.net/ (accessed November 2006).
65. Alpheus S. Williams, *From the Cannon's Mouth: The Civil War Letters of General Alpheus S. Williams* (Detroit: Wayne State University Press, 1959), 111, Letter to his daughter, 8 September 1862.
66. Basler, *The Collected Works of Abraham Lincoln*, vol. 5, p. 291.
67. Hattaway and Jones, *How the North Won*, 192.
68. *Official Records,* Series 1, vol. 11, part 3, p. 280, McClellan to Stanton, 30 June 1862.
69. Basler, *The Collected Works of Abraham Lincoln*, vol. 5, p. 298, Lincoln to McClellan, 1 July 1862.
70. Wert, *The Sword of Lincoln*, 118.
71. *Official Records,* Series 1, vol. 11, part 3, p. 281, McClellan to Thomas, 1 July 1862.
72. Ibid., Stanton to McClellan, 1 July 1862; Series 1, vol. 16, part 2, p. 88, Lincoln to Halleck, 2 July 1862.
73. Ibid., vol. 17, part 2, pp. 71–72, Halleck to Lincoln, 5 July 1862.
74. Ibid., vol. 11, part 3, p. 282, McClellan to Thomas, 1 July 1862.
75. Hattaway, *Shades of Blue and Gray*, 90.
76. *Report of the Joint Committee on the Conduct of the War*, vol. 1, p. 650, Burnside's testimony, 19 December 1862.
77. *Report of the Joint Committee on the Conduct of the War*, vol. 1, p. 650.
78. McClellan, *McClellan's Own Story*, 487–489.
79. Ibid.
80. Keyes, *Fifty Years' Observation of Men and Events Civil and Military*, 486–487.
81. Basler, *The Collected Works of Abraham Lincoln*, vol. 5, pp. 310–312.
82. *Official Records,* Series 1, vol. 11, part 3, pp. 313–314, Keyes to Lincoln, 10 July 1862.
83. John Pope, Report of Major-General John Pope, letter from the secretary of war in answer to resolution of the House of 18th ultimo, transmitting copy of report of Major General John Pope. March 3, 1863, p. 6.

84. *Official Records*, series 1, vol. 11, part 3, p. 314, Lincoln to Halleck, 11 July 1862.
85. Hattaway and Jones, "The War Board: The Basis of the United States First General Staff," 3.
86. Basler, *The Collected Works of Abraham Lincoln*, vol. 5, p. 323, 13 July 1862, Lincoln to McClellan.
87. Wert, *The Sword of Lincoln*, 131.
88. Niven, *The Salmon P. Chase Papers*, vol. 1, 349–350.
89. Ibid., 350.
90. Basler, *The Collected Works of Abraham Lincoln*, vol. 5, pp. 336–337.
91. Browning, *Browning Diary*, 565, Diary entry of Monday, July 28, 1862.
92. Welles, *Diary of Gideon Welles*, 121.
93. *Official Records*, Series 1, vol. 12, part 1, pp. 80–81.
94. Ibid., vol. 11, part 1, p. 81, McClellan to Halleck, 4 August 1862.
95. *Official Records*, Series 1, vol. 11, part 1, pp. 82–84, Halleck to McClellan, 6 August 1862.
96. Ibid., part 3, pp. 345–346, McClellan to Halleck, 1 August 1862.
97. Basler, *The Collected Works of Abraham Lincoln*. vol. 5, pp. 358–359, Address at a Union meeting, 6 August 1862.
98. *Official Records*, Series 1, vol. 11, part 3, pp. 337–338, Halleck to McClellan, 27 July 1862.
99. Niven, *The Salmon P. Chase Papers*, vol. 1, p. 363, Journal entry of 15 August 1862.
100. Hattaway and Jones, *How the North Won*, 205–235.
101. Niven, *The Salmon P. Chase Papers*, vol. 1, p. 350.
102. *Official Records*, Series 1, vol. 12, part 2 (Supp.) 1063, Porter to Burnside, 27 August 1862.
103. Ibid., 1069, Porter to Burnside, 29 August 1862.
104. Stephen R., Taffe, *Commanding the Army of the Potomac* (Lawrence: University of Kansas, 2006), 33–34.
105. Perret, *Lincoln's War*, 210.
106. Hay, *Letters of John Hay and Extracts from Diary*, vol. 1, p. 60.
107. Basler, *The Collected Works of Abraham Lincoln*, vol. 5, p. 399.
108. Peter Cozens and Robert I. Girardi, *The Military Memoirs of General John Pope* (Chapel Hill: University of North Carolina Press, 1998), 170.
109. John Hay, *Letters of John Hay and Extracts from Diary*, vol. 1, p. 61.
110. Niven, *The Salmon P. Chase Papers*, vol. 1, p. 370, Diary entry of 4 September 1862.
111. Walter N. Trenerry and Wallace J. Schultz, *Abandoned by Lincoln: A Military Biography of General John Pope* (Chicago: University of Illinois, 1990).
112. George B. McClellan, *Report of Major-General George B. McClellan Upon the Organization of the Army of the Potomac, Its Campaigns in Virginia and Maryland, from July 26, 1861, to November 7, 1862* (Boston: Office of the Boston Courier, 1864), 114.
113. *Official Records*, Series 1, vol. 12, part 3, p. 807.
114. Piatt, *Memories of the Men Who Saved the Union*, xxv.
115. Welles, *Diary of Gideon Welles*, 122.
116. Stoddard, *Lincoln at Work: Sketches from Life* (Boston: United Society of Christian Endeavor, 1900), 117–118.
117. Ibid., 120–121.
118. Ibid., 121–122.
119. Welles, *Diary of Gideon Welles*, 105.
120. Ibid., 109.
121. Hattaway and Jones, *How the North Won*, 240–241.
122. McClellan, *McClellan's Own Story*, 536.
123. *Official Records*, Series 1, vol. 19, part 2, p. 182, Halleck to McClellan, 5 September 1862.
124. Ibid., 169, Stanton to Halleck, 3 September 1862.
125. Ibid., Halleck to McClellan, 3 September 1862.
126. Ibid., 182, Halleck to McClellan, 5 September 1862.
127. Welles, *Diary of Gideon Welles*, 124.
128. Ibid., 124, 134.
129. Sears, *The Civil War Papers of George B. McClellan*, 428, McClellan to Mary Ellen McClellan.
130. *Official Records*, Series 1, vol. 19, part 2, p. 183, Pope to Halleck, Halleck to Pope, 5 September 1862.
131. Ibid., 189–190, McClellan to Halleck, 6 September 1862.
132. Ibid., 228, Banks to Heintzelman, 9 September 1862.
133. Ibid., McClellan to Heintzelman, 9 September 1862.
134. Ibid., 215, Stanton to Wool, 8 September 1862.
135. Hattaway and Jones, *How the North Won*, 242–244.
136. Basler, *The Collected Works of Abraham Lincoln*, vol. 5, p. 426.
137. Welles, *Diary of Gideon Welles*, 140, Diary entry of 19 September 1862.
138. David Donald, *Inside Lincoln's Cabinet: The Civil War Diaries of Salmon P. Chase* (New York: Longmans Green, 1954), 385–386.
139. Basler, *The Collected Works of Abraham Lincoln*, vol. 5, p. 434.
140. James M. McPherson, *Tried by War:*

Abraham Lincoln as Commander in Chief (New York: Penguin, 2008), 259.
141. William Whiting, *The War Powers of the President, and the Legislative Powers of Congress in Relation to Rebellion, Treason and Slavery* (Boston: John L. Shorey, 1862).
142. Arthur Meier Schlesinger, *The Imperial Presidency* (Boston: Houghton Mifflin, 1973), 63.
143. Whiting, *The War Powers of the President*, 10.
144. Basler, *The Collected Works of Abraham Lincoln*, vol. 5, pp. 388–389.
145. McClellan, *McClellan's Own Story*, 487–489.
146. *Official Records*, Series 3, vol. 2, part 1, pp. 584–585, General Order, No. 139, 24 September 1862.
147. *Official Records*, Series 1, vol. 24, part 3 (Vicksburg), 156–157, Halleck to Grant, 31 March 1863.
148. William F. Smith, *Autobiography of Major General William F. Smith, 1861–1864*, ed. Herbert Schiller (Dayton: Morningside, 1990), 57.
149. Smith, *Autobiography of Major General William F. Smith*, 57.
150. Snell, *From First to Last: The Life of Major General William B. Franklin*, 199.
151. Basler, *The Collected Works of Abraham Lincoln*, vol. 5, p. 442, Record of Dismissal of John J. Key.
152. Ibid., 508, Lincoln to Key, 24 November 1862.
153. John Hay, *Letters of John Hay and Extracts from Diary*, vol. 1 (Washington: Printed not published, 1908), 67–68, Diary entry of 26 September 1862.
154. *Official Records*, Series 1, vol. 19, part 1, p. 72, Halleck to McClellan, 6 October 1862.
155. Basler, *The Collected Works of Abraham Lincoln*, vol. 5, pp. 460–461, Lincoln to McClellan, 13 October 1862.
156. Ibid., 469–470.
157. John Hay, *Lincoln and the Civil War in the Diary and Letters of John Hay*, 133.
158. Joseph T. Glatthaar, *Partners in Command: The Relationships Between Leaders in the Civil War* (New York, Free Press, 1994), 93.
159. *Harper's Weekly*: A Journal of Civilization, 698, 1 November, http://www.sonofthesouth.net/ 1862 (accessed 29 November 2006).
160. Stephen W. Sears, *Controversies and Commanders*, 142–143.
161. John Cochrane, *American Civil War. Memories of Incidents Connected with the Origin and Culmination of the Rebellion that Threatened the Existence of the National Government* (New York: Rogers and Sherwood, 1879), 28–29.
162. Cochrane, *Memories*, 29–30.
163. Ibid., 30–31.
164. Ibid., 30.
165. Ibid., 31.
166. Ibid., 32.
167. Kelley, *Lincoln and Stanton: A Study of the War Administration of 1861 and 1862, with Special Consideration of Some Recent Statements of Gen. Geo. B. McClellan*, 75.
168. J.H. Stine, *History of the Army of the Potomac* (Philadelphia: J.B. Rodgers, 1892), 241.
169. McClellan, *McClellan's Own Story*, 650.
170. Stine, *History of the Army of the Potomac*, 242.
171. Brooks D. Simpson, "General McClellan's Bodyguard," in Gary W. Gallagher, *The Antietam Campaign* (Chapel Hill and London, University of North Carolina Press, 1999), 64.
172. Ibid., 66.
173. McClellan, *McClellan's Own Story*, 653.
174. Swinton, *Campaigns of the Army of the Potomac*, 228.
175. Thomas J. Rowland, *George B. McClellan and Civil War History* (Kent, Ohio: Kent State University Press, 1998), 159.

Chapter Six

1. *Report of the Joint Committee on the Conduct of the War*, vol. 1, p. 575.
2. Ibid., 578.
3. Ibid., 579.
4. Niven, *The Salmon P. Chase Papers*, vol. 1, pp. 398–397, Diary entry of 23 September 1862.
5. Walter H. Herbert, *Fighting Joe Hooker* (Lincoln: University of Nebraska Press, 1990), 117.
6. Meade, *Life and Letters of General George Gordon Meade*, vol. 1, p. 318, Letter dated 11 October 1862.
7. Ibid., 318–319, Letter to his wife 11 October 1862.
8. Herbert, *Fighting Joe Hooker*, 146.
9. Ibid., 148–149.
10. Ibid., 150–151.
11. Welles, *Diary of Gideon Welles*, 221.
12. Meade, *Life and Letters of General George Gordon Meade*, vol. 1, p. 332.
13. Stine, *History of the Army of the Potomac*, 246.
14. Swinton, *Campaigns of the Army of the Potomac*, 233.
15. *Official Records*, Series 1, vol. 21, pp. 46–47.
16. Stine, *History of the Army of the Potomac*, 247–249.
17. *Official Records*, Series 1, vol. 21, p. 47, Halleck to Stanton.

18. Stine, *History of the Army of the Potomac*, 244.
19. *Official Records*, Series 1, vol. 29, part 2, p. 565, Halleck to Burnside, 10 November 1862.
20. Ibid., 583–584, General Orders, Army of the Potomac, Number 184, 14 November 1862.
21. *Report of the Joint Committee on the Conduct of the War*, vol. 1, p. 657.
22. Snell, *From First to Last: The Life of Major General William B. Franklin*, 206.
23. Ibid., 207–208.
24. Basler, *The Collected Works of Abraham Lincoln*, vol. 5, pp. 514–515, Lincoln to Halleck, 27 November 1862.
25. Ibid., 509–510, Lincoln to Gen. Carl Schurz, 24 November 1862.
26. *Report of the Joint Committee on the Conduct of the War*, vol. 1, p. 672, Hooker's testimony.
27. Wert, *The Sword of Lincoln*, 204.
28. *Official Records*, Series 1, vol. 21, p. 66, Burnside to Halleck, 16 December 1862.
29. Ibid., 67, Burnside to Halleck, 17 December 1862.
30. Johnson, *Battles and Leaders of The Civil War: Retreat from Gettysburg*, vol. 3, "Franklin's 'Left Grand Division,'" by William Farrar Smith, 138.
31. Townsend, *Anecdotes of the Civil War in the United States*, 86.
32. *Report of the Joint Committee on the Conduct of the War*, vol. 1, pp. 673–676, Testimony of Halleck.
33. Snell, *From First to Last*, 228.
34. Perret, *Lincoln's War*, 231.
35. Thornton Kirkland Lothrop, *William Henry Seward* (Boston and New York: Houghton, Mifflin, 1898), 360.
36. Jamie L. Carson, Jeffery A. Jenkins, David W. Rohde, and Mark A. Souva, "The Impact of National Tides and District-Level Effects on Electoral Outcomes: The U.S. Congressional Elections of 1862–63," *American Journal of Political Science* 45, no. 4 (October 2001): 887–898.
37. Basler, *Collected Works of Lincoln*, vol. 5, pp. 510–511, Lincoln to Gen. Carl Schurz, 24 November 1862.
38. Perret, *Lincoln's War*, 231.
39. Welles, *Diary of Gideon Welles*, 194.
40. Beale, *Bates Diary*, 269, Diary entry of 19 December 1862.
41. Basler, *The Collected Works of Abraham Lincoln*, vol. 6, p. 9.
42. Bates, *Bates Diary*, 269.
43. McPherson, *Tried by War*, 146.
44. Beale, *Bates Diary*, 269, Diary entry of 19 December 1862.
45. Welles, *Diary of Gideon Welles*, 194.
46. Lothrop, *William Henry Seward*, 362.
47. Perret, *Lincoln's War*, 233.
48. Ibid.
49. Basler, *Collected Works of Abraham Lincoln*, vol. 6, p. 11, Letter to Chase, 20 December 1862.
50. Welles, *Diary of Gideon Welles*, 201–202
51. Basler, *Collected Works of Abraham Lincoln*, vol. 6, p. 12, Letter to Chase and Seward, 20 December 1862.
52. McPherson, *Tried by War*, 146.
53. John F. Reynolds, "Reynolds Diary," Letter to his sisters, 17 December 1862, (accessed 2 December 2009, http://library.fandm.edu/archives/Reynolds/JFR/inventory.html.
54. Rush C. Hawkins, "Why Burnside Did Not Renew the Attack at Fredericksburg," pp. 3–4, http://ehistory.osu.edu/osu/books/battles/vol3/index.cfm (accessed 3 December 2009).
55. Snell, *From First to Last*, 228.
56. Smith, *Autobiography of Major General William F. Smith*, 39.
57. Cochrane, *Memoirs*, 42.
58. Taaffe, *Commanding the Army of the Potomac*, 73.
59. *Official Records*, Series 1, vol. 21, pp. 868–870, Franklin and Smith to Lincoln, 20 December 1862.
60. Basler, *Collected Works of Lincoln*, vol. 6, pp. 16, 22 December 1862, Lincoln to Franklin and Smith.
61. Cochrane, *Memoirs*, 47.
62. *Official Records*, Series 1, vol. 21, p. 899, Letter dated 29 December 1862 to Hooker, who commanded Centre Grand Division and ordered the division be placed on 12 hours' notice for a march.
63. Cochrane, *Memoirs*, 31–32.
64. Niven, *The Salmon P. Chase Papers*, vol. 1, pp. 415, 423.
65. Cyrus B. Combstock, Memoir of John Newton, 1823–1895, pp. 235–236, http://books.nap.edu/html/biomems/jnewton.pdf (accessed 14 December 2009).
66. Cochrane, *Memoirs*, 48.
67. *Report of the Joint Committee on the Conduct of the War*, vol. 1, p. 731, Newton's testimony; Cochrane, *Memoirs*, 51.
68. Ibid., Newton's testimony.
69. Ibid., 741, Cochrane's testimony.
70. Ibid.
71. Ibid., 722, Burnside's testimony.
72. Ibid., 731, Newton's testimony.
73. Ibid.
74. Ibid., 711–712, Franklin's testimony.
75. Cochrane, *Memoirs*, 48.
76. Ibid., 50.
77. *Report of the Joint Committee on the Conduct of the War*, vol. 1, p. 731.
78. Cochrane, *Memoirs*, 48.

79. *Report of the Joint Committee on the Conduct of the War*, vol. 1, p. 58.
80. Ibid., 746, Cochrane's testimony.
81. Cochrane, *Memoirs*, 51.
82. *Report of the Joint Committee on the Conduct of the War*, vol. 1, p. 58.
83. Cochrane, *Memoirs*, 51.
84. *Report of the Joint Committee on the Conduct of the War*, vol. 1, p. 740, Newton's statement after he had read his testimony, 10 February 1863.
85. Cochrane, *Memoirs*, 51.
86. *Report of the Joint Committee on the Conduct of the War*, vol. 1, p. 58.
87. Cochrane, *Memoirs*, 51.
88. Ibid., 52.
89. *Official Records*, vol. 21, p. 900, Lincoln to Burnside, 30 December 1862.
90. *Report of the Joint Committee on the Conduct of the War*, vol. 1, p. 58.
91. *Official Records*, Series 1, vol. 21, p. 901, 30 December 1862, Parke to Hooker.
92. *Report of the Joint Committee on the Conduct of the War*, vol. 1, pp. 59, 718.
93. Ibid.
94. *Official Records*, Series 1, vol. 21, p. 941, Burnside to Lincoln, 1 January 1863.
95. Ibid.
96. *Report of the Joint Committee on the Conduct of the War*, vol. 1, pp. 59, 718.
97. McPherson, *Tried by War*, 157–158.
98. Emancipation Proclamation cited at "Emancipation Proclamation," http://www.archives.gov/exhibits/featured_documents/emancipation_proclamation/transcript.html (accessed 5 April 2010).
99. Taaffe, *Commanding the Army of the Potomac*, 76.
100. *Report of the Joint Committee on the Conduct of the War*, vol. 1, p. 59; *Official Records*, Series 1, vol. 21, p. 953, Halleck to Burnside, 7 January 1863.
101. Nevins, *A Diary of Battle*, 157–158.
102. *Official Records*, Series 1, vol. 21, p. 986, 20 January 1862, Special Orders, Headquarters Center Grand Division.
103. Swinton, *Campaigns of the Army of the Potomac*, 260.
104. John F Reynolds, "Reynolds Diary," Letter to his sister dated 23 January 1863, http://library.fandm.edu/archives/Reynolds/JFR/inventory.html (accessed 2 December 2009).
105. Meade, *Life and Letters of General George Gordon Meade*, vol. 1, p. 348.
106. *Report of the Joint Committee on the Conduct of the War*, vol. 1, p. 59.
107. Nevins, *A Diary of Battle*, 160.
108. McPherson, *Tried by War*, 162.
109. Swinton, *Campaigns of the Army of the Potomac*, 260–261.
110. Smith, *Autobiography of Major General William F. Smith*, 65–66.
111. Snell, *From First to Last: The Life of Major General William B. Franklin*, 248.
112. *New York Times*, "Loyalty of the West Point Graduates," 23 January 1863, "Disobedient and Unwilling Generals," 28 January 1863, "The Report of the War Committee: Its Revelations Regarding Gen. McClellan, Gen. Pope, Why McClellan was Not Before Displaced," 12 April 1863, http://query.nytimes.com (accessed 2 December 2009).
113. Sears, *Controversies and Commanders*, 67.
114. Gorham, *Life and Public Services of Edwin W. Stanton*, vol. 2, pp. 19–20.
115. Donald R. Jermann, *Fitz-John Porter, Scapegoat of Second Manassas: The Rise, Fall and Rise of the General Accused of Disobedience* (Jefferson, NC: McFarland, 2009), 216–220.
116. J. Gregory Acken, ed., *Inside the Army of the Potomac: The Civil War Experience of Captain Francis Adams Donaldson* (Mechanicsburg: Stackpole, 1998), 171.
117. Nevins, *A Diary of Battle*, 161.
118. *Report of the Joint Committee on the Conduct of the War*, vol. 1, p. 719.
119. *Official Records*, Series 1, vol. 21, pp. 998–999, 23 January 1863, Burnside to Lincoln.
120. Ibid.
121. *Report of the Joint Committee on the Conduct of the War*, vol. 1, p. 720.
122. Perret, *Lincoln's War*, 237.
123. Carl Schurz, cited in Bruce Catton, *The Army of the Potomac: Glory Road* (Garden City: Doubleday, 1952), 97.
124. *Official Records*, Series 1, vol. 25, part 2, p. 78.
125. Francis A. Walker, *History of the Second Army Corps in the Army of the Potomac* (New York: Charles Scribner's Sons, 1886), 198.
126. Basler, *Collected Works of Lincoln*, 78, Lincoln to Halleck, 25 January 1863.
127. Meade, *Life and Letters of General George Gordon Meade*, vol. 1, p. 351, Letter to his wife, 26 January 1863.
128. McPherson, *Tried by War*, 163.
129. Williams, *Lincoln and His Generals*, 210.
130. Ibid., 211.
131. Johnson, *Battles And Leaders of the Civil War*, vol. 3, *Retreat from Gettysburg*, "Hooker's Appointment and Removal," 240.
132. Browning, *The Diary of Orville Hickman Browning*, vol. 1, p. 619.
133. *Official Records*, Series 1, vol. 21, pp. 1008–1009, 29 May 1863, Halleck to Franklin.
134. Williams, *Lincoln and His Generals*, 206.
135. *Report of the Joint Committee on the Conduct of the War*, vol. 1, pp. 720–722.

136. *Official Records*, Series 1, vol. 25, part 2, p. 3, 25 January 1863.
137. Taaffe, *Commanding the Army of the Potomac*, 80.

Chapter Seven

1. Herbert, *Fighting Joe Hooker*, 48.
2. Milton H. Shutes, "'Fighting Joe' Hooker," *California Historical Society Quarterly* 16, no. 4 (December 1937), 304–320.
3. Ibid., 308.
4. Herbert, *Fighting Joe Hooker*, 49.
5. *Official Records*, Series 1, vol. 21, pp. 1004–5.
6. Ibid., 5, General Orders No. 1, 26 January 1863.
7. Basler, *Collected Works of Lincoln*, vol. 6, pp. 78–79.
8. Brooks, *Washington in Lincoln's Time*, 52–53.
9. Brooks, *Abraham Lincoln*, 356–357.
10. *Report of the Joint Committee on the Conduct of the War*, vol. 4, pp. 111–112.
11. *Official Records*, Series 1, vol. 25, part 2, p. 13, 7 January 1863, Halleck to Burnside.
12. Taaffe, *Commanding the Army of the Potomac*, 84–85; McPherson, *Tried by War*, 164.
13. Basler, *Collected Works of Lincoln*, vol. 6, pp. 132–133, Proclamation Granting Amnesty to Soldiers Absent Without Leave, 10 March 1863.
14. *Official Records*, Series 1, vol. 25, part 2, p. 51, General Orders No. 6, 5 February 1863.
15. *Official Records*, Series 1, vol. 24, part 3, p. 22, Halleck to Grant, 20 March 1863.
16. McPherson, *Tried by War*, 168–169.
17. Beale, *The Diary of Edward Bates*, 287.
18. Herbert, *Fighting Joe Hooker*, 182–183; Perret, *Lincoln's War*, 240.
19. Basler, *Collected Works of Abraham Lincoln*, vol. 6, p. 164.
20. See James M. McPherson, "Lincoln and the Strategy of Unconditional Surrender," in *Lincoln, the War President: The Gettysburg Lectures*, Gabor S. Boritt, ed. (New York: Oxford University Press, 1992), 45.
21. Basler, *Collected Works of Abraham Lincoln*, vol. 6, pp. 164–165.
22. William G. Le Duc, *This Business of War: The Recollections of a Civil War Quartermaster* (Minnesota Historical Society Press, 2004), 120.
23. Sears, *Chancellorsville*, 116.
24. *Official Records*, Series 1, vol. 25, part 2, pp. 199–200, Hooker to Lincoln, 11 April 1863.
25. Ibid., 214, Hooker to Lincoln, 15 April 1863, 9:15 p.m.
26. Ibid., Lincoln to Hooker, 15 April 1863, 10:15 p.m.
27. Ibid., 220–22, Stoneman to Brig. Gen. S. Williams, Assistant Adjutant-General, Army of the Potomac, 16 April 1863.
28. Sears, *Chancellorsville*, 127.
29. Basler, *The Collected Works of Abraham Lincoln*, vol. 6, p. 190, Hooker to Lincoln, 27 April 1863.
30. Cited in Hattaway and Jones, *How the North Won*, 380.
31. Hattaway and Jones, *How the North Won*, 380–381.
32. *Official Records*, Series 1, vol. 25, part 1, p. 171, General Orders Number 47, 30 April 1863.
33. Gambone, *Major General Darius Nash Couch*, 135.
34. Meade, *Life and Letters of General Meade*, vol. 1, p. 372, Meade to his wife, 8 May 1863.
35. Hattaway and Jones, *How the North Won*, 380–382.
36. Ibid., 383–384.
37. Taaffe, *Commanding the Army of the Potomac*, 97.
38. Meade, *Life and Letters*, vol. 1, p. 372.
39. John Bigelow, *The campaign of Chancellorsville: A Strategic and Tactical Study* (New Haven: Yale University Press, 1910).
40. Sears, *Chancellorsville*, 504–505.
41. Brooks, *Abraham Lincoln*, 357–358.
42. *Official Records*, Series 1, vol. 25, part 1, p. 171, General Orders No. 49, May 6 1863.
43. Basler, *Collected Works of Lincoln*, vol. 6, p. 210.
44. *Report of the Joint Committee on the Conduct of the War*, vol. 4, xlix.
45. Williams, *Lincoln and His Generals*, 243.
46. Meade, *Life and Letters of General Meade*, vol. 1, p. 372, Meade to his wife, 8 May 1863.
47. Basler, *Collected Works of Lincoln*, vol. 6, p. 202.
48. *Official Records*, Series 1, vol. 25, part 2, pp. 504–507, Halleck to Stanton, 18 May 1863.
49. Basler, *Collected Works of Lincoln*, vol. 6, p. 202.
50. Williams, *Lincoln and His Generals*, 245.
51. Swinton, *Campaigns of the Army of the Potomac*, 307.
52. Meade, *Life and Letters of General Meade*, vol. 1, p. 373, Meade to his wife, 8 May 1863.
53. T. Harry Williams, *Lincoln and His Generals*, 238.
54. Charles Benjamin, "Hooker's Appointment and Removal," in Johnson, *Battles and Leaders*, vol. 3, pp. 240–241.
55. Benjamin, "Hooker's Appointment and Removal," in *Battles and Leaders*, vol. 3, p. 241.
56. Meade, *Life and Letters of General Meade*, vol. 1, p. 373, Meade to his wife, 8 May 1863.

57. *Official Records*, Series 1, vol. 25, part 2, pp. 438–439.
58. Benjamin, "Hookers Appointment and Removal," in *Battles and Leaders*, 241.
59. Welles, *Diary*, 329, Diary entry of 15 June 1863.
60. Adam Gurowski, *Diary, from November 18, 1862, to October 18, 1863*, vol. 2 (New York: Carleton, 1864), 240–241.
61. *Official Records*, Series 1, vol. 25, part 2, pp. 473, 474.
62. Ibid., 14 May 1863, Lincoln to Hooker.
63. *Report of the Joint Committee on the Conduct of the War*, vol. 4, p. 151, Hooker's testimony.
64. A.M. Gambone, *Major General Darius Nash Couch: Enigmatic Valor* (Baltimore: Butternut and Blue, 2000), 137.
65. Ibid., 135.
66. Welles, *Diary*, 336, Diary entry of 20 June 1863.
67. *Report of the Joint Committee on the Conduct of the War*, vol. 4, p. 151, Hooker's testimony.
68. Meade, *Life and Letters of General Meade*, vol. 1, pp. 373–377.
69. Edward J. Nichols, *Toward Gettysburg: A Biography of General John F. Reynolds* (Philadelphia: Pennsylvania State University Press, 1958),181.
70. Nichols, *Toward Gettysburg: A Biography of General John F. Reynolds*, 181.
71. Meade, *Life and Letters*, vol. 1, p. 378, Letter of 19 May 1863.
72. Nichols, *Towards Gettysburg*, 181.
73. *Official Records*, Series 1, vol. 27, part 1, p. 30, Hooker to Lincoln, 5 June 1863.
74. Ibid., 34–35, Hooker to Lincoln, 10 June 1863.
75. Ibid., 35, Lincoln to Hooker, 10 June 1862.
76. Ibid., 38, Halleck to Hooker, 13 June 1863.
77. Ibid., 39, Lincoln to Hooker, 14 June 1863.
78. Ibid., 44, Hooker to Lincoln, 15 and 16 June 1863.
79. Ibid., 45, Hooker to Lincoln, 16 June 1863.
80. Herman Haupt, *Reminiscences of General Herman Haupt* (Milwaukee: Wright and Joys, 1901), 205.
81. Ibid., 205–206.
82. *Official Records*, Series 1, vol. 27, part 1, p. 45, Halleck to Hooker, 11:30 a.m., 16 June 1863.
83. Ibid., 45–46, Halleck to Hooker, 3:50 p.m., 16 June 1863.
84. Ibid., 46, Hooker to Halleck, 4:00 p.m., 16 June 1863.
85. Ibid., Hooker to Halleck, 7:30 p.m., 16 June 1863.
86. Ibid., 47, Hooker to Lincoln, 9:40 p.m., 16 June 1863.
87. Ibid., 45, Hooker to Lincoln, 11:00 a.m., 16 June 1863.
88. Ibid., 47, Halleck Hooker, 10:15 p.m., 16 June 1863.
89. Basler, *Collected Works of Lincoln*, vol. 6, pp. 281–282.
90. Ibid., 58–60, Hooker to Halleck, 26 June, 27 June.
91. Ibid., 60, Hooker to Halleck, 27 June.
92. Ambrose, *Halleck*, 135.
93. Welles, *Diary of Gideon Welles*, 348, Diary entry of 28 June 1863.
94. Ibid.
95. Ibid.
96. *Official Records*, Series 1, vol. 27, part 1, p. 61, Halleck to Meade, 27 June 1863.
97. Nichols, *Toward Gettysburg*, 220–223.
98. Meade, *Life and Letters*, vol. 1, p. 385, 13 June 1863.
99. Eleanor Reynolds cited in Nichols, *Toward Gettysburg*, 220–221.
100. *Official Records*, Series 1, vol. 27, part 1, p. 61, Halleck to Meade, 27 June 1863.
101. Ibid., 66–67, Meade to Halleck, 29 June 1863.
102. Ibid., 69, Haupt to Halleck, 30 June 1863.
103. Ibid., 70–71.
104. Ibid., 70, Halleck to Meade, 1 July 1863.
105. Ibid.
106. Basler, *Collected Works of Lincoln*, vol. 6, p. 312.
107. Ibid., 311.
108. Hattaway and Jones, *How the North Won*, 404–409.
109. McPherson, *Battle Cry of Freedom*, 665.
110. Wert, *Sword of Lincoln*, 305.
111. Stoker, *The Grand Design*, 302.
112. Hattaway and Jones, *How the North Won*, 415.
113. Swinton, *Campaigns of the Army of the Potomac*, 372.
114. McPherson, *Battle Cry of Freedom*, 663–664.
115. Ibid., 666.
116. *Official Records*, Series 1, vol. 27, part 3, p. 519.
117. Wert, *The Sword of Lincoln*, 305.
118. *Official Records*, Series 1, vol. 27, part 1, pp. 82–83, Halleck to Meade, 7 July 1863.
119. Ibid., 83, Lincoln to Halleck, 7 July 1863.
120. Ibid., 84, Meade to Halleck, 8 July 1863.
121. David H. Bates, *Lincoln in the Telegraph Office: Recollections of the United States Military Telegraphcorps During the Civil War* (New York: Century, 1907),156–157.
122. *Official Records*, Series 1, vol. 27, part 1, pp. 91–92, Meade to Halleck, 13 July 1863.

123. Ibid., 92, Halleck to Meade, 13 July 1863.
124. Ibid., Meade to Halleck, 14 July 1863.
125. Welles, *Diary,* 370–371, Entry of 14 July 1863.
126. *Official Records,* Series 1, vol. 27, part 1, p. 92, Halleck to Meade, 14 July 1863.
127. Ibid., 93, Meade to Halleck, 14 July 1863.
128. Williams, "The Committee on the Conduct of the War: An Experiment in Civilian Control," 153.

129. *Official Records,* Series 1, vol. 27, part 1, pp. 93–94, Halleck to Meade, 14 July 1863.
130. Meade, *Life and Letters,* 312, Appendix D, McClellan to Meade, 11 July 1863.
131. Hattaway and Jones, *How the North Won,* 465–479.
132. Taaffe, *Commanding the Army of the Potomac,* 144.
133. *Official Records,* Series 1, vol. 33, part 1, p. 663, Stanton to Foster, 10 March 1864, Stanton to Grant.

Bibliography

Primary Sources

Bates, David H. *Lincoln in the Telegraph Office: Recollections of the United States Military Telegraphcorps During the Civil War.* New York: Century, 1907.

Browning, Orville Hickman. *The Diary of Orville Hickman Browning.* Vol. 1, 1850–1864. Springfield: Illinois State Historical Library, 1925.

Cochrane, John. *American Civil War: Memories of Incidents Connected with the Origin and Culmination of the Rebellion That Threatened the Existence of the National Government.* New York: Rogers and Sherwood, 1879.

Cozens, Peter, and Robert I. Girardi. *The Military Memoirs of General John Pope.* Chapel Hill: University of North Carolina Press, 1998.

Dana, Charles A. *Recollections of the Civil War: With the Leaders at Washington and in the Field in the Sixties.* New York: D. Appleton, 1898.

De Joinville, The Prince. *The Army of the Potomac: Its Organization, Its Commanders and Its Campaign.* New York: Anson D.F. Randolph, 1862.

Franklin, William B. "The First Great Crime of the War." In *The Annals of the War.* J.M. Harper. London: Musson, 1913.

Gurowski, Adam. *Diary from November 18, 1862, to October 18, 1863.* Vol. 2. New York: Carleton, 1864.

Haupt, Herman. *Reminiscences of General Herman Haupt.* Milwaukee: Wright & Joys, 1901.

Hay, John. *Letters of John Hay and Extracts from Diary.* 3 vols. Washington: Printed not published, 1908.

———. *Lincoln and the Civil War in the Diary and Letters of John Hay.* Connecticut: Negro University Press, 1939.

Howard, Oliver Otis. *Autobiography of Oliver Otis Howard, Major General, United States Army.* New York: Baker & Taylor, 1907.

Joint Committee on the Conduct of the War. *Report of the Joint Committee on the Conduct of the War.* Washington: Government Printing Office, 1863.

Keyes, E.D. *Fifty Years' Observation of Men and Events Civil and Military.* New York: Charles Scribner's Sons, 1885.

Lincoln, Abraham. *Life And Works of Abraham Lincoln.* Vol. 6. State Papers, 1861–1865. Edited by Marion M. Miller. New York: Current Literature, 1907.

McClellan, George B. *McClellan's Own Story: The War for the Union; the Soldiers Who Fought It, the Civilians Who Directed It, and His Relations to It and to Them.* New York: C.L. Webster, 1887.

———. *Report of Major-General George B. McClellan Upon the Organization of the Army of the Potomac, Its Campaigns in Virginia and Maryland, from July 26, 1861, to November 7, 1862.* Boston: Office of the Boston Courier, 1864.

Meade, George C. *Life and Letters of General George Gordon Meade.* 3 vols. New York: Scribner's, 1913.

Myers, William Starr, ed. The *Mexican War Diary of George B. McClellan.* Princeton: Princeton University Press, 1917.

Nevin, Allan, ed. *The Diary of George Templeton Strong: The Civil War Years, 1860–1865.* 3 vols. New York: Macmillan, 1952.

Pease, Theodore, and James Randall, ed. *Diary of Orville Hickman Browning.* Vol. 1, 1850–1864. Springfield: Illinois State Historical Library, 1925.

Piatt, Don. *Memories of the Men Who Saved the Union.* New York and Chicago: Belford, Clarke, 1887.

Pope, John. Report of Major-General John Pope. Letter from the secretary of war, in answer to resolution of the House of 18th ultimo, transmitting copy of report of Major General John Pope. March 3, 1863. Laid on the table and ordered to be printed. Washington, 1863.

Porter, David D. *Incidents and Anecdotes of the Civil War*. New York: D. Appleton, 1885.

Official Records of the Union and Confederate Navies in the War of the Rebellion. Washington: Government Printing Office, 1894.

Official Records of the War of the Rebellion. Washington: Government Printing Office, 1880.

Seward, Frederick William. *Reminiscences of a War-Time Statesman and Diplomat, 1830–1915*. New York: G.P. Putnam's Sons, 1916.

Smith, William F. *Autobiography of Major General William F. Smith, 1861–1864*. Edited by Herbert Schiller. Dayton: Morningside, 1990.

Stanton, Edwin, M. *The Diary of a Public Man*. New Brunswick: Rutgers University Press, 1946.

Stedman, Edmund Clarence. *Life and Letters of Edmund Clarence Stedman*. New York: Moffat, 1910.

Swinton, William. *McClellan's Military Career Reviewed and Exposed: The Military Policy of the Administration Set Forth and Vindicated*. Washington: Samuel Towers, 1864.

Thayer, William Roscoe. *The Life and Letters of John Hay*. 2 vols. Boston and New York: Houghton and Mifflin, 1915.

Townsend, E.D. *Anecdotes of the Civil War in the United States*. New York: Appleton, 1884.

Williams, Alpheus S. *From the Cannon's Mouth: The Civil War Letters of General Alpheus S. Williams*. Detroit: Wayne State University Press, 1959.

Welles, Gideon. *Diary of Gideon Welles*. Boston and New York: Houghton, 1911.

Secondary Sources

BOOKS

Acken, J. Gregory, ed. *Inside the Army of the Potomac: The Civil War Experience of Captain Francis Adams Donaldson*. Mechanicsburg: Stackpole, 1998.

Ambrose, Stephen E. *Halleck: Lincoln's Chief of Staff*. Baton Rouge: Louisiana State University Press, 1962.

Baker, George E., ed. *The Works of William H. Seward*. 1853–1884. 5 vols. New York: AMS, 1972.

Basler, Roy P., Marion Dolores Pratt, and Lloyd A. Dunlap, ed. *The Collected Works of Abraham Lincoln*. 9 vols. New Brunswick, NJ: Rutgers University Press, 1953.

Beale, Howard K. *The Diary of Edward Bates, 1859–1866*. Washington: United States Printing Office, 1933.

Beatie, Russel H. *Army of the Potomac: Birth of Command, November 1860–September 1861*. Cambridge: Da Capo, 2002.

_____. *Army of the Potomac: McClellan Takes Command, September 1861–February 1862*. Cambridge: Da Capo, 2004.

_____. *Army of the Potomac: McClellan's First Campaign, March–May 1862*. Cambridge: Da Capo, 2007.

Bigelow, John. *The Campaign of Chancellorsville: A Strategic and Tactical Study*. New Haven: Yale University Press, 1910.

Brooks, Noah. *Abraham Lincoln*. New York: Fred DeFau, 1894.

_____. *Washington in Lincoln's Time*. New York: Century, 1895.

Brown, Richard D. *Major Problems in the Era of the American Revolution, 1760–1791*. Lexington: D.C. Heath, 1992.

Burlingame, Michael, ed. *With Lincoln in the White House: Letters, Memoranda, and Other Writings of John G. Nicolay, 1860–1865*. Carbondale: Southern Illinois University Press, 2000.

Catton, Bruce. *The Army of the Potomac: Glory Road*. Garden City: Doubleday, 1952.

_____. *Mr. Lincoln's Army*. Garden City: Doubleday, 1951.

Chambers, John Whiteclay. *Major Problems in American Military History*. Boston: Houghton Mifflin 1999.

Cohen, Eliot A. *Supreme Command*. New York: Free Press, 2002.

Conrad, Bryan, and H.J. Eckenrode. *George B. McClellan: The Man Who Saved the Union*. Chapel Hill: University of North Carolina Press, 1941.

Corwin, Edward S. *The President: Office and Powers, 1787–1957*. 4th ed. New York: New York University Press, 1957.

Coyle, David Cushman. *Ordeal of the Presidency*. Westport: Greenwood, 1960.

Cunliffe, Marcus. *Soldiers and Civilians: The Martial Spirit in America, 1775–1865*. Boston: Little, Brown, 1968.

Dana, Charles A. *Lincoln and His Cabinet*. "A Lecture Delivered Before the New Haven Colony Historical Society, Tuesday, March 10, 1896." Souvenir of the Thirteenth Annual Lincoln Dinner of the Republican Club of the City of New-York, 1899.

Davis, William C. *Battle at Bull Run*. Baton Rouge: Louisiana State University Press, 1977.

Dolce, Philip C., ed. *Power and the Presidency*. New York: Charles Scriber's Sons, 1976.

Donald, David. *Inside Lincoln's Cabinet: The*

Civil War Diaries of Salmon P. Chase. New York: Longmans Green, 1954.

Dougherty, Kevin, and Michael Moore. *The Peninsula Campaign of 1862: A Military Analysis.* Jackson: University Press of Mississippi, 2005.

Dupuy, R. Ernest, *Military Heritage of America.* New York: McGraw-Hill, 1956.

Fitzpatrick, John C. *George Washington Himself.* Westport: Greenwood, 1933.

Gallagher, Gary W., ed. *The Antietam Campaign.* Chapel Hill: University of North Carolina Press, 1999.

Galvin, John R. *The Minute Men: The First Fight; Myths and Realities of the American Revolution.* Washington: Pergamon-Brassey's, 1989.

Gambone, A.M. *Major General Darius Nash Couch: Enigmatic Valor.* Baltimore: Butternut & Blue, 2000.

Glatthaar, Joseph T. *Partners in Command: The Relationships Between Leaders in the Civil War.* New York: Free Press, 1994.

Gorham, George C. *Life and Public Services of Edwin W. Stanton.* 2 vols. Boston and New York: Houghton, Mifflin, 1899.

Goss, Thomas J. *The War Within the Union High Command: Politics and Generalship During the Civil War.* Kansas: University Press of Kansas, 2003.

Grimsley, Mark. *the Hard Hand of War: Union Military Policy Towards Southern Civilians, 1861–1865.* New York: Cambridge University Press, 1995.

Hassler, Warren W., Jr. *General George B. McClellan, Shield of the Union.* Baton Rouge: Louisiana State University Press, 1957.

Hattaway, Herman. *Shades of Blue and Gray: An Introductory Military History of the Civil War.* Columbia: University Press of Missouri, 1997.

Hattaway, Herman, and Archer Jones. *How the North Won: A Military History of the Civil War.* Urbana: University of Illinois Press, 1983.

Hay, John G. *Abraham Lincoln: A History.* Vol. 5. New York: Century, 1890.

Hearn, Chester G. *The Capture of New Orleans, 1862.* Baton Rouge: Louisiana State University Press, 1995.

Hennessy, John J. *Return to Bull Run: The Campaign and Battle of Second Manassas.* Norman: University of Oklahoma Press, 1993.

Herbert, Walter H. *Fighting Joe Hooker.* Lincoln: University of Nebraska Press, 1990.

Higginbottom, Don. "The Strengths and Weaknesses of the Militia." In *Major Problems in the Era of the American Revolution, 1769–1791.* Lexington: D.C. Heath, 1992.

Hitchcock, Ethan Allen. *Fifty Years in Camp and Field: Diary of Major General Ethan Allen Hitchcock, U.S.A.* Edited by W.A. Croffut. New York: G.P. Putnam's Sons, 1909.

Holbrook, Stewart H. *Lost Men of American History.* New York: Macmillan, 1946.

Huntington, Samuel P. *The Soldier and the State: The Theory and Politics of the Civil-Military Relations.* Cambridge: Belknap, 1957.

Hynes, Samuel. *The Soldiers' Tale: Bearing Witness to Modern War.* New York: Penguin, 1997.

Jermann, Donald R. *Fitz John Porter, Scapegoat of Second Manassas: The Rise, Fall and Rise of the General Accused of Disobedience.* Jefferson, NC: McFarland, 2009.

Johnson, Robert Underwood. *Battles and Leaders of the Civil War: Retreat from Gettysburg.* Vol. 3. New York: Century, 1887–1888.

Johnson, Timothy D. *Winfield Scott: The Quest for Military Glory.* Lawrence: University Press of Kansas, 1998.

Jones, Archer. *Civil War Command and Strategy: The Process of Victory and Defeat.* New York: Free Press, 1992.

Keegan, John. *The American Civil War: A Military History.* London: Vintage, 2010.

Kelley, W.M.D. *Lincoln and Stanton: A Study of the War Administration, 1861 and 1862, with Special Consideration of Some Recent Statements of Gen Geo B. McClellan.* New York: G. P. Putnam and Sons, 1885.

Le Duc, William G. *This Business of War: The Recollections of a Civil War Quartermaster.* Minnesota Historical Society Press, 2004.

Lothrop, Thornton Kirkland. *William Henry Seward.* Boston and New York: Houghton, Mifflin, 1898.

May, Ernest R., ed. *The Ultimate Decision: The President as Commander in Chief.* New York: George Brazillier, 1960.

May, Robert E. "An Officer Corps Responds to Opportunities for Expansion with Images of Heroic Expeditions." In John Whiteclay Chambers, *Major Problems in American Military History.* Boston: Houghton Mifflin, 1999.

McClure, A.K. *Abraham Lincoln and Men of War-Time.* 4th ed. Lincoln: University of Nebraska Press, 1892.

McPherson, James M. *Battle Cry of Freedom.* New York: Oxford University Press, 1988

_____. *Drawn with the Sword: Reflections on the American Civil War.* New York: Oxford University Press, 1996.

_____. "Lincoln and the Strategy of Unconditional Surrender." In *Lincoln, the War President: The Gettysburg Lectures.* Edited by Gabor S. Boritt. New York: Oxford University Press, 1992.

_____. *Tried by War: Abraham Lincoln as Commander in Chief.* New York: Penguin, 2008.

Myers, William Starr, ed. *The Mexican War Diary of George B. McClellan*. Princeton: Princeton University Press, 1917.

Neely, Mark E., Jr. "The Generalship of Grant and Sherman: Was the Civil War a Modern 'Total' War? A Dissenting View." In *Major Problems in American Military History: Documents and Essays*. Edited by John Whiteclay Chambers II and G. Kurt Piehler. Boston: Houghton Mifflin, 1999.

Nevins, Allan, ed. *A Diary of Battle: The Personal Journals of Colonel Charles S. Wainwright, 1861–1865*. New York: Da Capo, 1962.

Nichols, Edward J. *Toward Gettysburg: A Biography of General John F. Reynolds*. Philadelphia: Pennsylvania State University Press, 1958.

Niven, John, ed. *The Salmon P. Chase Papers*. Kent, OH: Kent State University, 1993.

Perret, Geoffrey. *Lincoln's War: The Untold Story of America's Greatest President as Commander in Chief*. New York: Random House, 2004.

Pratt, Fletcher, *Stanton: Lincoln's Secretary of War*. Westport: Greenwood, 1970.

Rafuse, Ethan S. *McClellan's War: The Failure of Moderation in the Struggle for the Union*. Bloomington: Indiana University Press, 2005.

_____. *A Single Grand Victory: The First Campaign and Battle of Manassas*. Wilmington: Scholarly Resources, 2002.

Randall, James G. *Lincoln, the President*. 4 vols. New York: Dodd, Mead, 1945–55.

Rowland, Thomas J. *George B. McClellan and Civil War History*. Kent, OH: Kent State University Press, 1998.

Schlesinger, Arthur M., Jr. *The Imperial Presidency*. Boston: Houghton Mifflin, 1973.

Sears, Stephen W. *Chancellorsville*. New York: Houghton Mifflin, 1996.

_____. *Controversies and Commanders: Dispatches from the Army of the Potomac*. Boston: Houghton Mifflin, 1999.

_____. *George McClellan: The Young Napoleon*. New York: Ticknor & Fields, 1988.

_____. *Landscape Turned Red: The Battle of Antietam*. New York: Ticknor & Fields, 1983.

_____. *To the Gates of Richmond: The Peninsula Campaign*. New York: Ticknor & Fields, 1992.

_____, ed. *The Civil War Papers of George B. McClellan: Selected Correspondence, 1860–1865*. New York: Ticknor & Fields, 1989.

Shy, John. "American Wars as Crusades for Total Victory." In *Major Problems in the Era of the American Revolution, 1769–1791*. Lexington: D.C. Heath, 1992.

Skelton, William B. *An American Profession of Arms: The Army Officer Corps, 1784–1861*. Lawrence: University of Press of Kansas, 1992.

_____. "An Officer Corps Responds to an Undisciplined Society by Disciplined Professionalism." In *Major Problems in American Military History*. Boston: Houghton Mifflin, 1999.

Snell, Mark A. *From First to Last: The Life of Major General William B. Franklin*. New York: Fordham University Press, 2002.

Stewart, Richard W. ed. *American Military History*. Vol. 1, *The United States Army and the Forging of a Nation, 1775–1917*. Washington, D.C.: Center of Military History, United States Army, 2005.

Stine, J.H. *History of the Army of the Potomac*. Philadelphia: J.B. Rodgers, 1892.

Stoddard, William Osborne. *Lincoln at Work: Sketches from Life*. Boston: United Society of Christian Endeavor, 1900.

Stoker, Donald. *The Grand Design: Strategy and the U.S. Civil War*. Oxford: Oxford University Press, 2010.

Swinton, William. *Campaigns of the Army of the Potomac*. New York: Charles B. Richardson, 1866.

_____. *McClellan's Military Career Reviewed and Exposed: The Military Policy of the Administration Set Forth and Vindicated*. Washington: Samuel Towers, 1864.

Taaffe, Stephen R. *Commanding the Army of the Potomac*. Lawrence: University Press of Kansas, 2006.

Tap, Bruce. *Over Lincoln's Shoulder: The Committee on the Conduct of the War*. Lawrence: University Press of Kansas, 1998.

Thomas, Benjamin P., and Harold M. Hyman. *Stanton: The Life and Times of Lincoln's Secretary of War*. New York: Alfred A. Knopf, 1962.

Trenerry, Walter N., and Wallace J. Schultz. *Abandoned by Lincoln: A Military Biography of General John Pope*. Chicago: University Press of Illinois, 1990.

Walker, Francis A. *History of the Second Army Corps in the Army of the Potomac*. New York: Charles Scribner's Sons, 1886.

Webb, Alexander Stuart. *The Peninsula: McClellan's Campaign of 1862*. New York: Charles Scribner's Sons, 1882.

Weigley, Russell F. *The American Way of War: A History of United States Military Strategy and Policy*. Bloomington: Indiana University Press, 1973.

_____. *A Great Civil War: A Military and Political History, 1861–1865*. Bloomington: Indiana University Press, 2000.

_____. "How Americans Wage War: The Evolution of National Strategy." In John Whiteclay Chambers, *Major Problems in American Military History*. Boston: Houghton Mifflin, 1999.

_____. *Towards an American Army*. New York: Columbia University Press, 1962.

Wert, Jeffrey D. *The Sword of Lincoln: The Army of the Potomac*. New York: Simon & Schuster, 2005.

Whiting, William. *The War Powers of the President and the Legislative Powers of Congress in Relation to Rebellion, Treason and Slavery*. Boston: John L. Shorey, 1862.

Williams, T. Harry. *The History of America's Wars*. New York: Alfred A. Knopf, 1981.

_____. *Lincoln and His Generals*. New York: Gramercy, 1952.

_____. *Lincoln and the Radicals*. Madison: University of Wisconsin Press, 1972.

_____. "The Military Leadership of North and South." In David H. Donald, ed., *Why the North Won the Civil War*. Baton Rouge: Louisiana State University Press, 1960.

Williams, Kenneth P. *Lincoln Finds a General: A Military Study of the Civil War*. New York: Macmillan, 1949.

Wilson, James Harrison. *The Life of Charles A. Dana*. New York: Harper, 1907.

Woodworth, Steven E. *Jefferson Davis and His Generals: The Failure of Confederate Command in the West*. Kansas: University Press of Kansas, 1990.

Journal Articles

Ambrose, Stephen E. "Lincoln and Halleck: A Study in Personal Relations." *Journal of the Illinois State Historical Society* 52, no. 1 (1908–1984). Lincoln Sesquicentennial, Spring 1959.

Carson, Jamie L., Jeffery A. Jenkins, David W. Rohde, and Mark A. Souva. "The Impact of National Tides and District-Level Effects on Electoral Outcomes: The U.S. Congressional Elections of 1862–63." *American Journal of Political Science* 45, no. 4 (October 2001).

Coffman, Edward M. "The Duality of the American Military Tradition: A Commentary." *Journal of Military History* 64, no. 4 (October 2000).

Cooling, Franklin B. "Civil War Deterrent: Defenses of Washington." *Military Affairs* 29, no. 4 (Winter 1965–1966).

Dwyer, Philip G. "Public Remembering, Private Reminiscing: French Military Memoirs and the Revolutionary and Napoleonic Wars." *French Historical Studies* 33, no. 2 (Spring 2010).

Epstein, Robert M. "The Creation and Evolution of the Army Corps in the American Civil War." *Journal of Military History* 55, no. 1 (January 1991).

Hacker, J. David. "A Census-Based Count of the Civil War Dead." *Civil War History* 57, no. 4 (December 2011).

Hattaway, Herman, and Archer Jones. "The War Board: The Basis of the United States First General Staff." *Military Affairs* 46, no. 1 (February 1982).

Meigs, Montgomery C. "General M.C. Meigs on the Conduct of the Civil War." *American Historical Review* 26, no. 2 (January 1921).

Morrisaon, James L., Jr. "Educating the Civil War Generals: West Point, 1833–1861." *Military Affairs* 38, no. 3 (October 1974).

Pierson, William Whatey, Jr. "The Committee on the Conduct of the Civil War." *American Historical Review* 23, no. 3 (April 1918).

Rafuse, Ethan S. "McClellan and Halleck at War: The Struggle for Control of the Union War Effort in the West, November 1861–March 1862." *Civil War History* 49, no. 1 (March 2003).

Reid, Brian Holden. "Historians and the Joint Committee on the Conduct of the War, 1861–1865." *Civil War History* 38 (December 1992).

Shutes, Milton H., "'Fighting Joe' Hooker." *California Historical Society Quarterly* 16, no. 4 (December 1937).

Sutherland, Daniel E. "Abraham Lincoln, John Pope, and the Origins of Total War." *Journal of Military History* 56, no. 4 (October 1992).

Weigley, Russell F. *The Journal of Military History* 57, no. 5. Special Issue: Proceedings of the Symposium on "The History of War as Part of General History" at the Institute for Advanced Studies, Princeton, New Jersey (October 1993).

Williams, T. Harry. "The Attack Upon West Point During the Civil War." *Mississippi Valley Historical Review* 25, no. 4 (March 1939).

_____. "The Committee on the Conduct of the War: An Experiment in Civilian Control." *Journal of the American Military Institute* 3, no. 3 (Autumn 1939).

Online

"American Presidents from Revolution to Reconstruction." http://odur.let.rug.nl/~usa/P/tj3/index.htm (accessed 5 September 2006).

"Century of Lawmaking for a New Nation: U.S. Congressional Documents and Debates, 1774–1875," Statutes at Large, 37th Congress, 1st Session, 294. http://memory.loc.gov/ammem/amlaw/lawhome.html (accessed 5 October 2007).

Combstock, Cyrus, B. "Memoir of John Newton, 1823–1895." http://books.nap.edu/html/biomems/jnewton.pdf (accessed 14 December 2009).

Emancipation Proclamation. http://www.archives.gov/exhibits/featured_documents/

emancipation_proclamation/transcript.html (accessed 5 April 2010).

Harper's Weekly: A Journal of Civilization. http://www.sonofthesouth.net/ (accessed 29 November 2006).

Hawkins, Rush C. "Why Burnside Did Not Renew the Attack at Fredericksburg." http://ehistory.osu.edu/osu/books/battles/vol3/index.cfm (accessed 3 December 2009).

Militia Act of 1792, Second Congress, Session I. Chapter XXVIII. http://www.constitution.org/mil/mil_act_1792.htm (accessed 25 August 2006).

New York Times. http://query.nytimes.com (accessed 2 December 2009).

Rafuse, Ethan S. "Typhoid and Tumult: Lincoln's Response to General McClellan's Bout with Typhoid Fever During the Winter of 1861–62." *Journal of the Abraham Lincoln Association* (Summer 1997). http://www.historycooperative.org/journals/jala/18.2/rafuse.html (accessed 5 February 2008).

Reynolds, John F. "Reynolds Diary." http://library.fandm.edu/archives/Reynolds/JFR/inventory.html (accessed 2 December 2009).

Taft, Horatio Nelson. "The Washington Diary of Horatio Nelson Taft." Manuscript Division, Library of Congress. http://memory.loc.gov/ammem/tafthtml/tafthome.html (accessed 3 January 2007).

Thatcher, James, M.D. "Military Journal." http://www.americanrevolution.org (accessed 16 May 2006).

Index

abolition 67–68, 76, 89, 91, 103, 113, 130
Adams-Onis Treaty 21
American "minute men" 9, 13
American Revolution 9, 15, 20, 30, 47
Anaconda Plan 43–45, 59, 69, 72–73
Andrew, Gov. John A. 67
Antietam, Battle 4, 99, 122, 126, 129–130, 135, 161, 173, 178, 185
Anti-Federalists 14
Ariel 112–113
army corps 83, 88, 93–95, 98, 106–108, 111, 121
Army of Northern Virginia (CSA) 51, 120, 169, 175
Army of the Potomac 2, 4, 8, 53, 58, 62, 66, 74, 86, 92, 94, 102–103, 105, 111; Chancellorsville 163, 166, 168, 171, 173–174; Fredericksbug 152–154, 156, 160, 162; Gettysburg 175–176, 181, 183, 185; Lincoln inspection at Harrison's Landing 113, 115, 119, 134–135, 137–138, 140–141, 143, 145, 150
Army of Virginia 110, 114–116, 119, 121, 134

Ball's Bluff 67
Baltimore 38–41, 47, 63, 75, 120, 122
Baltimore and Ohio Railroad 38, 89
Baltimore Riots, 1861 39–41
Banks, Gen. Nathaniel P. 63–64, 66, 94, 101–102, 104, 109, 121, 154
Barnard, Gen. John G. 48, 78, 93, 101
Bates, Atty. Gen. Edward 79, 81, 96, 160
Beauregard, Gen. Pierre G.T. 8, 19, 25–26, 29, 36, 43, 47–48, 60
Big Bethel 42
Bill of Rights 14
Black Hawk War 20
Blair, Postmaster General Montgomery 46, 84, 166
blockade, Union Naval 35, 43, 50, 76, 93, 182
Browning, Oliver Hickman 85, 153
Buchanan, Pres. James 34, 42, 51

Buell, Gen. Don Carlos 66, 69, 71, 80–81, 86, 90, 106, 137
Burnside, Gen. Ambrose 4, 8, 47, 84, 112, 114–116, 121, 129, 132, 134–138, 140–149, 151–154, 156, 158, 165, 174, 180, 182
Butler, Gen. Benjamin F. 33, 40–42, 47, 63

Calhoun, John C. 21–22, 29, 31
Cameron, Simon 37–38, 41, 61, 63–64, 66, 68, 71, 75–76, 83
Chambersburg 127, 175
Chancellorsville, Battle 4, 162–167, 169, 174
Chase, Secretary of the Treasury Salmon P. 37–38, 41, 77, 80–82, 84–86, 114–115, 117–119, 121, 128, 133, 140, 143–144, 153
Chickahominy River 108–109, 111
Chickamauga, Battle 179
citizen soldier 13, 31, 91
Clausewitz, Karl von 19, 45, 160
Cochrane, Brig. Gen. John 4, 127–128, 143–147, 151–152, 182
commander in chief, president as 3–4, 14, 33–34, 47, 53, 67, 73, 77, 80–81, 85, 96, 113, 119, 124–125, 130, 145, 147, 183, 185
conciliation policy (Union) 69, 76
Confiscation Act 47, 70, 139
Constitution 5, 14–15, 26, 29, 32–33, 38, 40, 46–47, 51, 53, 59, 68, 81, 115, 124, 147
Constitutional Convention in 1787 14
Continental Army 11–13, 29
Corps of Engineers 18, 21, 101
Couch, Gen. Darius 152, 159, 161, 163, 166–167, 173, 182
Crimean War 54
Crittenden-Johnson resolution 47

Davis, Jefferson 7–8, 24, 29, 34, 48, 51, 75
Democratic Party 138
Democrats 33, 42, 54, 89, 138
Department of Mississippi 97
Department of Missouri 71, 154
Department of Ohio 71

211

Department of the Potomac 53, 97
Department of the Rappahannock 104, 109
Department of the Shenandoah 104
Dix, Gen. John A. 42, 63-64

Emancipation 115, 124, 130, 185, 195
Emancipation Proclamation 114, 124-125, 147; preliminary 3, 122, 130, 185
expansible army 21-22, 27, 31

Fair Oaks, Battle 109
Federalists 14
filibusters 26
Florida 21, 23, 29, 43, 155
Fort Donelson 90-91
Fort Henry 90-91
Fort Sumter 1, 28-29, 36, 39, 139
Fortress Monroe 41, 87, 97, 10-104, 111, 117
Franklin, William B. 4, 37, 47, 66, 77, 82-86, 89, 93-94, 104, 106, 108, 118-121, 125, 134, 136, 141-144, 147-149, 152-154
Fredericksburg 96, 135-136, 143, 148, 158, 161-163, 169
Fredericksburg, Battle 4, 132, 135-137, 139, 141-142, 152-154, 156, 161, 177
Frémont, Maj.-Gen. John C. 64, 70-71, 109-110
French Revolution 16, 19

general in chief 3, 5, 7, 29, 34, 53-54, 61, 64, 66, 68-71, 73, 78-80, 86-87, 89, 95-97, 99-100, 102, 113-116, 119, 128, 130, 134, 143, 147, 149, 155, 158, 160, 164, 169, 181-184
general staff 18, 21, 100, 130
Gettysburg, Battle 2, 164, 175-177
Grant, Gen. Ulysses S. 1-3, 5, 24-25, 31, 50, 89, 90-92, 106, 116, 125, 144, 159, 177, 180

Habeas Corpus 40
Halleck, Gen. Henry W. 19-21, 27, 37, 51, 66, 71, 80-81, 86-87, 90-91, 97, 100, 112, 114-117, 119, 135, 155, 166, 169, 184
Hamilton, Alexander 14, 22
Hardee, William 18
Harpers Ferry 40, 46, 80, 93, 109, 122, 169-174
Harrison's Landing 112, 114-115, 132; letter 112-114
Haupt, Gen. Herman 135, 170
Hay, John 72, 106, 118, 126
Heintzelman, Gen. Samuel 47, 54, 66, 78-79, 94, 108-109, 113, 117, 121-122, 172
Hitchcock, Ethan Allen 99-102, 107-108, 130
Hooker, Gen. Joseph 129, 132-134, 138, 148-149, 151, 153-156, 158-159, 161-168, 170-171, 173, 178

Jackson, Andrew 17, 21-22
Jackson, Gen. Thomas J. "Stonewall" 42, 48, 72, 94, 101, 104, 109, 111, 116-117, 148, 162-163

Jefferson, Thomas 16
Johnston, Gen. Joseph E. 8, 47-49, 92, 96, 106, 109
Joint Committee on the Conduct of the War 49, 67, 78-79, 80-81, 88, 132, 138, 142, 144-145, 165, 178
Jomini, Gen. Antoine Henrei 18-21, 44-45, 48-49, 160

Kentucky 50
Key, Maj. John T. 126, 161
Key, Col. Thomas 68, 77, 79, 93

Lee, Robert E. 19, 25, 36, 51, 109-112, 116-117, 119-122, 126, 128, 130-131, 136-137, 148, 158-160, 162-164, 168-170-173, 175-179, 180, 185
limited war aims (Union) 43, 47, 66, 69, 71, 114
Lincoln, Abraham 3-6, 28,-32, 36-37; appoints Burnside 134, 136-140, 142-143; appoints Hooker 156, 158, 160-161, 165-167, 169, 171; appoints McClellan 51, 60-61, 64, 66, 68, 72-73, 76; Emancipation Proclamation 146-147, 152-154; fires McClellan 129; McClellan sick 79-80, 82, 85-88, 93-97, 100-104, 106-107, 109-113; preliminary Emancipation Proclamation 123-124, 126-128; sacks Hooker 173, 175, 177-178, 182-184; Second Manassas 118, 120-121; suspends Habeas Corpus 39-40, 42-46, 49-50

Madison, James 16-17, 33
Magruder, John B. 42, 105
Mahan, Dennis 18-21, 27, 88
Malvern Hill 111, 132
Manassas, First Battle 47-49
Manassas, Second Battle 117-120, 150
Manassas Junction 40-41, 88, 97, 101, 103
Manifest Destiny 22, 26
Maryland 32, 36, 38-39, 41, 45, 56, 62-64, 67, 80, 120-121, 168-169, 171, 175, 184
McClellan, George B. 19, 25-26, 33, 37, 42-43, 51-54, 56-59, 61-64, 68, 72, 77-79, 85, 89, 92-93, 96, 104, 111-112, 115, 118, 125, 129, 179, 184
McClure, Alexander 36
McDowell, Irvin 37, 43, 47-49, 66, 79-80, 84-85, 93, 103, 109-110, 118, 166, 168, 174-175, 178
Meade, Gen. George G. 76, 129, 133-134
Meigs, Quartermaster Gen. Montgomery 84-85, 101
Mexican War, 1846-47 20, 24-26, 29, 33, 37, 78, 94, 110, 155
Militia Act of 1792 15
militia tradition 9-10, 13-14, 21, 91, 100
Mississippi River 6, 32, 43, 72, 110, 159, 182
Missouri 32, 50, 58, 70-71, 80, 154

Mechanicsville, Battle 111
Merrimac 97
Monroe Doctrine 22
Mud March 148–149

Nashville 90
New Orleans 6, 17, 32, 58, 71–72, 107
New York Times 32, 150
Newton, Gen. John 4, 127, 143–147, 151, 182
Nicolay, John G. 50, 74, 106

officer corps 18–20, 22, 25–26, 28, 37, 54, 83, 86, 89, 91, 95, 127, 132, 134, 143, 146, 150–153, 156, 180, 182
on to Richmond strategy 45, 52, 69, 74–75, 131, 160, 182

Patterson, Gen. Robert 38–40, 47, 49
Peninsula Campaign 97, 103–112, 130, 132, 142, 144, 156, 169, 184
Pennsylvania 36, 38, 39, 42, 46, 60, 75, 127–128, 167–168, 171, 175, 177, 184
Philippi 42, 51
Pinkerton, Allan 122
political generals 33
Polk, James K. 24, 33
Polk, Leonidas 8
Pope, Gen. John 110–111, 114–121, 130, 134, 150–151, 153, 156
Porter, David D. 71–72
Porter, Gen. Fitz John 78–79, 89, 94, 103, 108, 111, 113, 117–118, 120–121, 129, 149–151, 159
Potomac River 61, 80, 87, 93, 96, 118, 127, 131, 177
president as commander in chief 3–6, 14, 33–34, 47, 53, 67, 73, 77, 80–81, 84–85, 96, 113, 119, 124–125, 130, 145, 147, 183, 185

Quaker gun 96
Quartermaster's Department 21

Radical Republicans 47, 67–69, 82, 88–89, 91, 95, 125, 134, 138, 140, 165, 183, 185
Rappahannock River 92, 96, 134, 137, 142–143, 179
regular army 14, 17–18, 21–22, 29, 31, 37, 46, 54
Report on the Reduction of the Army 21
Republican Party 37, 47, 83, 103, 108, 138
Reynolds, Gen. John F. 134, 141, 148, 159, 163, 166–168, 173–174, 176
Richmond, Virginia 8, 31, 41–43, 47, 51, 59, 69, 70–71, 74, 77, 82, 84, 88, 92, 97, 108, 111, 132, 183
Rio Grande 20

Schley, Frederick 63
Schurz, Gen. Charles 33, 152
Scott, Winfield 5, 7, 18, 22–25, 27, 29, 34–38, 40–47, 50–55, 56, 59, 61–62, 64, 68, 109, 182
Second Battle of Manassas or Bull Run 99, 117–120, 150
secretary of war 21, 34, 67, 100
Seminole War 20–21, 23
Seven Days' Battles 111
Seven Years War 11
Seward, William H. 28, 38, 61, 63–66, 68, 72, 81–82, 84, 92, 138–140, 145
Shenandoah Valley 42, 47–48, 51, 101–102, 104, 109, 112, 169
Sherman, Gen. William T. 3, 19, 31, 37, 47, 155
Shiloh, Battle 2, 106
slavery 1, 3, 6–7, 23, 28, 45, 47, 66–67, 69; arming 76, 79, 91–92, 103, 113–115, 124–128, 130, 147, 185
Smith, Gen. William Farrah 4, 89, 94, 107, 125, 138, 141–144, 147–149, 152, 154, 182
standing armies 9, 11, 16–17, 22–23
Stanton, Edwin M. 51, 76, 78, 83–85, 87–89, 93, 96, 99–100, 102–104, 106–108, 115–116, 119, 121–122, 128, 130, 135, 140, 146, 149–150, 152–153, 159, 162, 166
Stoddard, William 119
Stone, Gen. Charles P. 67
Stuart, Jeb 127
Sumner, Sen. Charles 67
Sumner, Gen. Edwin V. 37, 93–94, 103, 107–109, 113, 134–139, 141, 152–154, 167

Texas Revolution 23
Thayer, Sylvannus 18
Thomas, Col. Lorenzo 37, 56, 83, 100
Treaty of Guadalupe Hidalgo 25
Treaty of Paris (1783) 13

U.S. Military Academy at West Point 5, 7, 16, 18–20, 24–26, 29, 33, 37, 54, 66, 78, 83, 89, 92, 99, 110, 144, 150, 155
U.S. military tradition 4, 9, 11, 31, 54
U.S. Navy 50, 103–105
Urbanna Plan 78, 93

Vicksburg 72, 159
Vicksburg, Battle 176–177
Virginia 1, 36–38, 41–43, 45, 47, 50–52, 58, 63, 71, 74, 76, 78, 81, 84, 88, 92, 102, 109, 112, 137, 147, 149, 168

Wade, Benjamin 67–68, 79, 81, 139
Wadsworth, Gen. James S. 94, 102, 104, 143
Wainwright, Charles S. 148
war aims (Union) 1, 3, 5–6, 8, 19, 43, 45, 47, 67, 69, 71, 76, 91, 114, 124, 130, 181–182, 184
War Board 100, 102–103, 107, 114, 130
War of 1812 17–18, 21, 33
war power (of U.S. president) 5, 47, 124, 183

Washington, George 11–15, 20, 29, 87
Washington, D.C. 3, 28, 36, 38–41, 43–44, 47, 49–51, 53–54, 56, 60–65, 75, 77–78, 82, 84, 92–95, 97, 101–104, 109, 111, 113–115, 118, 120–123, 126, 128, 130, 134, 137, 143, 158, 160, 169, 173–175, 182

Welles, Gideon 45, 62, 64–65, 71–72, 119, 121–122, 139–140, 166, 173, 178
West Virginia 50
Williamsburg, Battle 107

Yorktown 103, 105–107, 132